Claud Mann's

TBS SUPERSTATION

DINNER & a movie

COOKBOOK

100 Favorite Recipes Served up by Claud Mann,
Your Chef Host on "Dinner & a Movie"

Written by Claud Mann, Kimberlee Carlson, and Heather Johnson

**Andrews McMeel
Publishing**

Kansas City

Library of Congress Cataloging-in-Publication Data on File
 03 04 05 06 LIB 10 9 8 7 6 5 4 3 2 1

Produced by Lionheart Books, Ltd.
Atlanta, Georgia 30341

Design: Carley Wilson Brown

Published by Andrews McMeel Publishing
an Andrews McMeel Universal company
4520 Main Street
Kansas City, Missouri 64111

Table of Contents

Chef's Introduction

In a nutshell, this is how it all went down. The year was 1994. I was a hard-working young restaurant chef minding my own business, just trying to bring home the bacon when the call came—the call every food service professional worth his salt waits for. It was the Big Cheese, legendary television producer and former Playboy Bunny, Kimberlee "Bunny" Carlson of TBS Superstation.

Cool as a cucumber, she asked me if I could develop some tasty recipes to complement the celebrated Turner movie library. She said this could be my gravy train if I could cut the mustard. Instantly intrigued, I responded, "I don't understand."

Then Bunny spilled the beans, explaining the concept. Captivating hosts to chew the fat while cooking a recipe thematically inspired by a mesmerizing movie. She seemed to think it would sell like hotcakes. Call me nutty as a fruitcake, but I decided right then and there that this was a pie I wanted my finger in. I walked out of the restaurant and never looked back. I had no way of knowing that I had hopped out of the frying pan and into the fire. That's right—it was back to the salt mines.

Now that I've gotten that off my chest, welcome to the new "Dinner & a Movie" Cookbook. The following recipes are some of our favorites, some of our viewers' favorites, and some that frankly have no business being seen by the public. In any case, our belief is that a recipe should be nothing more than a road map. Feel free to follow it, take a few side trips or head off in an entirely new direction. We just hope you have as much fun with these as we did.

Cheers,

Claud Mann

(The TBS Food Guy)

And now, although no one asked, I would like to leave you with:

Claud's **10** *Kitchen Commandments*

1. Keep your knives sharp. As a matter of fact, if all you have are cheap, dull knives, don't read any further until you've thrown them out and bought just one good one.

2. Get the kids into the kitchen to cook with you and really give them jobs to do. Remember—before TV, families used to cook together.

3. Never clean up if you can help it . . . hey, you did the cooking.

4. Make it a point to physically remove anyone from the kitchen who makes scornful remarks or backhanded inquiries about the fat, sugar, cholesterol or caloric content of any meal that you are preparing.

5. Always give yourself an extra hour. (When you're relaxed, you can have more fun.)

6. Constantly taste, taste, taste!

7. Get your sauté pans nice and hot and don't worry about a little smoke.

8. Discard bottled herbs and spices if purchased during a previous presidential administration. Smell them—they should have a discernable aroma. If not, might I suggest substituting pencil shavings, which are significantly cheaper and taste just about the same.

9. Whenever a guest offers to bring "a bottle of something," ask for a gallon of extra-virgin olive oil.

10. Always try to cook enough to offer a meal to a neighbor that lives alone. If you don't know them, it's a fine way to get started. (Plus, if more of us bothered to feed each other, the world would be a nicer place.)

Chapter 1

Appetizers Snacks & Lighter Fare

Austin Powers: International Man of Mystery 1997

For cheese fondue:

1/2 pound Gruyère cheese

1/2 pound Emmentaler cheese or your favorite English cheese

3 tablespoons flour

1 clove garlic

1 tablespoon butter

1 cup champagne or dry white wine

1/2 teaspoon white pepper

1 pinch cayenne pepper and nutmeg

1/2 teaspoon chopped lemon zest

2 tablespoons kirsch (cherry brandy)

1 French bread or baguette, cut into small cubes (each with a bit of crust attached)

For chocolate fondue:

1 cup heavy cream

1 pound chopped dark chocolate

1/4 cup chopped almonds

2 tablespoons orange liquor

Ladyfingers and plenty of fresh fruit, cut into bite-sized pieces

1 Swedish-made cheese enlarger

1 warranty card for Swedish-made cheese enlarger

1 book entitled "Swedish-Made Cheese Enlargers Are My Bag, Baby"

Oh, Fondue Me, Baby!

When WE host a happening fondue party, we observe the strict rules of the British Intelligence Fondue Training Center on Abbey Road: if your bread falls off its fork into the fondue pot, you're required to kiss the person to your right…or is it your left? When in doubt do what Austin Powers does…kiss everyone! Yeah, baby….

Cheese fondue:

1. Chop the cheese into small pieces then toss with the flour and set aside.

2. Slice the garlic in half; rub inside of your fondue pot, first with the cut sides of garlic, then the butter.

3. Place the pot over medium heat; add the champagne or white wine and heat until just barely boiling.

4. Add the floured cheese a handful at a time, stirring with a wooden spoon after each addition.

5. When the cheese is melted and creamy, add the white pepper, cayenne, nutmeg, and lemon zest. Stir in the kirsch just prior to serving.

Chocolate fondue:

1. Bring the cream to a simmer in the fondue pot. Add the chopped chocolate and stir until melted; then stir in the nuts and orange liquor.

2. Instruct your guests to spear the bread cubes, fruit, and ladyfingers with fondue forks or skewers. Swirl bread in the melted cheese; dunk fruit and ladyfingers in chocolate. Attempt to eat.

3. If said bread or fruit drops into fondue pot, remind guests that fondue etiquette requires them to kiss the person to their left.

4. Remind guests that, if kissing the guest to their left isn't their bag, they can opt to "Fon" do the dishes.

Yield: Serves 4-6

Do we make you hungry, baby?

Fondue was originally created by European goatherds to use up stale bread and old cheese.

Inside Scoop

Besides the more obvious nods to James Bond movies, *Austin Powers* contains references to a plethora of other '60s and '70s TV and films: The unique ring of Austin's picture phone is the same as the phone in *Our Man Flint*. Austin's exclamation when he enters the Electric Psychedelic Pussycat Swingers club, "It's my happenin', baby, and it freaks me out!" comes from *Beyond the Valley of the Dolls*. Many of the shots in the opening credits mimic The Beatles' movie, *Help!* Fembots were first seen in the TV show "The Bionic Woman." "The Look of Love" was the main song used in the seminal spy spoof movie, *Casino Royale*.

$\mathcal{B}$aby $\mathcal{B}$oom

For the seasonings:

3 tablespoons sugar

1 tablespoon salt

1/4 teaspoon chile paste

1/2 cup coconut milk

1/4 cup soy sauce

1/3 cup rice vinegar

1 tablespoon cornstarch

For the filling:

5 dried Chinese mushrooms

One 2-ounce package Chinese rice sticks

Peanut oil, as needed

1 tablespoon grated ginger root

1 tablespoon chopped garlic

1 finely diced serrano chile

1 cup crushed peanuts

1/2 cup finely diced celery

1/2 cup finely diced yellow onion

1/2 cup finely diced carrot

2 cups shredded napa cabbage

1/4 cup thinly sliced scallions

1/2 cup minced water chestnuts

1 cup chopped cilantro

1 package won ton or spring roll
   wrappers

1 egg, beaten

1 ripe au pair, in season

$\mathcal{O}$ffspring Rolls (a.k.a. "Little Bundles of Joy")

Like children, our offspring rolls require a little tender loving care … but with the proper nurturing, they'll grow up to be the kind of party food that'll make you proud.

1. Make the filling: Combine and whisk together the seasoning ingredients in a small mixing bowl. Set aside.

2. Place the dried mushrooms and rice sticks in separate bowls and cover with boiling water.

3. Allow the mushrooms to soak 15-20 minutes; drain, slice as thinly as possible, and set aside. Drain the rice noodles and set aside.

4. Place a wok or large cast iron skillet over medium heat and add 3 tablespoons of peanut oil. Add the ginger, garlic, serrano pepper, and peanuts and slowly stir fry for about a minute.

5. Add the celery, onion, and carrot and continue stir frying until they soften, about 2 minutes.

6. Mix in the Napa cabbage, scallions, water chestnuts, and sliced mushrooms. Continue cooking 3 to 4 minutes before raising the heat to high, whisking together the seasoning mixture and adding it all at once to the center of the pan. Cook and stir until the mixture thickens, about 3 minutes.

7. Spread out the hot mixture on a cookie sheet and allow to cool completely. Mix in the rice noodles and cilantro. Taste and adjust seasonings as desired.

8. Make the offspring rolls: Form 2 tablespoons of filling into a small cylinder and place it diagonally across the wrapper. Fold the point of the wrapper closest to you over the filling, tucking in the end. Brush the top corner with a little egg before folding in the sides and rolling up as tightly as possible.

9. Heat 2 inches of peanut oil in a heavy skillet over medium-high heat until one end of a roll dipped in the oil sizzles rapidly on contact.

10. Cook the offspring rolls in batches of five or six until golden, about 4 minutes. Turn once halfway through cooking.

11. Serve hot with Hoisin sauce, Chinese mustard or anything else that sounds tasty.

12. When it comes time to do the dishes, give yourself a time-out.

Yield: 20 rolls

Inside Scoop

When American soldiers returned home from World War II, the U.S. experienced an explosion of births, or a "baby boom." Sociologists define "baby boomers" as those Americans born from 1946 to 1964. Approximately 76 million Americans—29 percent of the population—were born during this 18-year period.

CHEW ON THIS

Enjoyed all over Asia, spring rolls are customarily served to celebrate the Chinese New Year, and with it, rebirth and the arrival of spring. A direct translation from the Chinese, *cheon guen*, the spring roll is a smaller and more delicate version of the better-known egg roll. Symbolizing wealth and prosperity, a plate of golden spring rolls is said to resemble a pile of gold bars.

Back to the Future

For the thyme and onion filling:
2 tablespoons extra virgin olive oil
1 tablespoon butter
1 medium white onion, thinly diced
2 medium red onions, thinly sliced
1 teaspoon light brown sugar
1 tablespoon fresh thyme, chopped
1/2 cup light-bodied red wine,
    Beaujolais is nice
Salt and pepper to taste

For the tart shell and toppings:
1 sheet frozen puff pastry dough
    (the most popular national brand
    contains two 10-inch sheets)
1 egg beaten with 1 tablespoon of cold
    water
1/2 cup grated Parmesan cheese
One 6-ounce jar artichoke hearts in
    water, drained and quartered
15 tasty black olives, pitted and
    chopped
A little thyme on your hands

Travelin' through Thyme and Onion Tart

Traveling through time is a breeze, if a few simple rules are followed:

1. Always reset your watch.
2. Never date your mom.
3. Never do anything that would cause you not to be born (see #2).

1. Time to make the filling: Heat the olive oil and butter in a large skillet on medium heat. Add the sliced onions and brown sugar; cook for 15 minutes, stirring often. Add the thyme and red wine and increase the heat to medium high. Continue cooking about 10 minutes, until the wine is reduced completely and the onions have the consistency of thick marmalade. Season to taste with salt and pepper. Set aside to cool.

2. Time to form the tart: Place a large cookie sheet on a rack in the lower third of the oven and preheat to 425°F. Lay out the puff pastry sheet flat on a lightly floured surface. Gently roll the dough to a 10-inch square, dusting with a little flour to avoid sticking. Transfer the dough to a well-buttered sheet of aluminum foil.

3. Using a small pastry brush paint a 1-inch border of the egg mixture around the perimeter of the pastry square. One at a time, fold over each egg-washed edge to create an inch-wide double thickness border around the tart; brush the egg mixture over the doubled edge. In the area inside the border, use the tines of a fork to lightly prick the dough at 1/2-inch intervals. This will prevent the bottom crust from puffing.

4. Time to fill: Sprinkle 1/4 cup of the Parmesan evenly over the fork-marked pastry base. Spread the cooled thyme and onion marmalade over the Parmesan and scatter the artichoke hearts and olives on top.

5. Time to bake: Carefully lift the tart by the edges of the foil and slide onto the hot cookie sheet. Bake for 30 minutes until puffy, crisp, and golden brown. Garnish with chopped thyme.

6. Thymely tip: If you suddenly realize that you have erred in one step of this recipe, and feel it absolutely necessary to travel back in time to correct it, don't get carried away and alter the course of gastronomic history. You might just return to find tonight's menu changed to corndogs and Jell-O®. Bon appétit!

Yield: One 8-inch tart.

Inside Scoop

Don't try this at home, kiddies! The filmmakers were at one time planning on making the time machine out of a refrigerator instead of a De Lorean.

FOOD FOR THOUGHT

An indispensable ingredient in stocks, soups, sauces, and rubs, thyme tops our list of culinary herbs. We're told the ancient Greeks arranged blooming thyme sprigs around the dead, believing that the soul of the deceased would dwell in its blossoms.

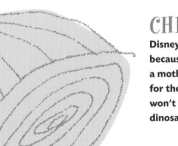

CHEW ON THIS

Disney passed on making this film because they considered the idea of a mother being attracted to her son too risque for their studio. Maybe that explains why they won't consider our screenplay for an animated dinosaur feature, "Oedipus T-Rex."

Earth Girls Are Easy 1988

Terrestrial Tarts with Loose Morels

If you think Earth girls are easy, come by the "Dinner & a Movie" test kitchen. We put out for all our guests . . . snacks, that is.

For the tarts:

6 sheets frozen filo dough (also spelled phyllo and fillo), defrosted

1/4 cup extra virgin olive oil

1 cup breadcrumbs

4 tablespoons mixed, minced, fresh herbs (chervil, Italian parsley, tarragon, thyme, etc.)

For the *loose* morels:

1 cup chicken or beef broth

1/4 cup vermouth

1/4 cup dried morel mushrooms

5 tablespoons butter

2 cups fresh, wild, freewheeling mushrooms (morel, chanterelles, shiitake, oyster, etc.)

2 cups white mushrooms

3 tablespoons minced shallots

1 tablespoon minced garlic

1/2 cup good-quality, dry red wine

3 tablespoons whipping cream

Salt and pepper to taste

1 probe, well chilled

Q: What do earth girls call a guy built like a mushroom?

A: A fungi

1. These tarts are easy: Preheat oven to 375°F. Lay out one piece of filo on a cutting board (keep the remaining pieces covered with a damp cloth or they will dry out and crack). Brush lightly with olive oil and sprinkle with breadcrumbs and herbs.

2. Repeat the process with the remaining filo sheets. Cut the layered filo rectangle into 8 equal pieces and transfer each to an ungreased cookie sheet.

3. Bake for 10-15 minutes, until brown and crisp.

4. Never forget your morels: Combine chicken broth and vermouth in a small saucepan and bring to boil. Add the dried morels; remove from heat and let soak for 20-30 minutes.

5. Remove morels from broth mixture and squeeze out excess liquid. Slice thinly and set aside, reserving broth for later.

6. Slice the fresh mushrooms thinly and set aside.

7. Heat 3 tablespoons of the butter over medium heat in a large sauté pan and add the reconstituted mushrooms. Sauté for 2

minutes; add the sliced mushrooms and sauté for 5 minutes, stirring often.

8. Stir in the shallots, garlic, wine, and reserved broth. Bring to a boil, reduce heat to low and simmer for 10-15 minutes.

9. Add the cream; season to taste with salt and freshly ground pepper. Keep warm until use; just before serving, whisk in the remaining 2 tablespoons of butter.

10. Place one filo square on a plate, spoon the mushroom mixture over and top with another filo square. Garnish with chopped, fresh herbs and serve.

11. Lead your space friends to the sink and introduce them to an important custom reserved for only the most honored guests . . . the dishes.

Yield: Serves 4

CHEW ON THIS

Geena Davis may be easy but don't cross her. In 1999, she placed 24th out of 28 semifinalists for the Olympic archery team. A member of MENSA—the society for those with genius-level I.Q.s—Davis is also no pushover in the brains department.

FOOD
FOR THOUGHT

Earth girls would do well to know that, while loaded with flavor, mushrooms have practically no fat, sodium, or cholesterol and are super low in calories. These edible fungi are packed with essential minerals that work to neutralize those pesky, cell-damaging free radicals. Recent Japanese studies have also proven that shiitake mushrooms in particular may significantly reduce serum cholesterol levels.

Field of Dreams
1989

1 ¼ cups lukewarm water

1 teaspoon sugar

1 tablespoon active dry yeast

1 ½ teaspoons salt

4 cups unbleached, all-purpose flour

1 tablespoon olive oil

4 teaspoons baking soda mixed with
  1 quart water

1 egg, beaten with 2 teaspoons water,
  kosher salt, sesame seeds, poppy seeds

1 pinch hitter

Batter-up Ballpark Pretzels

If you bake them, they'll say yum . . .

1. Combine the water, sugar, and yeast in a large mixing bowl and set aside in a warm spot. After 10-15 minutes, the mixture should begin to foam and bubble.

2. Add the salt and half of the flour and mix well with a wooden spoon. Turn the dough out onto a clean, floured surface and gradually knead in just enough of the remaining flour to form a smooth and elastic dough.

3. Continue to knead the dough for another 5 minutes before transferring to a clean bowl oiled with a few drops of olive oil. Turn the dough in the bowl to coat all sides evenly with oil.

4. Cover the bowl with a clean kitchen towel and set in a warm, draft-free place until doubled in bulk, about half an hour. Preheat the oven to 450°F. Punch the dough down and roll into a large log. Divide into 12 even pieces, then roll each piece into a 16-18-inch rope.

5. Shape the pretzels into any shapes that come to mind. To form a traditional pretzel shape, simply tie the dough into a loose knot pinching the ends across the loops.

6. Combine the baking soda and the water in a small saucepan and

bring to a boil. Using a slotted spoon, carefully lower each pretzel in the boiling water until it begins to float, about 15 seconds.

7. Drain each pretzel and transfer to a greased baking sheet, brush lightly with the egg-water mixture and sprinkle generously with kosher salt, sesame, and poppy seeds.

8. Cover the pretzels with a cloth and allow to rise again, about 5 minutes. Bake in preheated 450°F oven for about 15 minutes or until golden brown.

9. After dinner, fill the sink with hot soapy water and hope that someone will come.

Yield: Makes enough for the whole team

CHEW ON THIS

In the 1982 novel, *Shoeless Joe*, upon which *Field of Dreams* was based, the main character, Ray Kinsella, goes looking for real-life author/recluse J. D. Salinger. The producers of the film created a fictional reclusive author after Salinger—reportedly furious over his inclusion in the novel—threatened legal action. Guess that means we should stop working on our screenplay for *Catcher in the Rye Crisp*.

FOOD FOR THOUGHT

According to our sources at the mall, the word pretzel is derived from the archaic German *brezitella* meaning "little arm" or "little branch." As early as 600 A.D., monks would twist and bake bits of scrap dough as a reward to children who learned their lessons. The shape of the dough is said to represent the arms of a child folded across her chest in prayer while the three open spaces are symbolic of the holy trinity.

Flashdance

1983

For the buns:
3/4 cup lukewarm water
1 tablespoon active dry yeast
2 tablespoons sugar
1 tablespoon vegetable oil
1 tablespoon sesame oil
2 ½ cups flour

For the pork:
8 ounces pork tenderloin, cut in
   1/4-inch cubes
2 tablespoons soy sauce, mixed with
   1 tablespoon corn starch
1 tablespoon dry sherry
2 scallions, minced
1 teaspoon grated ginger
1 teaspoon minced garlic
2 tablespoons hoisin sauce
1 tablespoon sugar
1 tablespoon peanut oil
1 sweatshirt, strategically ripped

Jennifer's Steamin' Pork Buns (with Oh, What a Filling)

We guarantee that once you bite through this steamy bun and into the succulent pork within, you'll want to cut the necks out of all your T-shirts, slip on a pair of leg warmers, and douse yourself with a bucket of cold water.

1. Get those buns moving: In a small bowl, combine the warm water, yeast, sugar, and oils. Whisk vigorously and set aside in a warm place until the yeast begins to bubble, about 10 minutes.

2. Sift 2 cups of flour into a medium mixing bowl. Gradually pour in the water and yeast mixture, stirring with a wooden spoon until the dough forms a cohesive mass.

3. Turn the dough out onto a lightly floured surface and knead for 5 minutes, adding only as much flour as needed to keep the dough from sticking.

4. Place the dough in an oiled bowl, cover with plastic wrap and set aside in a warm spot until double in bulk, about 45 minutes.

5. While the dough rises, combine the pork with the soy, sherry, scallion, ginger, garlic, hoisin sauce, and sugar.

Tasty Tip
Don't have a steamer? Improvise with a colander or flat strainer balanced on ramekins (small oven-proof bowls).

6. Heat peanut oil in a wok or heavy skillet over high heat. Add the pork mixture and stir fry 2-3 minutes. Remove from heat and cool to room temperature.

7. Remove dough to a lightly floured board and roll into a cylinder, 2 inches wide and 12 inches long. Cut into 12 pieces; flatten each piece into a 3-inch disc.

8. Place 2 tablespoons of filling in the center of each disc. Gather the dough around the filling in small pleats; twist and pinch together to seal.

9. Place each of the buns on a small sheet of foil or parchment, cover with a damp cloth and let rise 30 minutes in a warm spot.

10. Arrange in a single layer on a plate or steamer basket and steam 10-15 minutes over rapidly boiling water. Eat warm or let cool to room temperature, wrap, and refrigerate.

11. End up with pork buns of steel? Don't fret if your buns don't puff as proudly as you'd like, they'll still be hot and tasty (and you can always call in your pork bun stand-in for the close-ups).

Yield: 12 steaming buns

Never Talk to Strangers

1 teaspoon minced fresh oregano

1 teaspoon minced fresh thyme

2 tablespoons minced parsley

1 teaspoon crushed red pepper

1 pinch saffron threads (optional)

2 cloves garlic, peeled and mashed
with a fork

4 tablespoons red wine

1/4 cup olive oil

1 pound beef fillet, sliced into
matchstick-sized pieces

2 red bell peppers, thinly sliced

2 green bell peppers, thinly sliced

1 large red onion, thinly sliced

2 tablespoons sherry vinegar or
balsamic vinegar

Sea salt and fresh ground pepper

1 large tomato, peeled, seeded,
and chopped

2 tablespoons sweet Spanish paprika

2 tablespoons finely chopped prosciutto

1 ½ pounds of your favorite pizza dough

10 Spanish green olives, pitted and sliced

3 eggs, hard-boiled and sliced

1 egg

1 teaspoon turmeric

1 pair tight jeans and an irresistibly
sexy accent

Spanish Beefcake

Here at "Dinner & a Movie," we believe strangers are just friends we haven't met yet…especially if they look like Antonio Banderas. So throw caution to the wind and invite someone new over for supper. There's only a slight chance that your tall, dark, handsome dinner companion is a dangerous psycho killer, and we feel it's worth the risk.

1. Preheat oven to 450°F. In a large bowl, combine the oregano, thyme, parsley, crushed red pepper, saffron, and garlic. Add the wine and 1 tablespoon of the olive oil. Mix the sliced meat in with the seasoning mixture, tossing to coat evenly. Cover and refrigerate at least 30 minutes and up to 2 hours.

2. In a large bowl, toss the sliced peppers and onion with the vinegar and 1 tablespoon of the olive oil. Transfer to a cookie sheet, season with salt and pepper and roast 30 minutes.

3. Heat the remaining oil in a large sauté pan over medium heat. Drain the marinade from the meat and sauté briefly until the meat is no longer pink, but not yet fully cooked. Remove meat from pan and set aside.

4. Add the chopped tomato, paprika, and any remaining marinade to the hot pan. Cook 5 minutes, then remove from heat and stir in the roasted vegetables, prosciutto, and the half-cooked beef fillet. Check and adjust seasonings and set aside to cool to room temperature.

5. Divide the dough in two and roll out each half into a 15-inch disc. Place one disc on a parchment-covered cookie sheet and spread the cooled filling over the top, leaving an uncovered border of at least an inch around the edges. Place the egg slices and olives evenly over the top. Cover with the second disc and pinch the edges together. Whisk the turmeric and egg together and brush the top and sides lightly with the mixture.

6. Reduce oven temperature to 350°F and bake 30-40 minutes until crust is golden brown. Serve warm or at room temperature. (Alternatively, you may make small empanadas, turnover style, and deep-fry until crisp.)

7. After dinner, when safely alone, slip into your tightest black rubber gloves, put on "Ravel's Bolero" and let those naughty dishes know who's boss.

Yield: Serves 8 as an appetizer or 4 as a main course

Inside Scoop

After gaining international attention starring in *Women on the Verge of a Nervous Breakdown*, *Tie Me Up/Tie Me Down* and other films by legendary Spanish director Pedro Almodovar, Antonio Banderas first became familiar to many Americans as the object of Madonna's unrequited crush in her 1991 concert documentary *Truth or Dare*. Banderas made his official American debut in 1992's *The Mambo Kings*.

CHEW ON THIS

Our Spanish Beefcake is a proud and strutting example of tapas, a word used to describe any number of small, delectable dishes served in bars throughout Spain. Derived from the Spanish *tapar* meaning "to cover," tapas may have originally been as simple as a thin slice of ham, bread or cheese placed over one's wine glass to keep the flies out. Our local bartender just uses a fly-swatter, then passes out bowls of peanuts.

Saturday Night Fever

For the marinara:

One 28-oz can Italian plum tomatoes, cut in quarters

2 tablespoons extra-virgin olive oil

3 anchovy fillets, chopped

2 cloves garlic, peeled and thinly sliced

Chopped parsley

Freshly ground black pepper

For the mozzarella:

6 sheets frozen filo dough (also spelled phyllo and fillo), defrosted

3 tablespoons extra-virgin olive oil

1 cup bread crumbs

1/4 cup finely shredded fresh basil

Twelve 1-ounce packages part-skim mozzarella (also labeled string cheese)

Whole fresh basil leaves for garnish

1 disco ball

Tony Manero's Mozzarella Marinara

The year was 1977. You had a different date every Saturday night. You could eat plate after plate of deep-fried cheese in little Italian restaurants into the wee hours. You could wear white polyester and still feel good about yourself. Times have changed. We watch our cholesterol and the last thing we want on a Saturday night is a fever. Well, we can't help you with your love life or your fashion sense, but we can offer you this example of "Heart Smart Disco Fare℗" that may help keep you ha, ha, ha, ha stayin' alive.

1. Prepare for a hot night: Preheat oven to 325°F. In a large mixing bowl, combine the tomatoes, olive oil, anchovies, and garlic. Spread out the contents of the bowl on a large cookie sheet and roast for 30 minutes, stirring once or twice. Transfer to the work bowl of a food processor or blender. Pulse quickly 3-4 times. The sauce should be somewhat chunky. Season with chopped parsley and freshly ground black pepper to taste. Cover and keep warm.

2. Dress up the mozzarella: Increase the oven temperature to 375°F. Lay out 1 piece of filo on a clean, dry surface. (Keep the remaining pieces covered with a damp cloth until use or they will dry out and crack.) Cut 2 strips, 6-7 inches wide, from the first sheet. Lay the strips side by side and brush both sides of each strip lightly with olive oil.

3. Sprinkle 1 tablespoon of bread crumbs and 1/2 teaspoon of basil evenly over the top of each strip. Center 1 piece of cheese at the end of the filo strip closest to you and roll up tightly. The filo-wrapped cheese should resemble a small cigar. Fold the ends under, sprinkle with bread crumbs, and place on an ungreased baking sheet. Repeat the process for each piece of the remaining cheese. Bake for 10 minutes until "cigars" are hot and crispy.

4. Strut your stuff: Lay out 6 warmed plates and make a pool of marinara in the center of each. Place 2 mozzarella "cigars" over the sauce and garnish with a basil leaf.

5. After dinner, lead your dance partner to the sink for a hot and soapy solo.

Yield: Serves 6 as an appetizer.

"I remember the old days at the five-four...no shoes, no shirts, lots of service..."
—*Larry De Laguardia (D&aM's ubiquitous appliance repairman)*

Olive Oil Fact #57
Olive oil is made up of nearly 75 percent mono-unsaturated fat, the type of fat that actually helps to lower high cholesterol levels in the body. It also contains elements believed to prevent cancer and slow the aging process. Some say it also aids in the ability to learn complex dance routines.

Inside Scoop
Saturday Night Fever was the late, great film critic Gene Siskel's favorite film. He had reportedly seen the movie 17 times and at one time had owned the famous white suit. When last auctioned in 1995, the suit sold for $145,000.

Thelma & Louise

1991

For the tomatillo sauce:
1 pound tomatillos, husked
4 cloves garlic, peeled
2 jalapeño peppers
1/4 teaspoon salt
1/2 teaspoon ground cumin
1/4 cup chopped cilantro

For the hot peppers:
8 fresh pasilla or poblano chiles
1 pound boneless lamb loin chops
1/4 cup extra-virgin olive oil
1 teaspoon freshly ground black pepper
1/2 teaspoon oregano, chopped fresh
1/2 pound tasty, semi-soft cheese, i.e.
   Gouda, Jarlsberg, or Port-Salut, cut
   into little, finger-sized pieces
1 cup all-purpose flour
2 eggs, beaten
Plenty of gas money and
   a Texas-free Atlas

Alternate Ingredients

Goldie Hawn and Meryl Streep were
originally up for the roles of Thelma and
Louise and Billy Baldwin was slated to
play Brad Pitt's part.

Two Hot Peppers on the Lamb

Blowing up trucks, knocking over liquor stores and running from the law can sure make you hungry. If you feel like driving off a cliff, maybe you just need a good meal. . . .

1. Too hot to handle: Heat an ungreased griddle or cast-iron skillet over medium-high heat. Place the tomatillos, garlic, and jalapeño on the griddle and roast for about 10 minutes, until the skins are blistered and dark brown.

2. Transfer mixture to a blender and add the salt, cumin, and cilantro. Blend for no more than 5-10 seconds, leaving the sauce a little chunky. Transfer to a small saucepan and keep warm.

3. From the frying pan to the fire: Place the peppers directly over a high flame or under the broiler, turning occasionally until the skins begin to blister and blacken on all sides. Place the roasted peppers in a paper bag and allow to sit for 15 minutes. Feel free to pass the time by taking pot shots at passing vehicles. (Big rigs with "Honk if you're Horny" bumper stickers are especially fair game.)

4. Scrape off the burnt skin under cold running water and carefully slice a small lengthwise slit down the side of each pepper. Scrape out the seeds and pith.

5. We're on the lamb: Trim the lamb of excess fat and cut into long, thin pieces. Place the lamb strips in a small mixing bowl and toss with 2 tablespoons of the olive oil, black pepper, and oregano.

6. Heat a large, heavy skillet over medium-high heat until quite hot, add a few tablespoons of olive oil and quickly add the lamb strips. Sauté until the lamb begins to get brown and crisp around the edges. (Make sure to have the exhaust fan on or a window open. If the pan is hot enough, oil tends to smoke.)

7. Stuff each pepper with a piece of cheese and a few crispy lamb strips.

8. Cut to the chase: Wipe the skillet with a paper towel. Coat the bottom with olive oil and place over medium-high heat. Dust each pepper with flour, dip in beaten egg, and sauté until golden brown on all sides, turning as needed. (But never into Texas.)

9. For each serving, fling 2 hot peppers into a fiery pool of tomatillo sauce, garnish with a cilantro sprig, and never look back.

10. Desperate clean-up tip: Don't. Given the choice between a) futilely tackling the towering mountain of cheese-and-grease encrusted dishes you're about to face and b) peacefully plummeting off an impossibly high cliff, the decision seems obvious . . . Buckle up!

Yield: 4 servings

Inside Scoop

Director Ridley Scott was all set to hire a body double for the sexier parts of that infamous love scene between Geena Davis and Brad Pitt until Davis reportedly informed him no double would be necessary.

CHEW ON THIS

Archeologists have found evidence of lamb's popularity at prehistoric dinner parties given as early as half a million years ago in the caves of Peking Man. But on Monday nights, did they watch "Dinner & a Cave Drawing"?

FOOD FOR THOUGHT

A general rule of thumb: The smaller the chili pepper the hotter it is. The ancient Aztecs used chilies as a form of torture for captured enemy warriors and adulterous wives. Why not turn the tables and use them on abusive husbands. A little more pepper, dear?

Turner & Hooch

1/4 cup brown rice
2 cups whole-wheat flour
1/4 cup wheat germ
1/4 cup bulgur wheat
2 cups all-purpose flour
1 cup corn meal
1/2 cup whole oats
1/4 cup oat bran
1/4 cup rye flour
1/2 cup powdered milk
2 tablespoons brewer's yeast
1 tablespoon garlic powder
1 tablespoon baking powder
1/4 cup vegetable oil or bacon
  drippings
3 eggs, beaten
2 cups beef broth
1 cup finely grated cheddar cheese
1/4 cup chopped parsley
1 copy Rin Tin Tin's autobiography,
"Because We Can"

K-9 Grain Dog Biscuits

*C'mere, boy. C'mere, boy. Sit up. Roll over. Make biscuits.
Good dog!*

1. Cook the brown rice as per package instructions. Set aside to cool.

2. In a large mixing bowl, combine whole-wheat flour, wheat germ, bulgur wheat, all-purpose flour, corn meal, whole oats, oat bran, rye flour, powdered milk, brewer's yeast, garlic powder, and baking powder.

3. Add the oil or bacon drippings to the dry mixture and stir together until no large lumps remain.

4. In a small bowl, combine the beaten eggs, beef broth, cheese, and chopped parsley.

5. Add the egg mixture to the K-9 grain mixture and stir well to create a cohesive dough. Turn the dough out onto a clean, floured surface and knead 2-3 minutes.

6. Preheat oven to 300°F. Divide the dough into quarters; roll 1 quarter out to a thickness of 1/2-inch. Use a cookie cutter or paring knife to cut out nervous little mailmen, beckoning fire hydrants, expensive shoes, harmless kittens, or any other shape your dog finds uniquely irresistible. Repeat with the remaining dough, combining and re-rolling the scraps.

Inside Scoop

We're pleased to know
Tom Hanks' father was a cook.

7. Bake the K-9 grain treats on a parchment-lined cookie sheet for 1 hour. Turn off heat and let the treats remain in the oven another 30 minutes, until dry and crisp.

8. To clean up:

(a) Place dirty bowls and utensils on floor.

(b) Whistle for dog.

(c) Return freshly licked dishes to cupboard.

Yield: Makes about fifty 2-inch treats

FOOD FOR THOUGHT

In one scene of this film, the Tom Hanks character rewards Hooch (the dog) with chocolate chip cookies. Most dog owners know that chocolate contains theobromine, a compound proven to be highly toxic to dogs. Even small amounts of chocolate can cause vomiting and nausea. Larger doses may progress to cardiac arrhythmia, seizures, and even death. Because dogs have such a sweet tooth, you dog owners should be especially careful at Christmas time not to leave boxes of candy under the tree. Now that we think of it, Hanks probably knew this and was simply tired of being upstaged by a canine.

Dog Eat Dog?

Why the heck you ask, would anyone make dog food? After reading the label, we recently looked up the definition of *by-products* and immediately got to work on this recipe. Ol' Shep may not know the difference ... but then again, he's never sat through *Soylent Green*. (That probably goes without saying as so few German Shepherds are rabid Charleton Heston fans.)

The War of the Roses

Mouth-watering Kathleen Turnovers

1989

Can you blame us? "Mouth-watering Michael Douglases" just didn't sound as good.

For the pastry:
1 ½ cups all-purpose flour, sifted
1 cup cake flour, sifted
1/4 teaspoon salt
1 teaspoon sugar
6 tablespoons chilled vegetable shortening
1/2 cup cold butter, cut into small pieces
1/3 cup cream cheese, softened
1-2 tablespoons ice water, as needed
1 egg, beaten (for egg wash)

For the spinach filling:
1/2 pound frozen spinach, chopped
2 scallions, chopped
1/4 cup chopped fresh parsley
1/4 cup chopped fresh dill
1/2 cup walnut pieces
3 tablespoons olive oil
1/2 onion, diced
1 cup feta cheese, crumbled
1/4 cup cottage cheese
1 egg
Pinch nutmeg

For the apple filling:
2 baking apples, peeled, cored, and thinly sliced
1 teaspoon lemon juice
1/4 cup golden raisins
1/2 cup cranberry juice
1/2 teaspoon ground cinnamon
1/4 cup powdered sugar
1 tablespoon butter
A good divorce attorney

CHEW ON THIS

At the age of 47, Kathleen Turner rejuvenated her sexy image with a starring role as the lustful Mrs. Robinson in a popular Broadway stage version of *The Graduate*. The play, though panned by critics, was a hit with audiences. We're sure it had nothing to do with Turner's daring full-frontal nudity.

1. Make the pie crust: In a medium bowl, mix together the flours, salt and sugar. Add the shortening and using a pastry blender or two knives, work it into the flour until it resembles coarse cornmeal. Add butter and continue cutting it in until the bits are no larger than small peas. Add the cream cheese one tablespoon at a time, mixing with a fork after each addition to moisten the dough evenly. If the dough still feels dry, add ice water, a few drops at a time. Using your hands, gently shape the dough into a disc. Wrap with plastic wrap and refrigerate at least 20 minutes.

2. Make the spinach filling: Squeeze excess water from the spinach and toss with the scallions, parsley, dill, and walnuts in a large mixing bowl.

3. Heat the olive oil in a large skillet over medium heat, add the onion and sauté until translucent, about 5 minutes. Stir in the spinach mixture and remove from heat to cool.

4. Mix together the cheeses, egg, and nutmeg in a small mixing bowl. Stir the cheese mixture into the spinach mixture, check seasonings, and set aside.

5. Make the apple filling: Combine the apples, lemon juice, golden raisins, cranberry juice, cinnamon, powdered sugar, and butter. Bring to a boil, reduce heat and simmer for 10-15 minutes until thickened. Remove from heat and set aside to cool.

6. Make the spinach turnovers: Line 2 large baking sheets with parchment paper and preheat the oven to 400°F.

7. Cut the dough into two equal pieces; wrap and return one piece to the refrigerator. Dust a clean work surface with flour and roll the dough out into a rectangle measuring approximately 12 x16 inches. Trim any ragged edges and quarter the dough into four 6 x 8-inch pieces.

8. Spoon 4 to 5 tablespoons of filling onto each rectangle, brush the edges with a little egg wash and fold over to enclose the filling. Crimp the sealed edges gently with the tines of a fork and brush the tops with egg wash. Transfer the turnovers to a prepared baking sheet and bake for 20-25 minutes, or until golden.

9. Make the apple turnovers: Roll out the remaining dough to a thickness of about 1/8-inch (a little thicker than a quarter). Use a 5- or 6-inch round cutter to cut out 4 rounds and fill each with 1/4 cup of apple filling. Egg wash the inside edges, fold over, and seal as with the spinach turnovers.

10. Brush the top of each turnover with egg wash and dust with a little sugar; transfer to a baking sheet and bake 20 minutes, until golden.

11. Before diving into the snacks, have each guest sign a prenuptial agreement forfeiting all rights to leftovers.

Yield: 8 Turnovers

FOOD FOR THOUGHT

When it comes to turnovers, the possibilities are endless. Whether steamed, baked, or fried, filled with truffles, curry, apricots, or fried pork, the ubiquitous and flexible turnover makes gratifying appearances throughout the world.

Napped Through History?

The real War of the Roses happened in the late 1400s when two English families—the Yorks and the Lancasters—fought over the crown. Since the Lancaster family's heraldic badge was a red rose and the York's was a white rose, the thirty-year conflict became known as the War of the Roses. Don't worry, this won't be included on the test.

Inside Scoop

Director Danny DeVito had to fight to maintain the dark ending of this film. Not surprisingly, Twentieth Century Fox wanted to change it to something happier.

When Harry Met Sally

1989

What Am I, Chopped Liver?

For the topping:
1 pound fresh chicken livers
1 tablespoon chopped shallots
1 tablespoon chopped garlic
4 tablespoons olive oil
2 eggs
2 onions, finely chopped
1 large leek, finely chopped
1 tablespoon red wine vinegar
2 tablespoons chopped parsley
Salt and freshly ground black pepper
1 very close friend of the opposite sex

We'll have what she's having . . .

1. Rinse the liver in cold water and place in a mixing bowl with the shallots, garlic, and 2 tablespoons of olive oil. Cover and refrigerate 20 minutes.

2. Place the eggs in a medium saucepan and cover with 2 inches of cold water. Place the pan over high heat and bring to a boil. As soon as the water comes to a boil, remove pan from heat, cover and let sit 10 minutes. Transfer the hot eggs to a bowl of ice water until cool to the touch. Peel, finely chop, and set aside.

3. Heat remaining olive oil in a large sauté pan over medium-high heat. Sauté the chicken livers for 2 minutes on each side. Transfer the liver to a plate; add the chopped onions, leeks, and vinegar to the hot pan and sauté about 3 minutes, until golden brown.

4. Return the liver to the pan with the onions and leeks; reduce heat to medium and continue cooking 5 minutes.

5. Combine the liver mixture in the work bowl of a food processor and chop to desired consistency. Transfer to a bowl and stir in the chopped egg and parsley. Season to taste with salt and freshly ground black pepper.

6. After dinner, pose this question to your guests: "Can men and women do the dishes without sex getting in the way?"

Yield: Makes 1–1 1/2 pounds

Inside Scoop

Director Rob Reiner kept this movie "all in the family." His mother plays the woman offering the witty comeback, "I'll have what she's having" after Meg Ryan demonstrates her faking prowess at Katz's Deli. Reiner and Billy Crystal have been friends since Crystal guest-starred as Reiner's best friend on an episode of "All In the Family."

Nosh On This

A key ingredient in traditional chopped liver recipes, schmaltz, meaning rendered chicken fat, is also commonly used in English to describe something overly sentimental or corny. Other Yiddish terms commonly used in English include:

Bupkis – zilch
Chutzpeh – brazenness
Cockamamie – ludicrous
Drek – shoddy merchandise
Glitch – malfunction
Klutz – clumsy person
K'vetsh – whine, complain
Maven – an expert
Mentsh – special man
Mish mash – hodgepodge
Nosh – snack
Putz – a jerk
Schlep – drag or haul
Schlock – junk
Schmoe – (see schmuck)
Schmooze – network, chat
Schmuck – a fool
Schmuts – dirt
Schpiel – sales pitch
Schtik – a routine
Tush – butt

Young Guns II

1990

Yer gonna need:

1 whole fresh duck foie gras (Alias "Duck Liver" 1—1 ½ pounds)

4 slices smoked bacon

1 russet potato, peeled and sliced thinly

1 shot whisky (feel free to substitute sarsaparilla if your gang nickname is "Peach Fuzz")

4 ears of sweet corn freshly cut from the cob

1/3 cup heavy cream

1 teaspoon chopped fresh thyme

2 tablespoons butter

1 leather cell phone holster for lightning-quick access to agent, personal manager, and publicist

1 silver spoon, lodged firmly in mouth

Inside Scoop

After learning to ride horses for *Young Guns*, Keifer Sutherland grew to love the sport so much, he took up calf roping as a hobby.

Quick Draw Foie Gras

Maybe no cowboy worth his "sel de mer" would sit down to a mess of fancy goose liver for supper, but if your daddies are Hollywood big guns and you've grown up eatin' on Rodeo Drive (and not on the rodeo circuit), this'd be your idea of downhome cookin'.

1. Hone your chef's knife to a razor sharpness, season your skillet to a gun-barrel black sheen, and get ready to stare culinary death in the face.

2. Soak the foie gras in a bowl of ice-cold, lightly salted water for 20 minutes.

3. Rinse well, gently pull off any large pieces of fat, cover, and refrigerate.

4. Cook the bacon until crisp, set aside and reserve the fat.

5. Heat a heavy skillet over medium-high heat, add half of the bacon grease and sauté the potatoes until crisp and golden. Transfer to a cookie sheet, season with salt and pepper, and keep warm in a 250°F oven.

6. Add the whisky, corn, cream and thyme to the hot skillet and reduce the heat to medium. Cook 5 minutes. Remove from heat and stir in the butter until incorporated. Keep warm until use.

7. Slice the liver into 1/2-inch slices and season with salt and pepper.

8. Heat a dry, cast-iron skillet over medium-high heat until very, very hot. Quickly and accurately sear the foie gras for no more than 45 seconds on each side.

9. Alternate the sautéed foie gras and warm potato slices over a few spoonfuls of the corn-whisky sauce and threaten to shoot anyone who doesn't beg for seconds.

Yield: Serves 4 as an appetizer

FOOD FOR THOUGHT

If cooking for your local PETA chapter, you should know that cooking foie gras would be faux pas. Only those of us who put our appetites before our ethics can handle the lowdown on foie gras. Its exact translation is "fat liver" and never were truer words spoken. The livers of these ducks or geese get really big—three pounds or so—because the birds are force-fed, fattened, and not allowed to exercise for about four to five months. Once the livers are taken from the birds—notice how we glossed over the details there—they are marinated, cooked, and seasoned and, despite their inauspicious beginnings, are undeniably delicious. If the idea of foie gras is too much for you to handle, feel free to use traditionally grown chicken or duck livers as a tasty substitute.

Son of a Gun
Both Emilio Estevez and Keifer Sutherland have famous actor fathers. Estevez's dad is Martin Sheen and Sutherland's dad is Donald Sutherland.

Chapter **2**

Soups Salads & Sandwiches

4 squab

1/2 cup dry vermouth

Sea salt and black pepper

4 sprigs fresh tarragon

1 stick butter

24 whole, peeled cloves garlic

1 cup sliced brown crimini mushrooms

1 cup sliced oyster mushrooms

1 cup sliced shiitake mushrooms

1 cup low-salt chicken broth

3 tablespoons fresh-squeezed
lemon juice

3/4 cup extra-virgin olive oil

2 cups roughly torn sourdough bread

1 cup Italian parsley leaves

1 cup fresh mint leaves

2 cups watercress

1 new identity

Stool Pigeons

The term "stool pigeon" comes from the practice of tying decoy pigeons to a stool to attract live birds. The criminal element adopted the phrase to describe police informants or "squealers." Serve this delicious squab salad to your guests and we predict you'll only hear squeals of delight and you certainly won't have to tie your guests to their stools. Although, as a good host, you should always offer to push their stools in.

1. Preheat oven to 400°F. Season squab inside and out with vermouth, salt, and pepper. Place a few tarragon sprigs in each squab. Fold the wing tips back and tie the legs closed.

2. Combine the butter and whole garlic cloves in a small sauce pan over low heat. Once the mixture melts and separates, carefully skim the surface and remove and discard the foamy top layer.

3. In a large ovenproof sauté pan over medium-high heat, brown the squab and garlic cloves in 2 tablespoons of the clarified butter. Transfer the pan to the preheated oven and roast for 10–15 minutes, until the thickest part of the thigh reads 160°F on an instant-read thermometer.

4. Transfer the squab and garlic to a platter and keep warm. Add 1 tablespoon of clarified butter to the hot sauté pan; add the mushrooms and season with salt and pepper. Place the pan in the oven and roast 20 minutes until mushrooms are soft-ened, but not shrunk. Transfer the mushrooms to the platter with the squab and set aside.

5. Add 1 cup of chicken stock to the hot pan scrape with a wooden spoon to loosen any browned bits stuck to the pan. Place over medium-high heat and reduce the stock to 2 tablespoons, then whisk in the lemon juice and olive oil, season to taste, and transfer mixture to a small bowl.

6. Spread the bread on a baking sheet and toast until crisp, about 10 minutes.

7. In a large mixing bowl, toss the parsley, mint, water-cress, roasted garlic, and mushrooms. Add the toasted bread. Place a mound on each plate and top with a pigeon and a spoonful of lemon dressing.

8. After dinner, place your dishes in the "wetness" protection program . . . a.k.a. the sink.

Yield: Serves 4

Did You Know...

Popular in Victorian England, pigeon—or squab, as it's often called—is made with young birds that have never flown and are therefore very tender. One of the few types of poultry that really doesn't taste like chicken, this rich, flavorful, single-serving-sized bird is, in our opin-ion, more than ready for a comeback.

CHEW ON THIS

A recipient of five Oscar® nominations, including one for *The Client*, Susan Sarandon has won only once, in 1995, for *Dead Man Walking*, directed by her longtime partner, Tim Robbins. Sarandon and Robbins met while making the hit film *Bull Durham*. "Dinner & a Movie" would like to give Susan Sarandon our DAAMY™ award for "Best Use of Citrus in a Drama" for her erotic cleansing rituals in 1980's *Atlantic City*. Susan, please contact TBS Food Guy Claud Mann to collect your reward.

Dirty Dancing

For the smoldering loins:

2 pork tenderloins

1/2 cup good quality soy sauce

2 teaspoons chopped, canned chipotle
  pepper (smoked Mexican jalapeño
  peppers, found in most supermarkets)

1 tablespoon chopped garlic

2 teaspoons crushed oregano

3 tablespoons peanut oil

2 tablespoons brown sugar

1 life (you had the time of)

Accessorize, people!:

2 red or yellow bell peppers, thinly
  sliced

1 red onion, thinly sliced

1 fennel bulb, thinly sliced

3 scallions, sliced in half

1 cup tasty black or green olives,
  pitted and chopped

4 freshly baked Italian or French rolls

A cold shower

1 expandable dance belt

Bumpin' Grinders

*Go back to your playpen, baby. We'll call you when you're old
enough for a bumpin' grinder.*

1. Work those loins: Place the pork loins, soy sauce, chipotle, garlic, oregano, peanut oil, and brown sugar in a zip lock plastic bag
or non-reactive container and refrigerate at least 20 minutes and
no more than 12 hours.

2. Preheat the oven to 500°F.

3. Remove the pork from the marinade and place on an oiled rack
set in a shallow roasting pan. Reserve the marinade for use later.

4. Roast the tenderloins in the upper third of the pre-heated
oven for 15 minutes; turn over and roast an additional 10–15
minutes. (If using an instant read thermometer, it should read
at least 150°F.) Allow your meat to rest at least 10 minutes before
slicing (ouch).

5. While your meat rests, heat a dry cast iron skillet over medium-
high heat until quite hot; add the bell peppers, onion, fennel, and
scallions to the hot pan and cook about 3 minutes until softened
and fragrant; add the reserved marinade and a few tablespoons of
water. Reduce the heat to medium and simmer gently for 5 minutes.

6. Split the rolls lengthwise, leaving a hinge; brush with a little
olive oil, and toast on a dry griddle until crisp and warm.

7. Rhythmically and suggestively pack each roll with plenty of smoldering loin; accessorize with the bell pepper sauté and chopped olives.

8. Tell your guests that although dancing should be dirty, dishes shouldn't; and offer to teach them all a new move . . . "The Dishwater Dip!"

Yield: 4 Servings

CHEW ON THIS

It's not just a movie, it's a phenomenon! Made for $6 million, the movie grossed an astonishing $170 million and has spawned two successful soundtracks, a concert tour, a TV series, and a Broadway musical. Audience interest inspired a 10th anniversary re-release of the movie in 1997, and plans for a much-hailed sequel are currently in the works.

FOOD FOR THOUGHT

Depending on where you hail from, you might call this sandwich a sub, a po boy, or a grinder. One thing we can all agree on is Patrick Swayze's ability to bump and grind. After learning the craft from his dancer/choreographer mom, Swayze went on to perform with several ballet companies, including the Joffrey. His first professional gig was as Prince Charming in "Disney on Parade."

Inside Scoop

One of our favorite "Dinner & a Movie" guests, *Dirty Dancing* choreographer Kenny Ortega won an Emmy® Award for his choreography of the opening ceremony of the 2001 Winter Olympics.

Dracula: Dead and Loving It 1995

10 whole black peppercorns
1 tablespoon salt
15–20 whole cloves garlic, peeled
1 pound tuna steak
2 green onions, thinly sliced
1/4 cup finely chopped red onion
1–2 tablespoons sambal chile paste
1 teaspoon lemon zest
1 tablespoon mayonnaise
2 tablespoons extra-virgin olive oil
8 slices sourdough bread
1 ½ cups crumbled feta cheese
1/4 cup chopped cilantro
1 steel mesh turtleneck

Nosferatuna Melts

(A wolf howls in the distance) Leesten to thee cheeldren of thee night . . . vat muzeek day make! *Contrary to popular belief, they're not howling for blood, they're just politely asking for seconds on these tasty tuna treats.*

1. In a large saucepan, bring 2 or 3 inches of water to a boil; add the peppercorns, salt, and garlic; boil for 5 minutes.

2. Add the tuna steak to the boiling water, reduce heat, and simmer no more than 4 minutes.

3. Remove the tuna and immediately immerse in ice water until cool.

4. Slice tuna as thinly as possible and set aside.

5. Strain the garlic from the water and chop as finely as possible.

6. Combine the tuna with the chopped garlic, green and red onion, chili paste, lemon zest, mayonnaise, and olive oil and mix together well.

7. Preheat oven broiler on high.

8. Top each piece of sourdough with the tuna mixture, and top with crumbled feta.

9. Broil the Nosferatuna melts just long enough to warm the feta (2 to 3 minutes). Garnish with cilantro and serve with ice-cold beer (or body temperature Bloody Marys).

CHEW ON THIS

Long regarded as a vampire deterrent, it's been said that garlic first sprouted in the Garden of Eden in the footprints of Lucifer. Believed to have curative powers, garlic was used by the British Army during WWI to treat both tuberculosis and infections in the field.

10. Once dinner is over, quickly and mysteriously retire to your coffin, leaving your dishes for Renfield. (If you don't have a Renfield, any dinner guest who eats bugs and calls you Master will do.)

Yield: 4 servings

FOOD
FOR THOUGHT

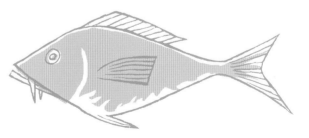

How do you ID a vampire?
a) Their driver's license is more than 200 years old.
b) No one appears in the photo.

Inside Scoop

Before making his 1968 film directorial debut with the comedy classic, *The Producers*, Mel Brooks enjoyed a very successful career in television as a writer and performer on Sid Caesar's "Your Show of Shows" and as a creator of the hit spy parody show, "Get Smart." Brooks is so closely associated with comedy that when he produced the melancholy drama *The Elephant Man* in 1989, he had his name removed from the movie's publicity so people wouldn't come expecting to laugh. Brooks directed this Dracula spoof as a companion piece to his *Young Frankenstein*.

Dumb and Dumber 1994

Soup on a Stick

For the soup:

1 pound large shrimp

4 pounds chicken backs and necks

2 thin slices fresh ginger

1/2 teaspoon black peppercorns

2 scallions, cut into 2-inch pieces

3 cloves garlic, peeled & crushed

1/4 cup dried mushrooms

4 quarts cold water

1 teaspoon salt

For the stick:

1 pound beef tenderloin, well trimmed

1 pound pork tenderloin, well trimmed

1 pound skinless boneless chicken
  breasts

8-ounces firm tofu, cut into 1-inch cubes

1 English cucumber, cut in 3/4-inch cubes

6 scallions, cut in 2-inch pieces

For service:

3 tablespoons soy sauce

2 tablespoons sesame oil

1 teaspoon chile paste

2 teaspoons white vinegar

1/2 Napa cabbage, thinly sliced

1/2 pound baby spinach, stems removed

In case of dumb kitchen accidents:

  1 phone book to look up the number
  for 911

You don't have to be the sharpest tool in the shed to make a darn good soup on a stick. Just try to follow this simple recipe and look up any big words.

1. Try to make the soup: Peel and devein the shrimp. Arrange on a platter, cover, and refrigerate. Combine shrimp shells with the chicken backs, ginger, peppercorns, scallions, garlic, and mushrooms in a large, heavy pot. Cover with cold water and bring to a rapid boil over high heat. Skim the surface to remove any scum that floats to the top. Partially cover the pot, reduce heat, and cook at a low simmer for at least 1 hour, preferably 2. Strain liquid through a fine strainer into a large bowl; skim off any fat that rises to the top, salt to taste, and set aside. Important: avoid submerging head or extremities in the broth until it has cooled.

2. Try not to hurt yourself: Slice the beef, pork, and chicken breast across the grain as thinly as possible and arrange on a platter. (When slicing the meats, may we suggest a knife?)

3. In a small bowl, mix together the soy sauce, sesame oil, chili paste and white vinegar. In a medium bowl, toss together the Napa cabbage and spinach.

4. Try to serve dinner: Place an electric skillet or wok in the center of the table and bring the broth to a simmer. Arrange the uncooked foods around the simmering broth and ask the dumbest person present to please come forward. (If everyone steps forward, pick the person with the cleanest hands.) Explain slowly and clearly that they have the great honor of preparing the soup for everyone and that you're genuinely sorry they won't have the time to eat.

5. Have Mr. Lucky begin preparing the skewers by alternating the tofu, cucumber, and scallions with little rolled-up slices of meat on each skewer. (Draw a simple diagram if necessary.) Submerge the skewers in the simmering broth just long enough to cook the meat, about 2 minutes.

6. Using a fork, push the cooked meat and vegetables off the skewers and into soup bowls. Put a handful of cabbage and spinach mixture in each bowl. Top with a ladleful of hot broth and a dollop of chili-soy sauce.

Yield: 6–8 servings

Smart & Smarter

Here's a handy dandy entertaining tip: throw a soup on a stick party. You make the basic broth then invite all your friends to bring their favorite pricey meats and vegetables already skewered and ready for the pot.

Inside Scoop

Farrelly Brothers projects mean big dating opportunities for Jim Carrey. During the shoot for this movie, it was Lauren Holly. On *Me, Myself and Irene*, it was Renée Zellweger. Apparently, there's no truth to the rumor that Zippy the Dog was wearing an engagement ring at the end of *Ace Ventura: Pet Detective*.

"The larger the bra-size, the smaller the IQ."
—*Rush Limbaugh*

Ferris Bueller's Day Off *1986*

Can't Go to School, I Falafel

For the falafel mixture:

1/4 cup bulgur wheat

2 cups canned garbanzo beans, aka chickpeas or ceci beans

2 teaspoons cumin

1 teaspoon coriander

1/2 teaspoon ground turmeric

1/8 teaspoon cayenne

1 tablespoon chopped garlic

1 tablespoon lemon juice

1 teaspoon salt

1/4 cup parsley

1 piece pita bread, finely chopped

Peanut oil, for frying

For the tahini sauce:

1 cup sesame paste

1 cup water

3 tablespoons lemon juice

2 teaspoons garlic

Salt to taste

Suggested garnishes:

Lettuce, tomatoes, pepperoncini, radishes, sprouts, more pita bread, a note from your mom.

We would never condone playing hooky—at least not in print—but sometimes you need a break. This recipe is so simple, it's like taking a night off from cooking.

1. Cover the bulgur wheat with warm water and soak for 20 minutes.

2. Drain the soaked bulgur and combine with the garbanzos, cumin, coriander, turmeric, cayenne, garlic, lemon juice, and salt in the work bowl of a food processor. Pulse 2 or 3 times, until well chopped but not puréed.

3. Transfer to a mixing bowl; stir in the parsley and chopped pita bread and refrigerate at least 20–30 minutes.

4. Combine the tahini sauce ingredients in a food processor and blend until smooth. Refrigerate until use.

5. Heat peanut oil in a heavy saucepan or deep fryer until 350–360°F. Wet hands and shape the falafel mixture into small balls about the size of a small walnut.

6. Fry the balls, a few at a time, until crisp and golden, about 3 minutes. Serve immediately in a warmed pita pocket with tahini sauce and garnishes of choice.

7. When it's time to clean up, call in sick.

Yield: Serves 4

Make Snacks, Not War…

Add another obstacle to Arab-Israeli peace. While this humble snack has been enjoyed for centuries all over the Middle East, many Arabs are steamed that Israel has recently designated the falafel as its own national dish. Gaining enough popularity to actually be called "the Israeli hotdog," this tasty repast has even been celebrated in a popular Israeli song titled "And We Have Falafel" which proclaims: "It used to be when a Jew came to Israel he kissed the ground and gave thanks/Now as soon as he gets off the plane he has a falafel." Either way, all we are saying is give chickpeas a chance.

CHEW ON THIS

Though Matthew Broderick became engaged to his *Ferris Bueller* co-star Jennifer Grey after they made this film together, he didn't actually make it to the altar until 1997 when he married "Sex & the City" star Sarah Jessica Parker.

Inside Scoop

If Ferris' high school looks familiar, that's probably because it was the setting for another John Hughes movie, *The Breakfast Club*. For the record, it's Glenbrook North High School in Illinois. The north Chicago suburbs where Hughes has shot so many of his movies are informally known as the "John Hughes Back Lot."

A Few Good Men 1992

1 pound dried black beans
2 red onions
1 whole head garlic
1 green bell pepper, finely diced
2 smoked ham hocks
1 bay leaf
2 teaspoons cumin
1 tablespoon chopped fresh thyme
   or oregano
1 quart chicken broth
1/2 cup sherry vinegar
1 teaspoon fresh oregano
3 tablespoons dry sherry
Salt and black pepper, to taste
1 kitchen code of honor, held with
   conviction

Inside Scoop

Best known as the creator of the Emmy®-award winning TV show, "The West Wing," writer Aaron Sorkin got the idea for *A Few Good Men* from a conversation he had with his older sister, Deborah, a Navy lawyer who had investigated a case similar to the one portrayed.

You Can't Handle the Soup!

Sure you'd like a hot, steaming bowl of Cuban black-bean soup. Everyone does! But are you ready to pick through the beans? Chop the onions 'til tears pour out of your eyes? Grind spices 'til your fingers are raw? The price of soup doesn't come cheap.

1. Pick through beans and discard any that are broken; also discard pebbles or any object that does not appear to be a bean. Rinse well; transfer to a large pot and cover with cold water. Bring to a boil; remove from heat and let soak for 30 minutes.

2. Finely chop one of the onions and slice the garlic head in half. Add these to the beans and then add the bell pepper, ham hocks, bay leaf, cumin, and thyme. Add the chicken broth and as much cold water as needed to cover the mixture by 2 inches. Return to a boil; reduce heat and simmer until the beans are tender (at least an hour). Stir every 20 minutes to prevent the bottom from scorching. Remove garlic and discard.

3. While the soup cooks, slice the remaining onion very thinly;

place in a bowl and toss with sherry vinegar. Add the oregano and a pinch of salt; set aside.

4. When the beans are soft enough, remove and puree 2 cups, then stir back into the soup. Add the sherry and a grinding of black pepper. Remove the ham hocks; chop and set aside. Check the soup for seasoning.

5. Serve the soup as is or over white rice. Garnish with chopped ham hock and sliced, marinated red onion.

6. After dinner, announce with quietly seething anger and unbridled contempt that any guests not reporting for KP duty will be given a kitchen "code red."

Yield: Serves 6–8

Archeological excavations of prehistoric kitchens offer evidence that black beans—also known as Turtle, Black Spanish, Tampico, or Phaseolus Vulgaris (our favorite appellation)—are thought to have originated over 7,000 years ago in Southern Mexico. Apparently they keep well.

CHEW ON THIS

The Guantanamo Bay naval base is the oldest U.S. base outside the continental U.S. and the only one in a communist country. The U.S. leases the 71-square-mile tract from Cuba for a whopping $4,085 per year. If you wonder why Cuba allows us to continue this arrangement—despite hostile relations between our countries—it's because one of the terms of the lease requires that the U.S. and Cuba must mutually consent to terminate the agreement.

The Great Outdoors

Campfire Grilled Vegetable Salad

2 red bell peppers
2 yellow bell peppers
2 Japanese eggplants
2 small yellow squash
2 small zucchini
1 red onion
2 bunches leeks
1 cup extra-virgin olive oil
1/4 cup flat leaf parsley, chopped
8–10 cloves garlic, minced
1/4 cup cider vinegar
2 teaspoons cumin seed, toasted and ground
Salt and pepper
1 bottle calamine lotion
1 set sheet music to "Kumbaya, Kumbaya"
1 very long extension cord for television

FOOD FOR THOUGHT

Want a grilled vegetable soup instead of salad? After the vegetables have been grilled and cut into pieces, cover with a rich chicken or vegetable stock and simmer for 20 to 30 minutes. Season to taste with salt and pepper and garnish with chopped parsley.

Nothing beats the wilderness for getting away from it all. You leave the workaday week behind to rough it, commune with nature, and enjoy all the sounds of the forest: the wind in the trees, the hoot of an owl, the babbling brook, the theme song from "Dinner & a Movie" blasting from the surround-sound of the giant plasma-screen TV you packed in with you to the campsite. Sure, getting back to nature is great, but you can't miss the show.

1. Prepare the Salad Fixin's. Cut the peppers in half lengthwise, slice off the white membrane, and remove the seeds.

2. Slice the Japanese eggplant, yellow squash, and zucchini lengthwise, into 1/2-inch slices.

3. Peel the red onion and slice into 1/2-inch rounds.

4. Trim the root bundle and the dark green ends from the leeks, slice in half lengthwise, and rinse well in an icy mountain stream (or under the tap). Wrap the leeks in foil and set aside.

5. In a small bowl, whisk together the olive oil, parsley, and garlic. Brush the sliced vegetables lightly with the mixture.

6. Prepare a good-sized charcoal or mesquite fire. Allow it to burn down to ash-topped coals before arranging the coals evenly throughout the firepit. Look around for a wire brush to clean the grill for about a minute before giving up and using a paper towel like always.

7. Working in batches, grill the vegetables on both sides until nicely marked. Depending on the intensity of the fire, figure about 2 to 3 minutes per side, with the exception of the leeks, which should cook for 5 minutes in their foil jackets before being unwrapped and grilled.

8. Cut the grilled vegetables into 2-inch to 3-inch pieces and place in a large mixing bowl. Add the vinegar and cumin to the olive oil mixture and whisk together before pouring the dressing over the warm vegetables and tossing. Transfer to a platter, season with salt and pepper, and serve.

9. Experts agree: For the best flavor when cooking outdoors, always use as much "borrowed" wood as possible from neighboring cabins and campsites.

Yield: Serves 4–6

Inside Scoop

Both Dan Aykroyd and John Candy are alumni of the Second City comedy troupe's Canadian branch in Toronto. Your comedic education won't be complete until you've seen Candy and other Second City Toronto alums on the classic sketch comedy show "SCTV," available at a video store near you. Dr. Tongue, we love you!

CHEW ON THIS

Next time you invite guests over for a BBQ, here's a way to keep from having hungry people lurking around hating you whilst waiting for the coals to be ready. Wow your guests by carefully using a hair dryer to blow the coals to perfection in as little as five minutes. If they still hate you after this trick, don't blame us.

Grumpy Old Men 1993

Young at Hearts of Romaine Seizure Salad

For the dressing:

8 anchovy fillets (reserve oil)

1 egg yolk (or substitute 1 tablespoon mayonnaise)

1 ½ teaspoon Dijon mustard

1 tablespoon garlic, finely chopped

1 teaspoon freshly ground black pepper

2 tablespoons fresh lemon juice

1 teaspoon red wine vinegar

1 teaspoon Worcestershire sauce

1 cup good Parmesan cheese, freshly grated

3/4 cup pure olive oil (not extra-virgin)

2 tablespoons ice water

For the croutons:

2 tablespoons pure olive oil

2 tablespoons reserved anchovy oil

1 tablespoon garlic, finely chopped

1 teaspoon fresh thyme, chopped

1 baguette, cut into 1/4-inch cubes

Salt and pepper to taste

For the salad:

6 hearts of Romaine, washed and chilled

1 bone to pick

1 grudge held, with gusto

What the hell are you lookin' at, Wisenheimer?! You've never seen a foolproof recipe for a perfect Caesar salad? Well shut your pie hole and maybe you'll learn something. In our day, people used to walk ten miles through the snow for a good Caesar . . .

1. *Dressing, I'm supposed to make dressing?* In a medium mixing bowl, mash half of the anchovy fillets. Add the egg yolks, mustard, garlic, black pepper, lemon juice, vinegar, Worcestershire, and 1/2 cup of the grated Parmesan. Whisk all ingredients together, making sure to complain audibly if the movement causes any pain.

2. *All this exercise can't be good.* Add the olive oil in a slow steady stream while whisking constantly. (If you haven't alienated everyone within earshot, it's a good idea to ask someone to help by trickling in the oil a little at a time while you whisk.) Keep whisking until all the oil has been emulsified and the dressing (and most likely your whisking arm) is quite stiff. If the dressing gets a little too thick, whisk in a couple of tablespoons of ice water.

3. *What's with the fancy toast on my salad?* Combine the anchovy oil, olive oil, garlic, thyme, salt, and pepper in a large skillet and place over medium heat. Add the croutons and toss to coat with the oil. Continue cooking until the croutons begin to turn golden brown, stirring constantly.

4. *My heart, it's my heart!* Tear the hearts of Romaine into bite-sized pieces or larger, depending on the fit of your dentures.

5. *Sorry, false alarm . . . (not that you care).* Toss the hearts with a ladleful of the dressing. Pile onto chilled plates and top with warm croutons, anchovies, and grated Parmesan. (Feel free to serve with any fresh grilled catch from recent ice-fishing excursions.)

6. *Goodness, what a lovely evening this has been!* Muster all available acting prowess and make the transformation into "chipper and adorable curmudgeon" just long enough to recruit plenty of help with the dishes. Then kick everybody out and watch the lottery results!

Yield: 4–6 servings

FOOD
FOR THOUGHT

Culinary legend has it that the classic Caesar salad was a spur of the moment creation of restaurateur Caesar Cardini of Tijuana, Mexico in 1924. Running out of normal menu items, he instructed the wait staff to take those now famous ingredients out to the dining room and ceremoniously prepare them tableside with a flourish. The International Society of Epicures in Paris would later name his salad "greatest to originate from the Americas in 50 years." Apparently they hadn't tasted our cousin Bunny's Chocolate Calamari Roll-ups.

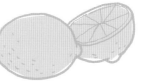

No Prescription Necessary

Forget the Viagra, the anchovies in a traditional Caesar salad are believed to have aphrodisiacal properties. (FYI...so do pomegranates, watercress, dates, chocolate, pickles, asparagus, and, of course, snails. That would explain those yearnings while gardening.)

Inside Scoop

Including *Grumpy Old Men*, Jack Lemmon and Walter Matthau starred in 12 movies together including their signature roles in *The Odd Couple*. Both funny guys in real life, Walter Matthau often claimed his real name was Walter Matasschanskayasky, but after his death it was revealed that he invented this name to sound more exotic. His real real name is allegedly Walter Matthow.

This recipe contains raw eggs which may be harmful to anyone very old, very young, or with health problems. If you're concerned, try substituting one tablespoon of mayonnaise for each egg yolk.

CHEW ON THIS

Today, one in eight Americans is over 65, but by the year 2030 the number will be one in four. We've seen the future and it's really grumpy.

Look Who's Talking

1989

Oh, Clam-Up Chowder!

3 cups water

2 cups clam juice

2 bay leaves

3 cloves garlic, peeled and crushed

3 sprigs fresh thyme

8 pounds littleneck or cherrystone clams

1/2 cup diced bacon

2 tablespoons butter

1 onion, diced medium

2 stalks celery, diced medium

3 tablespoons all-purpose flour

2 pounds small red potatoes, diced medium

1/4 cup chopped parsley

1–2 cups cream or half & half

Black pepper to taste

1 tiny ball gag

Clams keeping you up nights with their incessant yammering? Here's a delicious way to shut them up.

1. Combine the water, clam juice, bay leaves, garlic, and thyme in a large pot over high heat and bring to a boil.

2. Add clams; cover and cook until clams are just opening, about 5–7 minutes. Remove from heat, and when the clams are cool enough to handle, shuck over the pot to collect juices. Strain the liquid into a medium saucepan and keep warm until use.

3. Chop the clam meat and set aside.

4. Cook the bacon over medium heat until crisp. Pour off and discard the grease, then add the butter, onion, and celery, and cook 5 minutes until soft and translucent.

5. Add the flour to the bacon and onion mixture and continue cooking 2 more minutes, without browning. Stir often.

6. Whisk in the hot clam broth and then add the potatoes. Cook until the potatoes have softened, but are not falling apart. Add the reserved minced clams, parsley, cream, and black pepper. Serve immediately.

7. After dinner, cast your friends in the lead roles of your fabulous new movie "Look Who's Washing."

Yield: Serves 6–8

Spill The Beans

Not surprisingly, director Amy Heckerling came up with the idea for *Look Who's Talking* while she was pregnant.

FOOD
FOR THOUGHT

When you buy live clams at a fish market, generally they'll be given to you in a plastic bag. If you leave them in the bag and put them in the refrigerator, they're going to suffocate because they need oxygen—they're alive. Putting them in water won't work either because that also doesn't provide enough oxygen. What you need to do is put them in a dry bowl, cover them with a damp cloth and pop them in the fridge. They'll live for days, happy as clams. What's the dead giveaway of a deceased clam? It doesn't open when you cook it. If this happens to you, we recommend a timely burial . . . in your trashcan.

$\mathcal{M}$edicine $\mathcal{M}$an
1992

$\mathcal{M}$iraculously Cured Salmon Salad

For the salmon:

1/4 cup kosher salt

1/4 cup brown sugar

2 teaspoons ground coriander

1 teaspoon cracked black pepper

Zest and juice of 1 orange

Four 8 ounce salmon fillets

1/3 cup each: hickory chips, raw brown rice, and brown sugar

1 tablespoon loose tea

For the sauce:

2 firm, ripe tomatoes, diced

2 cloves garlic, finely chopped

2 jalapeño chiles, finely chopped

2 tablespoons coconut milk

Juice of 2 limes

2 tablespoons dende oil (use peanut oil if unavailable)

1/4 teaspoon salt

For the salad:

1 can hearts of palm, thinly sliced

1/2 cup coarsely chopped cilantro

1/2 cup coarsely chopped parsley

1 onion, thinly sliced

1 quart Ben and Jerry's® "Rain Forest Crunch"

Open wide and say mmmmm . . . Sean Connery plays a hard-drinking rogue doctor searching for an Amazon miracle cure. You won't have to search any further for the cure to hunger. This delicately smoked salmon is delicious and making it doesn't hurt a bit. If you doubt our diagnosis, get a second opinion.

1. Combine the salt, sugar, coriander, black pepper, orange zest, and juice in a small mixing bowl.

2. Rub the salt mixture evenly over both sides of the salmon fillets, cover, and refrigerate 30 minutes.

3. Meanwhile, place the wood chips in a small bowl and cover with hot water.

4. Make the sauce: Combine all sauce ingredients in a small saucepan; heat and keep warm over a very low heat.

5. Line a large, heavy pot that has a tight fitting lid with aluminum foil.

6. Place the soaked wood chips, brown rice, brown sugar, and tea in the pot; lightly oil a wire rack and set it inside the pot, over the chips.

7. Scrape off all excess salt mixture from the salmon and arrange the fillets on the oiled rack.

8. Cover the pot tightly and place over medium heat.

9. When the pot just begins to smoke, reduce the heat to low and continue smoking another 15–20 minutes, until salmon is firm to the touch.

10. Toss together the hearts of palm, cilantro, parsley, and onion.

11. Serve the salmon warm over the palm heart salad and spoon the warm dressing over each fillet.

Yield: 4 servings

Inside Scoop

When John McTiernan was scouting locations for *Medicine Man*, he returned to Borneo's rain forest where he'd shot most of *Predator* five years earlier. Ironically, the forest had already vanished, just as the *Medicine Man* script predicted. Our solution: eat more wild salmon. A significant percentage of rain forest deforestation is for beef production.

Rain Forest-Saving Tip #237

Don't stand in front of the refrigerator with the door open for more than 45 minutes at a time.

No Prescription Necessary

Due to thousands of years of natural selection, wild salmon provide far greater amounts of Omega-3 fatty acids than farmed salmon. Not only do these miraculous oils provide richer flavor, but numerous studies suggest that Omega-3s can reduce serum cholesterol, lower blood pressure, aid bone growth, fend off breast cancer, and bolster the immune system.

CHEW ON THIS

Curing food, whether by smoke, salt, or acid, is one of the oldest and tastiest forms of food preservation. Speaking of tasty preservation, Sean Connery was born more than seven decades ago in Scotland.

National Lampoon's Vacation 1983

Road Trip Tri-Tip Sandwich

Life on the road can leave you with a hunger the size of The Giant Ball of Twine. Especially after unexpected detours to The House of Mud, The Corn Palace, Fluker's Worm Farm and Ye Olde Trailer Park O' Trashy Relatives. Keep up your strength with a juicy barbecue sandwich that's spicy enough to stop highway hypnosis and get you back on the road to wherever it is you're going.

CHEW ON THIS

This film was based on the article "Vacation '58," by writer/director John Hughes. It appeared in the September 1979 issue of *National Lampoon*.

For the tri-tip:
One 2–3 pound beef tri-tip or sirloin tip roast
1 tablespoon each: ground black pepper, ground oregano, ground cumin, celery salt, garlic powder, and paprika
4 large seeded hamburger buns

For the sauce:
2 tablespoons butter
1 medium onion, diced
4 cloves garlic, finely chopped
1 teaspoon dry mustard
4 tablespoons brown sugar
1 teaspoon instant coffee
1–2 tablespoons hot pepper sauce
2 cups tomato sauce
2/3 cup cider vinegar
Salt and pepper to taste

For the slaw:
4 tablespoons almond slivers, toasted
1/4 cup olive oil
2 tablespoons toasted sesame oil
3 tablespoons lemon juice
1/2 teaspoon mustard seed
1/2 teaspoon celery seed
1/2 head red cabbage, thinly sliced
2 ripe tomatoes, diced
3 ears fresh corn, cut from the cob
3 scallions, thinly sliced
Salt and black pepper to taste
Unfoldable road maps, ancient flares, and the most current hours of operation for Wally World

1. Fasten your seatbelts, check the mirrors and preheat the oven to 350°F.

2. "Are we there yet?" In a small bowl, combine the black pepper, oregano, cumin, celery salt, garlic powder, and paprika.

3. Rub the spice mix well into the meat and place the roast fat-side-up in a foil-lined pan. Bake for 45 minutes to an hour in the pre-heated oven, or until the internal temperature in the thickest part of the meat reads 120°–125°F.

4. While the tri-tip cooks, make the BBQ sauce. In a medium saucepan, over medium heat, melt the butter and sauté the onions and garlic until soft and golden.

5. Add the mustard, brown sugar, and instant coffee to the saucepan and cook for one minute, stirring constantly.

6. Stir in the hot pepper sauce, tomato sauce, and vinegar. When the mixture comes to a boil, reduce the heat and simmer 30 minutes. Check and adjust seasonings.

7. Remove the meat from the oven and let rest a few minutes before slicing thinly across the grain and returning to the roasting pan.

8. Slather the meat with plenty of warm sauce and return to the oven, then prepare the slaw.

9. In a large bowl, mix almonds, olive oil, sesame oil, lemon juice, mustard seed, and celery seed. Add the chopped cabbage, tomatoes, corn, and scallions. Season to taste with salt and pepper. Toss and refrigerate until serving.

10. Heat the buns, pile high with barbecued beef, smother with gobs of warm sauce and arrange entire meal precariously onto flimsy paper plates. Hop into the family wagon (beginning, yet again, another rousing chorus of "99 Bottles of Beer on the Wall") and get back on the open road, secure in the knowledge that your upholstery will never, ever look the same again.

Yield: 4 servings

Tri-Tip Tip

Practically unknown outside of California, the tri-tip wasn't popular until the early 1950s. A Santa Maria butcher reserved the triangular shaped tip of the bottom sirloin usually doomed to be ground into hamburger. He slow-roasted it, gave samples to his customers and called it tri-tip. The rest is history.

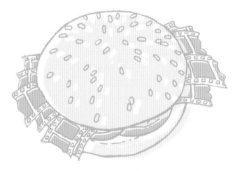

Inside Scoop

The Griswolds' original vacation destination was scripted as Disneyland, but it was changed to the fictitious Wally World when Disney objected to the finale in which the theme park is closed for repairs when the Griswolds arrive. They argued that the happiest place on earth is open 365 days a year. Do we take that to mean that nothing ever HAS to be repaired? That is a magic kingdom!

An Officer and A Gentleman 1982

Drop & Give Me 20 Bean Salad
(with Moody & Misunderstood Zack Mayo)

For the Zack mayo:

2 egg yolks
1/2 teaspoon Dijon mustard
1/2 teaspoon salt
2 tablespoons chopped chives
2 tablespoons chopped fresh dill
1 tablespoon fresh chervil
1 teaspoon red wine vinegar
1 ½ cups canola oil
2 tablespoons lemon juice
Salt and pepper to taste

For the 20 bean salad:

4 eggs
4 small red potatoes
10 green beans, trimmed
10 yellow wax beans, trimmed
1 head Boston or bibb lettuce
3 large tomatoes, quartered
1 can oil-packed solid white tuna
1/2 cup brine-cured olives
1/4 cup toasted almonds
1 large chip on shoulder

This recipe contains raw eggs which may be harmful to anyone very old, very young or with health problems.

Sound off, soldiers!
I don't know but I been told!
Eskimo Pies are really cold!
I don't know but I been taught!
Julia Child's really hot!

—New Recruit Chant from Claud Mann's Cooking Boot Camp

1. You eye ballin' me, boy?: Combine egg yolks, mustard, salt, chives, dill, chervil, and vinegar in the work bowl of a food processor.

2. Process at high speed while adding the oil a few drops at a time. Add the lemon juice and correct seasonings to taste. Cover and refrigerate.

3. You're not worthy to boil the eggs!: Place the eggs in a medium saucepan and cover with cold water. Bring to a boil, remove from heat, cover and let stand for 25 minutes. Peel and quarter when cool enough to handle.

4. Prep the veggies ... Now prep them again, AND DO IT RIGHT!: Fill a small saucepan with cold water and a pinch of salt, slice the potatoes into slices 1/4-inch thick, dropping the slices into the water as you work.

5. Bring the potatoes to a simmer and cook 3 to 4 minutes, until tender. Drain, toss with a few drops of olive oil and refrigerate.

6. Cook the beans in lightly salted boiling water until tender, about 5 minutes. Immediately refresh by plunging into ice water until cool to the touch.

7. You're never gonna get through this salad; why don't you quit now, and make it easy on everyone? Arrange lettuce on plates and top decoratively with the eggs, potatoes, beans, tuna, tomatoes, olives and almonds.

8. We suggest serving the dressing on the side. (Not everyone can tolerate the same amount of Zack Mayo.)

9. Wait until it's time to do the dishes, then dramatically announce you've decided to D.O.R., and head for the hills. Dis-Missed!

Yield: 4 servings

FOOD FOR THOUGHT

Richard Gere owes John Travolta for three big breaks in his career. *Days of Heaven*, *American Gigolo*, and *An Officer and A Gentleman* were all turned down by Travolta before being offered to Gere. We can only assume Gere would like to thank Travolta for NOT passing on "The Boy in the Plastic Bubble."

Inside Scoop

Some ingredients need a little encouragement to mix. Vinegar and oil, for instance, need an egg to emulsify into a delicious mayonnaise. From all reports, Deborah Winger and Richard Gere didn't exactly mix well off-screen either, yet their on-screen chemistry—especially in the racy love scenes—made film history. Perhaps they were emulsified by their mutual need for a hit film.

Raiders of the Lost Ark 1981

Extra Cheesy Spielburgers

Starring (in order of appearance):

2 pounds either beef chuck, top round, chicken or turkey thighs, or lean lamb, very cold

1/4 cup crushed ice

1/4 cup chopped scallions

2 tablespoons chopped parsley

1 teaspoon freshly cracked black pepper

Kosher salt to taste

1 pound sharp cheddar, thinly sliced

2 tablespoons butter

2 cups sliced mushrooms

2 tablespoons peanut oil

1 beefsteak tomato, sliced

1 white onion, thinly sliced

1 small head romaine lettuce

Condiments galore

4 buns (plus 2 bun stand-ins)

Inside Scoop

During filming in Tunisia, nearly everyone in the cast and crew got sick except Spielberg. He reportedly avoided illness by eating an endless stream of canned Spaghetti-Os® he had brought with him.

Rumor has it that Steven Spielberg might be a "Dinner & a Movie" fan. And Steven, we're big fans of yours. Hey, we work on a cooking show. Knowing which side our bread is buttered on is practically our business. We like Steve, hopefully he likes us, and . . . hopefully . . . he'll like one of those 14 action-packed, food-adventure scripts we've got in our bottom drawer.

As long as you're here, let me pitch this . . . it all starts when a TV chef discovers a mystical golden strainer empowered with the ability to separate not only egg yolks but good from evil . . .

1. Pre-production: After casting the role of "leading meat" for your extravaganza, contact the representing agent and begin negotiations. (Scale plus 10% and a few points on the meal should secure the deal.) Cut the meat into 1–2-inch pieces and transfer to a food processor. Add the crushed ice and using short pulses, grind the meat to the consistency of coarse hamburger. Don't overgrind (or over direct) or the meat will become tough. Transfer to a mixing bowl, add the scallions, parsley and black pepper; mix together well.

2. Divide the meat into 4 equal pieces. Form each piece into a virtual blockbuster of a burger, each one more fantastic and wildly successful than the one before it. (If really aspiring to greatness, try forming the patties around a fat chunk of cheese...who cares if it throws you over budget and behind schedule, this is your vision, dammit!) Season both sides of the patties with kosher salt and refrigerate.

3. Sauté the mushrooms in butter (assuring them privately all the while that they are the real stars of this meal.) Season with salt and pepper and set aside.

4. Production: Heat a heavy cast-iron skillet over a medium-high heat until very hot. Quickly brush the pan with peanut oil and ask the assistant director to call for the patties.

5. After the patties have walked through the blocking and are comfortable with their motivations, shout ACTION! and thrust them into the pan. The scene should last about 4 minutes; flip them and do the reversals, then top each burger with as much cheese as you can get away with.

6. Continue working until each burger is cooked precisely the way you want it . . . if you want "rare," yell CUT now! . . . if you feel "medium" will help skew a larger, younger audience, then continue cooking 2 minutes longer.

7. Smother each burger with sautéed mushrooms and excruciatingly obsequious accolades (making a mental note to phone their agent and kvetch about how impossible they were to work with).

8. Post-production: Give yourself a pat on the back and exit stage right before someone directs you to do the dishes.

Yield: 4 servings

Lactose Intolerant? Read no further...

If you doubt how much people love cheese, consider this: FIVE of the twenty top-grossing movies of all time were directed by Steven Spielberg.

CHEW ON THIS

No one disputes that the hamburger was named for the famous seaport town of Hamburg, Germany. However, the first U.S. appearance of this quintessentially American, bun-encased, handheld banquet is a subject of sizzling debate. Although many food historians theorize burgers were born during the 1904 St. Louis World's Fair—Louisiana Purchase Exposition, we decided to resolve this once and for all. Alas, after a sea of condiments and countless root beers, we were too bloated and sleepy to reach an official consensus.

Spaceballs

1987

A long time ago, in a galaxy far, far away...

6 large beets, washed and trimmed
3 large cloves garlic, peeled
2 tablespoons olive oil
1 small onion, sliced thinly
2 leeks, white part only, finely chopped
1 Granny Smith apple, peeled, cored, and diced
1 small turnip, diced
2 cups chicken stock or water
Juice of 1/2 lemon
3 tablespoons rice wine vinegar
Salt and pepper to taste
1 cup sour cream
Juice and zest of 1 orange
2 tablespoons toasted walnuts
2 tablespoons chopped fresh dill
Plenty of chutzpah
2 cinnamon rolls and some bobby pins

The Beet Goes On

Always cook beets unpeeled with the root and 2 inches of the tops still attached. This prevents the loss of flavor and nutrients. Ironically, beets were originally grown for the part most people throw out today, their green tops. We say chop those tops and cook 'em like kale or chard.

May the Borscht Be with You

A long time ago (almost as long as it's been since my ungrateful son last visited me) in a galaxy far, far away (almost as far as I'd travel for a delicious bowl of beet soup)...

1. Place the beets and garlic cloves in a pot; cover with cold water and bring to a boil. Reduce the heat and simmer, uncovered for 30–45 minutes, until the beets are tender.

2. While the beets cook, heat the olive oil in a large, heavy saucepan over medium-low heat. Add the sliced onion, leeks, green apple, and turnip. Cook slowly until tender, about 15 minutes.

3. Rinse the beets under running water until cool to the touch; the peel should slide off easily. Cut into quarters.

4. Working in 2 to 3 batches, place the beets, garlic cloves, onion mixture, and chicken stock in a blender or food processor and process until smooth.

5. Season with the lemon juice, rice wine vinegar, salt and pepper. Cover and chill the soup.

6. Combine the sour cream and the orange juice and zest and set aside.

7. Ladle the soup into chilled bowls, completing each serving with a dollop of orange cream and a sprinkling of walnuts and dill.

8. So why aren't you eating? . . . Eat!

Yield: 4 servings

Inside Scoop

At one time Mel Brooks was the social director and resident comic at Grossinger's, the famous Jewish resort in the Catskills. Grossinger's and other Jewish hotels formed the legendary "Borscht Belt" which became the training ground for top comedians during its heyday of the '50s and '60s.

CHEW ON THIS

After the release of the *Star Wars* prequel *Phantom Menace*, video rentals of *Spaceballs* went up a reported 73 percent.

Top Gun

For the stew:

One 4-pound pork shoulder butt

4 cups chicken stock

2 yellow onions, quartered

2 heads garlic, cut in half crosswise

3 bay leaves

Cold water, to cover

Two 30-ounce cans white hominy, drained

For the picante sauce:

1 cup dried chiles

2 ½ cups water

1/2 teaspoon salt

2 tablespoons white vinegar

For the garnishes:

3 roma tomatoes

2 white onions

3 avocados

6 lemons

1/4 head red cabbage

1 bunch cilantro

2 bunches radishes

4 jalapeño peppers

Whole oregano

1 virile, suitably masculine, animal-inspired nickname (appropriately, Chef Claud's moniker is food inspired—when things get too hot in the kitchen, he only answers to "Daikon".)

Pentagon "Pork Barrel" Pozole

The phrase "pork barrel politics" comes from the pre-Civil War era practice of distributing salt pork to the slaves from huge barrels. By 1870, congressmen were referring regularly to dipping into the "pork barrel" to obtain our tax dollars for often unnecessary projects in their home districts. Of course we're not saying the Top Gun program was unnecessary. Any program that could inspire another testosterone-fueled blockbuster replete with power ballad is worth whatever price we have to pay. If the Cold War did nothing else, it gave the world "Take My Breath Away" and gave us a compelling reason to make one of our favorite Mexican soups.

1. Make the stew: Trim pork butt of excess fat and cut into four pieces. Rinse meat with cold water and transfer to a large stockpot.

2. Add the chicken stock, quartered onion, garlic, and bay leaves. Add enough cold water to just cover the meat and bring to a boil.

3. Reduce the heat to a simmer and cook for 45 minutes, occasionally skimming off any fat or scum that rises to the top.

4. Make the picante sauce: Combine the dried chiles, water, salt and vinegar in a small saucepan over medium-high heat. Boil for five minutes, transfer to a blender jar, and puree. Strain into a bowl and set aside.

5. Prepare the garnishes: Dice the tomatoes, onions, and avocado; quarter the lemons; chop the cabbage and cilantro; thinly slice the radishes and jalapeños.

6. When the meat begins to soften and fall apart, add the hominy and return to a simmer.

7. Salt to taste and ladle into the largest bowls you can find.

8. Season individually at the table with lemon and salsa picante and garnish with abandon.

9. (Remember to retain and scrutinize your grocery bill. If you're paying any more than $1,500 per pound for onions, you should have your lobbyist call their lobbyist and work something out.)

Yield: 6–8 servings

CHEW ON THIS

Some estimates put the cost of the Cold War at $8 trillion.

A key ingredient in Mexican folk dishes like pozole and menudo, hominy was one of the first foods the colonists appropriated from the Native Americans. Consisting of dried white or yellow corn kernels with the hull and germ removed, whole hominy is commonly used in soups and casseroles and ground hominy is used to make that most revered American folk dish, grits.

Inside Scoop

Technically, Tom Cruise is not quite tall enough to be a navy pilot. Their minimum height is 5 feet, 8 inches, and Maverick reportedly squeaks in at 5 feet, 7 inches.

Trading Places

1983

Celery Root of All Evil Soup with Pork Belly Croutons

For the vegetable stock:

2 tablespoons olive oil

2 leeks, thinly sliced

5 cloves crushed, unpeeled garlic

1 ½ teaspoons salt

2 stocks celery, roughly chopped

1 fennel bulb, sliced

1/2 bunch parsley stems

5 whole black peppercorns

1 bay leaf

1/2 cup white wine

1 ½ quarts cold water

For the soup:

1 large celery root (also called celeriac), peeled and diced

1 medium leek, thinly sliced

1 medium yellow onion, thinly sliced

1 medium yellow potato, peeled and sliced

1 sprig each: thyme and tarragon, tied together with a piece of string

1/2 pound pork belly (bacon), diced

2 cups cubed French bread

1/2 cup cream

Salt and pepper to taste

An uncanny, innate sense of global commodities

Dan Aykroyd and Eddie Murphy live out a nature vs. nurture experiment in this 1983 comedy classic. We contend that all good things come not just from nature or nurture but from a combination of the two. Celery root, for instance, was created by nature but with a little nurturing can be made into this delicious soup.

1. Combine the olive oil, leeks, garlic and salt in a stock pot over medium-low heat. Cook slowly without browning for 10 minutes.

2. Add the celery, fennel, parsley stems, peppercorns, bay leaf and white wine; cook until the wine reduces by half, then cover with the cold water and bring to a boil.

3. Once the stock reaches a boil, reduce the heat and simmer uncovered anywhere from 30-45 minutes (although a longer cooking time generally yields a more highly flavored stock, there is no penalty for early withdrawal).

4. Strain the vegetable stock into a large saucepan. (You may skip steps 1-4 if using a canned stock...not as rich but a recommended stock option.)

5. Combine the celery root, leek, onion, potato and the bundled herb sprigs with the vegetable stock.

6. Cover and simmer until the vegetables are quite soft, about 30 minutes.

7. Meanwhile, call your broker. If pork bellies are up, proceed to the next step. (If pork bellies are down, consider diversifying your ingredients and attempting this recipe during the next fiscal year.)

8. Fry pork belly until crisp; drain all but one tablespoon of grease from the pan and stir in bread cubes. Cook, stirring often until golden brown. Set aside.

9. Remove the bundled herbs from the soup; working in batches, puree mixture in a food processor or blender. (Always use caution when blending hot liquids.)

10. Stir in the cream; check and correct seasonings to taste. Cover and keep warm.

11. Call your guests to the table. If their interest remains at an all time high, divide soup into four bowls, garnish with pork belly croutons and ask yourself again: "How can anything so inherently evil taste so good?"

Yield: 4 servings

FOOD FOR THOUGHT

Celery root or *celeriac* is simply a variety of celery grown for its large, flavorful root. Until the 17th century, it was considered to be a powerful aphrodisiac and used primarily as a marital aid. It can be eaten raw, made into soup or steamed and pureed. Like any other root vegetable, anything you can do with a carrot you can do with a consenting celeriac, depending on the laws in your county.

Inside Scoop

Beginning his career as a stand-up comedian when he was just 16, Eddie Murphy made his television debut as a part-time player during the disappointing 1980 season of "Saturday Night Live." He quickly became the cast's break-out performer though he was only 19 at the time.

CHEW ON THIS

Apparently, piggish behavior is nothing new to the New York Stock Market. History tells us that founding city fathers were having so much trouble with marauding hogs they built a long wall across town. Today, we know it as Wall Street. (Maybe the wall should go back up?)

Chapter **3**

Pasta
Side Dishes
et al.

Airplane!

1980

Thai Noodles with Airplane Nuts

When we think flying, we think nuts. This high-flying recipe uses plenty of 'em, and, surely, with the cost of airline tickets, these crunchy, in-flight treats don't come cheap. So next time you fly, hold onto your nuts. And—yeah, we know—don't call you Shirley.

For the noodles:

- 2 chicken breasts, skinless and boneless
- 2 tablespoons dry sherry
- 3 tablespoons soy sauce
- 1/4 cup peanut oil
- 5 cloves garlic, finely chopped
- 1 serrano or jalapeño pepper, finely chopped
- 1 tablespoon shredded pickled ginger
- 2 eggs, beaten
- 1/2 yellow bell pepper, sliced into 1/2-inch strips
- 1/2 pound spaghetti or vermicelli
- 1 cup mung bean sprouts
- 1 cup (or 8 flight-sized bags) plain peanuts, coarsely chopped
- 1 tablespoon ketchup
- 2 tablespoons Thai fish sauce (if unavailable, use anchovy paste)
- 1 tablespoon sugar
- 3 scallions, cut into 1-inch lengths

For the garnish:

- 1/4 cup coarsely chopped mint leaves
- 1/4 cup cilantro leaves
- 3 limes, cut into quarters
- 1 teaspoon red pepper flakes
- 1/4 cup crushed peanuts
- 1 air-sickness bag (for leftovers)

1. Slice the chicken into thin strips and place in a small bowl. Add the sherry and half of the soy sauce. Cover, set aside, and remember, everyone is counting on you.

2. Cook the pasta al dente. Rinse well in cold water, drain, and set aside.

3. Prepare and lay out all ingredients where they can be reached quickly during the stir fry. Avoid touching eyes and sensitive areas of self and others after cutting chile peppers.

4. Using a wok or large cast-iron skillet, heat the peanut oil on high heat. Add the garlic, serrano pepper, and pickled ginger, and stir fry until light brown and fragrant.

5. Drain excess marinade from chicken and add to the wok along with the beaten eggs. Stir fry for 2 minutes and remember, everyone is counting on you.

6. Run cold water on any blistered areas of face or hands from oil splatters in steps 4 and 5.

7. Add the bell pepper, pasta, and half of the bean sprouts. Stir fry for another minute, and remember, everyone is counting on you.

8. Add the remaining soy sauce, peanuts, ketchup, fish sauce, and sugar. Cook for another minute, stirring often.

9. Mix in the scallions and transfer to a serving platter. Garnish with the remaining bean sprouts, fresh mint, cilantro, lime quarters, red pepper flakes, and peanuts.

10. At this point, your guests may begin to smell something wonderful coming from the kitchen and wonder what it is. (A large room with pots, pans, and a stove, but that's not important right now.)

Yield: 4 servings

Inside Scoop

Before the Farrelly Brothers, the Hudlin Brothers, or the Coen Brothers hit the film-making scene, the Zucker Brothers (along with their friend Jim Abrahams) had already proven that brotherly bonds could produce big box office. *Airplane* set the standard for a string of successful Zucker/Abrahams film parodies, including *Naked Gun* and *Hot Shots*. To get a first-hand glimpse of this writing-producing-directing team at work, catch their cameo appearance in the beginning of the film as the ground crew that directs the plane into the window.

CHEW ON THIS

Peanut oil is the oil most often used by Chinese chefs for wok cooking because it can be heated to well over 400° F before it smokes or burns.

The 'Burbs

For the cheese sauce:

3 cups whole milk
1/2 onion
1 bay leaf
2 whole cloves
1/2 cup butter
1/4 cup shallots, minced
1/3 cup flour
1 teaspoon dry mustard
1/8 teaspoon white pepper
1 tablespoon Worcestershire sauce
1 teaspoon chopped fresh thyme
1/8 teaspoon nutmeg
1/8 teaspoon cayenne
1/2 teaspoon salt

For the filling:

16 ounces dry macaroni
1 ½ cups grated Gruyere or
    Swiss cheese
2 cups grated cheddar cheese
1 ½ cups grated Parmesan cheese
1/2 cup bread crumbs
1 dirty little secret

Classic "Cul de Sac" Mac 'N' Cheese

. . . or as we like to call it, Dr. Klopeck's What's-That-Smell-in-the-Basement Hackaroni Casserole.

1. Preheat the oven to 375°F. Butter a 3-quart casserole.

2. Cook the macaroni al dente (a minute or two less than the package instructions). Rinse in cold water, drain, and set aside.

3. Make the cheese sauce: Pour the milk into a small saucepan. Tack the bay leaf to the onion with the cloves and place in the milk. Slowly bring the milk to a simmer on a medium-low heat.

4. Melt 1/2 of the butter in a medium saucepan over medium heat. Add the chopped shallots and cook until soft. Add the flour, dry mustard, and white pepper and cook another 3 minutes, stirring often.

5. Slowly add the hot milk to the butter and flour mixture, whisking constantly. Stir in the Worcestershire; transfer the clove-studded onion and simmer at least 20 minutes (stirring occasionally), until sauce is thick and creamy.

6. Remove from heat, discard the onion, and stir in 1/2 cup each of the grated cheddar and Gruyere. Whisk in the fresh thyme, nutmeg, cayenne, and salt.

7. Mix and bake: Turn the cooked, drained macaroni into the buttered casserole, add the hot cheese sauce, and stir together. Stir in 1/2 cup of the Parmesan and the remaining cheddar and Gruyere.

8. Sprinkle with the rest of the Parmesan cheese and the bread crumbs; dot with the remaining butter and bake uncovered in the upper third of the preheated oven for 30 minutes, or until brown and bubbly.

Yield: 8 servings

FOOD FOR THOUGHT

Suburbs began in the 1800s when improvements in transportation allowed people to live farther away from their work.

Cheese Fact #73

Legend has it that the first cheese probably was made by accident. In the Middle East, milk was commonly stored in bags made from animal intestines, which naturally contain rennet, the enzyme responsible for separating milk into curds and whey.

Comfort Food

As the world becomes a more frightening place, many Americans are returning to familiar, hearty food as a means of escaping a daily onslaught of national security issues, economic instability, and the dawning realization that neither party in government has a clue. Trendy restaurants nationwide have followed suit, and chic menus now offer meat loaf, pot roast, and mac 'n' cheese at prices that would make anyone need comfort.

CHEW ON THIS

Actress Carrie Fisher enjoyed a typical suburban upbringing—if you consider Beverly Hills a suburb and a famous actress mom and infamous crooner dad to be typical. Lucky for her, she had the grounding influence of stepmother Elizabeth Taylor to help keep her down to earth.

Inside Scoop

Tom Hanks was the first actor to win back-to-back Academy Awards® for Best Actor since Spencer Tracy did it in 1937 and 1938. Hanks won for *Philadelphia* and *Forrest Gump*. Tracy won for *Captains Courageous* and *Boys Town*.

Coal Miner's Daughter 1980

Butcher Holler Ham Hocks and Collards

1 tablespoon butter or olive oil

6 cloves garlic, peeled and crushed

3 smoked ham hocks (about 2 pounds)

1–2 quarts water or chicken stock

2 pounds collard greens

2 quarts water plus 1 tablespoon salt

4 cups fresh or frozen black-eyed peas

1 teaspoon freshly ground black pepper

1/2 teaspoon red pepper flakes

1 teaspoon chopped fresh thyme

2 teaspoons brown sugar

1 tablespoon cider vinegar

The desire to make it big . . . as big
   as your hair

Inside Scoop

Born in Butcher Holler, Kentucky, Loretta Lynn got married when she was 13 years old but didn't hit it big on the country music scene until she was 29. Lynn handpicked Sissy Spacek to portray her in this film. In addition to winning the Best Actress Oscar® for *Coal Miner's Daughter*, Spacek was also nominated for a Grammy for her rendition of the film's title song.

*This recipe was born
from a coal miner's table.
You watched it on "Dinner & a Movie"
if you've got cable . . .*

1. Heat the oil or butter in a large, heavy saucepan over medium heat. Add the garlic and ham hocks, and sauté until golden brown.

2. Cover with water or chicken stock and bring to a boil. Reduce heat and simmer 45 minutes to an hour.

3. While the hocks simmer, wash the greens thoroughly and remove the toughest part of the stems.

4. Bring 2 quarts lightly salted water to a boil in a large pot. Add the greens, stir, and cover; cook about 2 minutes, then transfer to a colander.

5. Rinse greens with cold water to stop the greens from cooking. Squeeze out excess water and coarsely chop. Set aside.

6. When the ham hocks begin to tender up some, take them out and pull off all the meat you can, chop it up, and add it back.

7. Give the bones to the dogs.

8. Add the black-eyed peas, black pepper, red pepper flakes, thyme, brown sugar, cider vinegar, and collards. Continue cooking at a simmer for about 20 minutes. Adjust seasonings to taste, and serve with hot, buttered cornbread.

9. Pick the biggest hussy at the table and tell her she's not only woman enough but actually welcome to take your man as long as she does the dishes first.

Yield: 4 servings

CHEW ON THIS
Spacek's first film appearance was as an extra in Andy Warhol's *Trash*.

They're Playing Our Song
The "Dinner & a Movie" theme song is "Beans & Cornbread" by Louis Jordan.

FOOD FOR THOUGHT

Tradition requires Southerners to eat black-eyed peas—which are really beans—on New Year's Day for good fortune in the coming year. No one is definite about the origins of this ritual but legend has it that it will ensure money in your pocket all year long. The black-eyed peas symbolize coins, the greens symbolize paper money, and the ham hocks come from pigs, the only animals that can't look back.

$\mathcal{D}$eceived

1991

1 cup cashews
1/2 cup walnuts
1/2 cup pine nuts
2 tablespoons butter
1 cup finely chopped leeks
1 tablespoon finely chopped garlic
1 cup chopped white mushrooms
1/2 ounce dried wild mushrooms,
    soaked in 1/2 cup warm water and
    finely chopped
Salt and pepper to taste
1 tablespoon each: chopped fresh
    parsley, thyme, and basil,
1 cup cooked brown rice
1/2 cup Grape Nuts™
1 cup cottage cheese
3 eggs, beaten
1/4 cup ketchup or tomato sauce
1 Acme brand "Fake Your Own
    Death Kit ⓉⓂ "

$\mathcal{S}$uper $\mathcal{E}$xtra $\mathcal{M}$eaty $\mathcal{M}$eatloaf

This classic thriller features Goldie Hawn as a wife who's been dealt the ultimate deception. But don't worry, we would never deceive you. We're TV people. You can trust us. This is the meatiest meatloaf ever. It's positively chock full of delicious, juicy, life-giving Meaty-Meat™. Would we lie to you? Of course not, we're TV people.

1. Toast the cashews, walnuts, and pine nuts on a baking sheet at 350°F for 10 minutes.

2. Coarsely chop the cashews and walnuts (leave the pine nuts whole) and set aside.

3. Sauté the leeks in butter until softened, but not brown. Add the garlic and reduce the heat to medium.

4. Add the chopped mushrooms and the mushroom-soaking liquid and cook over medium heat about 10 minutes. Season with salt and pepper to taste.

5. Transfer the hot mixture to a large mixing bowl and add the herbs, toasted nuts, brown rice, Grape Nuts™, cottage cheese, and eggs, and mix well.

6. Butter a 1½ quart baking dish or loaf pan and fill with the mixture and bake for 60 minutes. The top should be firm and nicely brown, but not burned. (Brush with tomato sauce or ketchup for the final 20 minutes, if desired.)

We Don't Know Who To Believe Anymore

Fooled you! Her real name is Goldie Studlendgehawn.

7. Serve up your meatless meatloaf secure in the knowledge that even your most carnivorous guest may be deceived by its hearty goodness.

8. Deploy your Acme brand "Fake Your Own Death Kit®" proving you'll do whatever it takes to avoid doing the dishes.

Yield: Serves 600

FOOD FOR THOUGHT

Where's the beef? Everywhere, apparently! If you think you're a vegetarian, you'd better think again. Less than 50 percent of an average steer ends up as retail beef cuts. The remainder ends up as (among other things) cosmetics, toothpaste, chalk, shampoo, car tires, explosives, buttons, violin strings, crayons, sporting equipment, and insulin.

Mushroom Tip #27

If you think commercial mushrooms are raised in fertilizer, you've been deceived. Fact is, these mushrooms are grown in sterile hothouse environments, so there's no need to soak or rinse them heavily with water before cooking. Mushrooms will absorb the excess water and ultimately lose flavor. So a simple wipe from front to back will do.

Groundhog Day

5 large russet potatoes
Olive oil to coat
1/2 cup sour cream or yogurt
1/2 cup of your favorite cheese (white cheddar, fontina, goat cheese, etc.)
1/2 cup chopped chives or green onions
2 tablespoons butter
2 tablespoons olive oil
4 whole, peeled cloves garlic
2 small Japanese eggplant (or 1 very small globe eggplant) thinly sliced
2 small zucchini or yellow squash, sliced thinly
1 large ripe tomato, chopped
1/2 cup olives, thinly sliced
Salt and freshly ground black pepper
All the time in the world

Bing!

The star of an amazing variety of films including *Mississippi Burning*, *Thelma & Louise*, and *Memento*, busy actor Stephen Tobolowsky also co-wrote the screenplay for *True Stories* with his college classmate, playwright Beth Henley and David Byrne, former member of the band The Talking Heads. His turn as *Groundhog Day*'s hapless insurance agent Ned Ryerson will always be our favorite though. Are we right or are we right? Ri-ri-ri-ri-right!

Déjà Vu Twice-Baked Potatoes

You wake up. You bake the potatoes. You bake the potatoes again. You eat the potatoes. They're delicious! You wake up. You bake the potatoes. You bake the potatoes again. You eat the potatoes. They're delicious! You wake up . . .

1. Preheat the oven to 425°F.

2. Scrub potatoes well under cold running water.

3. Dry and coat lightly with olive oil and place on the middle rack of the preheated oven. Bake for 25 minutes, then puncture the tops and continue baking another 30 minutes or until tender.

4. Allow the potatoes to cool, then slice the top quarter off each. Scoop out the flesh into a bowl and set the empty shells aside.

5. Combine the sour cream, cheese, and chives with the potato, and mash together. Season to taste with salt and freshly ground black pepper. Dot with butter, return to the oven, and bake another 15 minutes.

6. While the potatoes bake a second time, heat olive oil and garlic cloves in a sauté pan over medium high-heat.

7. As soon as the garlic begins to brown, remove it and set aside. Add the eggplant and zucchini slices and sauté 2 minutes. Add the tomato and olives, and reduce heat to low. Chop and add the reserved garlic; salt and pepper to taste.

8. Top the twice-baked potatoes with the vegetable sauté and more cheese. Serve immediately.

9. Repeat steps 1 through 8.

Yield: Serves 4

Inside Scoop

Groundhog Day was actually filmed in Woodstock, IL rather than the real Punxsutawney, PA. Harold Ramis selected Woodstock as the location because his parents lived nearby and he could spend time with them during the shoot. There's now a plaque that reads "Bill Murray stepped here" on the curb where Murray continually stepped into a puddle.

No Prescription Necessary

In this existential classic, Bill Murray's character confronts the same question homemakers face everyday: How do you do the same thing day after day without wanting to kill yourself? We're not sure what the answer is, but making potatoes is a good start. A complex carbohydrate, potatoes facilitate the production of serotonin which may not change your life but will certainly make you feel better about the life you have.

FOOD FOR THOUGHT

It is common knowledge that potatoes should be stored in a cool, dark location. However, the average refrigerator is just a little too cold for proper potato storage. Some of the starches in potatoes will actually convert to sugar when refrigerated for any length of time. Because sugar caramelizes at high heat, your fries might just burn before getting crisp.

CHEW ON THIS

The French translation of déjà vu is "already seen."

$\mathcal{M}$oonstruck

1987

$\mathcal{W}$hen the $\mathcal{M}$oon $\mathcal{H}$its $\mathcal{Y}$our $\mathcal{E}$ye $\mathcal{L}$ike a $\mathcal{C}$heese $\mathcal{P}$izza $\mathcal{P}$ie

The cast (in order of appearance):

3/4 cup lukewarm water

1 tablespoon active dry yeast

1 tablespoon honey

1/4 cup yellow corn meal

2 teaspoons salt

8 tablespoons extra-virgin olive oil

2 cups unbleached all-purpose flour

2 pounds ripe roma tomatoes, or
   one 28-ounce can Italian tomatoes,
   well drained

3/4 pound Mozzarella cheese, coarsely
   grated

1/4 cup freshly grated Parmesan cheese

1 small handful fresh basil or oregano,
   roughly chopped

1 copy "La Boheme" by Giacomo Puccini

CHEW ON THIS

"That's Amore" was one of the most popular singles of 1954. It was #16 on the
Billboard Chart of the year. For seafood
enthusiasts, try singing "That's Amore"
with these alternate lyrics: *"When an
eel's in the reef with a big set of teeth,
that's a moray . . ."*

The opera "La Boheme" figures so heavily in the plot and atmos-
phere of this movie, we thought it essential to use it as our soundtrack while preparing the dish. So crank up that CD (or album if
you're old school), fire up your oven, grease your baton, and get
ready to conduct your own rendition of pizza and Puccini.

Act I: Put on your favorite recording of La Boheme (*preferably
with Montserrat Caballé and Placido Domingo*). Combine the
yeast, honey, corn meal, and half of the water. Whisk together and
set aside in a warm spot until the mixture begins to foam, about
20 minutes. (*At this point, the seamstress Mimi enters, probably
coughing.*)

Add the remaining water, salt, and 2 tablespoons of the olive oil,
and mix well with a wooden spoon. Mix in one cup of the flour and
transfer to a floured working surface. Gradually knead another half-
cup of flour to create a soft, elastic dough. (*Rodolpho lights Mimi's
candle in more ways than one—they have fallen helplessly in love.*)

Act II: Continue kneading 8 to10 minutes, adding only as much
flour as needed to keep the dough from sticking. Remember: the
moister the dough, the crispier the crust. (*Christmas Eve in the
Latin quarter . . . the flirtatious and scheming Musetta attempts to
win back Marcello . . . he falls easily under her spell*).

Transfer the dough to a bowl oiled with 1 tablespoon olive oil and turn a few times to coat all sides of the dough. Cover the bowl with a towel or plastic wrap and set in a warm, draft-free place until the dough has doubled in size, about 45 minutes to an hour. (*The mysteriously wealthy Alcindoro returns to the café from his ill-fated shoe hunt to find that Musetta has ditched him, leaving only the unpaid check.*)

Act III: Peel the tomatoes, slice lengthwise, and squeeze out as much juice as possible. Cut each half into thin strips; sauté in 2 tablespoons olive oil over medium heat for about 10 minutes and set aside. If using canned tomatoes, make certain to squeeze out excess juice before sautéing. (*The poet Rodolpho is already unreasonably jealous and Mimi just doesn't seem to be getting over that nasty cough.*)

Preheat oven to 475°F. Whether using a pizza stone, ceramic tile, or baking sheet, make sure that it is in the oven while preheating. Toss the grated mozzarella with the remaining olive oil and set aside. (*Mimi bids a tearful farewell to Rodolpho, Musetta and Marcello break up over Musetta's flirting . . . Rodolpho and the fragile Mimi decide to give it another go.*)

Act IV: Punch down the dough, form into a ball, and flatten on a floured surface. Using a rolling pin, roll out until the dough is anywhere from 10 to 14 inches in diameter. A smaller diameter will produce a thicker, more bread-like crust; a larger diameter will yield thinner, more crispy crust. (*Although Rodolpho and Marcello are heartbroken and miss Mimi and Musetta beyond words, they still manage to force down an impromptu feast with Colline and Schaunard.*)

Transfer the dough onto a baker's peel or pizza paddle sprinkled generously with corn meal; spread the tomato mixture evenly across the top of the pizza; slide into the hot oven; bake for 10 minutes. (*Mimi really is not taking care of herself . . . Musetta sells her earrings for medicine . . . Colline sings a moving farewell to his favorite trench coat.*)

Remove the pizza from the oven just long enough to top with the mozzarella and Parmesan; return to the oven and bake another 10 minutes. Garnish with fresh basil or oregano and serve at once. (*Mimi and Rodolpho recall all the good times . . . Mimi slips away . . . Rodolpho's anguished cries fill the air.*)

Yield: Makes 1 big pizza pie

Inside Scoop

When Cher accepted her Best Actress Academy Award® for this film, she remembered to thank her hair and make-up people but forgot to thank director, Norman Jewison, and writer, John Patrick Shanley. Luckily, Shanley wasn't forgotten by other Academy voters. He won both the Academy Award® for Best Screenplay and a Writer's Guild Award for the film. Cher felt so bad about the oversight, she took an ad out in *Variety* to thank her forgotten coworkers later that week.

FOOD FOR THOUGHT

Pizza was popularized in the U.S. by soldiers who had encountered it in Italy while fighting in World War II, but it's been around for a lot longer than that. Food historians tell us that the earliest antecedent of today's pizza was most likely made from garbanzo flour, dates, and cheese. These early pies were popular among the foot soldiers of Darius the Great (King of Persia 521–486 B.C.) and were baked upon their shields over campfires.

Pretty Woman

1990

1/3 cup extra-virgin olive oil
1 onion, peeled and chopped
1 carrot, cut into small dice
4 garlic cloves, peeled and minced
6 anchovy fillets, mashed
1/4 teaspoon crushed red pepper
1/2 cup dry red wine
3 pounds ripe tomatoes or
   one 28-ounce can peeled plum
   tomatoes, drained and chopped
1 ½ cups flavorful black olives,
   pitted and halved
3 tablespoons large capers, drained
2 tablespoons chopped parsley
Salt and pepper
1 pound angel hair pasta
Address of the nearest free clinic

Julia's Angel Hair Puta-Nesca

In this 1990 inspirational Cinderella story, Julia Roberts' stunning debut made quite an impression on young girls everywhere. Her realistic portrayal of a beautiful, bright-eyed, healthy, well-adjusted prostitute not only proved that profit and passion go hand-in-hand, but also gave the oldest profession a well-needed boost.

1. Heat the olive oil in a medium saucepan over medium-low heat. Add the onion and carrot, and cook very slowly until the onion becomes soft and translucent, about 10 minutes. Add the garlic, anchovies, and crushed red pepper; continue cooking until the garlic just begins to turn golden. (Don't let it brown.)

2. Add the red wine and raise the heat to medium-high. Simmer until the wine is almost completely reduced. Stir in the tomatoes, olives, and capers. Reduce heat to medium and cook uncovered for 20 minutes, stirring often. (While the sauce simmers, bring 5–6 quarts of water to a boil in a large pot or Dutch oven.)

3. When the sauce has thickened, stir in the chopped parsley, and season to taste with salt and pepper. Add more red pepper flakes if desired.

4. When the water boils, add 2 tablespoons of salt and return to a boil. Add the pasta and stir immediately to prevent sticking.

Cover the pot until the water returns to a boil again; then remove cover and cook until pasta is al dente, stirring often.

5. Drain pasta in a colander over a large pasta bowl. Pour out the water and wipe the bowl with a towel before transferring the pasta to the warmed bowl. Immediately ladle the sauce over the pasta. Toss and serve in shallow bowls.

6. Play a "trick" on your guests: Ask your guests if they know what the oldest profession really is (cooking, of course). Anyone who doesn't get the right answer must immediately begin the second oldest: (Dishwashing).

Yield: 4–6 servings

Inside Scoop

An earlier version of the *Pretty Woman* script was titled *$3,000* in honor of the fee Gere's character pays Roberts to stay with him for the week. This script featured Gere's character ending the relationship with Roberts' character by throwing her out of his car, driving off, and leaving her by the side of the road.

CHEW ON THIS

You probably already know, prostitution is only legal in the U.S. in certain counties in Nevada. (Now, don't try to tell us you don't know which counties.)

The Quick and the Dead 1995

Spaghetti Western

2 pounds skirt steak

1 shot whisky

2 tablespoons peanut oil

1 pound ground pork

1 cup whole milk

Salt

2 to 3 dried New Mexico chiles

1 cup chopped onion

1 or 2 small jalapeño peppers,
   seeded and finely diced

1 cup chopped celery

1/2 cup chopped carrot

1 cup chopped bell pepper

1 tablespoon minced garlic

1 tablespoon ground cumin

1 tablespoon ground coriander

1/2 teaspoon chili flakes

1/2 teaspoon oregano

1 teaspoon sage

1 cup beer

2 cups canned Italian tomatoes,
   with juice

One 6-ounce can roasted chiles, chopped

1 cup beef stock

1 bay leaf

1 pound spaghetti or linguine

1 big beef (to settle with a bad guy)

The term "Spaghetti Western" was coined to describe the stylish westerns made by Italian directors in the mid-to-late '60s. The best known of these directors, Sergio Leoni, put these films—and star Clint Eastwood—on the map with A Fistful of Dollars in 1964. If a stylish blend of the Italian and the Western deserves its own film genre, it certainly deserves its own genre of food. We've combined a hearty pasta with the savory goodness of western chili to make a spaghetti dish that'll knock the spurs off your Versace boots.

1. Chop the beef into small pieces by hand, toss with the whisky, and set aside for 10 minutes.

2. In a large Dutch oven, heat one tablespoon of the oil over medium-high heat until just shimmering. Brown the beef and pork in three or four batches. Drain and discard fat from the Dutch oven, and reduce heat to medium. Return all the browned meat to the pot, add the milk and a pinch of salt, and simmer until the milk has cooked away completely, then remove from heat.

3. Heat a dry skillet over medium-high heat and toast the dried chiles for 2–3 minutes. When cool enough to handle, break open peppers and remove the seeds, membrane, and stems. Place chiles in food processor or coffee grinder and pulverize. Set aside.

4. Heat the remaining oil in a separate cast iron skillet over medium heat. Add the onion and jalapeño pepper, and sauté until the onion becomes translucent; add the celery, carrot, and bell pepper, and continue cooking 2 minutes, stirring often. Add the garlic, cumin, coriander, ground roasted chiles, chili flakes, oregano, and sage to the skillet; cook 1 minute, stirring frequently to avoid scorching.

5. Add the beer; let it cook until it has evaporated, then add the tomatoes with their juice and the canned chiles. Stir well with a wooden spoon, scraping the bottom and sides to loosen any tasty bits stuck to the skillet. Transfer contents of the skillet to the Dutch oven and place over medium-high heat. Add the beef stock and bay leaf to the Dutch oven, stirring well to mix all the ingredients and bring to a low boil. Immediately reduce heat to low, half cover the pot and simmer from 1 to 2 hours, until the meat is tender.

6. Bring 6 quarts of water to boil in a large pot, add two tablespoons of salt, and return to a boil. Add the pasta all at once and stir immediately to prevent sticking. Cover the pot until the water returns to a boil again, then uncover and stir until the pasta is al dente, stirring often.

7. Drain the pasta in a colander over a large pasta bowl. Dump out the water and wipe the bowl with a towel before transferring the pasta to the warmed bowl. Immediately ladle the sauce over the pasta. Toss and serve in shallow bowls.

8. After the last of your guests has ridden off into the sunset, adjust your hat, strap on your sponge, and walk bravely into the kitchen for a real showdown . . .
with the dishes!

Yield: Plenty (6–8)

FOOD FOR THOUGHT

There are over 600 shapes of pasta throughout the world. When pairing the shape with the sauce, remember, the thicker the sauce, the thicker the pasta should be. Large tubes and pasta with holes or ridges stand up to chunky sauces particularly well.

Inside Scoop

Is it too late for us to join the European union? Sharon Stone and Russell Crowe shot a love scene for this film which Stone and director Sam Raimi later decided to cut. While the scene never appeared in the film's American release, it IS included in international versions. How many Euros would you pay to see that?

Scrooged

1988

You will receive visits from these ingredients:

3 cups unbleached, all-purpose flour
2 tablespoons salt
1 teaspoon ground sage
4 large eggs
Cold water, as needed
1 stick cold butter, cut into
  small pieces
1 cup chopped pecans
2 ounces bourbon
2 tablespoons chopped parsley
Plenty of leftovers, such as turkey,
  duck, delicious stuffing, sweet
  potatoes, cranberry relish, etc.
1 easy-to-follow personal past

Inside Scoop

Take a good look at those street carolers insulted by Bill Murray's character in the movie. That's jazz great Miles Davis along with fellow musicians David Sanborn, Larry Carlton, and Paul Shaffer.

The Ghost of Christmas Past-a

Are repeated nightly visitations to your holiday leftovers haunting you with heartburn? Here's a tasty way to recycle them . . . God bless us everyone!

1. Place flour, salt, and sage in food processor. Turn on machine and add the eggs in a slow, steady stream. Continue processing until dough just begins to form a rough ball. Add a touch of water only if the dough hasn't begun to come together and still looks dry. Stop processor and feel the dough; it should hold together well but not be sticky.

2. Transfer to a lightly floured surface and knead by hand another 5–10 minutes, until supple and smooth. Cover with a kitchen towel or plastic wrap and let the dough rest at least 15 minutes before proceeding.

3. Divide pasta dough into four equal parts and roll as thinly as possible either with a rolling pin (good luck) or preferably a hand-cranked pasta machine. Dust the pasta sheets with a little flour if they become too sticky to handle. A standard hand-cranked pasta machine produces a sheet about 4 inches wide and 12 inches long.

4. Arrange your leftovers (I mean tasty pasta fillings) within reach, and lay the pasta strips across a lightly floured work surface. Place little mounds of different fillings about 2 inches apart and an inch from the bottom edge of the pasta.

5. Brush the bottom edge with water and fold the top over, lining up the edges. Press down lightly to seal the seam. Cut out individual raviolis by trimming along the sealed seam and in between the mounds of filling with a fluted pastry wheel or a crimp sealer. Toss raviolis with flour and keep refrigerated until use.

6. Place 1 teaspoon butter and the chopped pecans in a medium sized saucepan over medium heat. Once the pecans just begin to brown and become fragrant, add the bourbon and ignite to burn off the alcohol. (Make certain to close the bottle and place away from the flame before doing so.) Remove from heat and add the cold butter a little at a time, whisking and swirling the pan constantly. Keep warm over a low heat but don't boil or the sauce will break.

7. Bring 2 large pots of lightly salted water to a boil; divide the ravioli between the pots and boil about 4 minutes (until they float to the top and the doubled pasta edges are cooked al dente). Remove from the water with a slotted spoon and transfer to warm plates. Spoon pecan-bourbon sauce over the top and garnish with chopped parsley and a dollop of cranberry relish.

8. After you've finished your third supernaturally large helping of Ghost of Christmas Past-a, announce with overly cheery Yuletide sentiment that you finally think you fully understand and are indeed ready to embrace the true spirit of holiday giving. Feel free to illustrate this point by first giving some lucky guest your favorite sponge, then giving them your lucky dishtowel, and, finally, giving them directions to the sink. BAH HUMBUG!

Yield: Serves 4

Learn From Your Past-a Mistakes

Sometimes the simplest things seem the most difficult. Follow a few simple rules for perfect pasta:

1. Use a pot large enough for the volume of water necessary. A pound of pasta serves 4 to 6 and requires at least 1 gallon of water.

2. Add 1 to 2 tablespoons of salt for each pound of pasta. It's best to add the salt after the water comes to a full boil.

3. Once the salted water is at a full boil, add the pasta all at once and stir immediately to avoid clumping. Cover briefly and return to a boil, then uncover and stir often while cooking.

4. Different shapes and brands of dried pasta require substantially different cooking times. Most fresh pasta cooks in just a couple of minutes, or until it floats to the surface.

5. Be prepared to drain the pasta in a colander the very instant it seems perfect to you. Have the sauce ready; toss pasta and sauce together immediately. Allowing the pasta to sit without sauce for any length of time will result in a shameful mess.

Staying Alive
1983

Italian Scallion Risotto

For the vegetable stock:

2 tablespoons olive oil

1 onion, quartered

2 carrots, coarsely chopped

2 stalks celery, coarsely chopped

15 cloves unpeeled garlic, crushed

2 cups coarsely chopped tomatoes

1/2 bunch parsley stems

5 whole black peppercorns

1 bay leaf

2 quarts cold water

1/2 cup dried mushrooms (morel or shiitake preferably)

For the risotto:

2 tablespoons butter

2 tablespoons olive oil

1/2 teaspoon kosher salt

1/2 cup finely chopped yellow onion

2 cups Arborio rice (an Italian short grain rice)

2 yellow squash

1 cup good quality dry champagne

1/2 bunch scallions, thinly sliced on the diagonal

1 cup freshly grated good Parmesan cheese

Freshly ground black pepper

1 large dance bag

1 burning desire to make it big

5-6-7-8 . . . One good Italian stallion deserves another. In this 1983 Sylvester Stallone-directed sequel to Saturday Night Fever, *our hero, Tony Manero, follows his muse out of the neighborhood disco and makes the logical leap . . . to starring on Broadway! For our recipe, we auditioned hundreds of rice dishes but only this risotto had the right culinary choreography to make the cut. And, like Tony, it can really fill out a dance belt.*

1. Combine the olive oil, onion, carrot, celery, and garlic in a stockpot over medium-low heat. Cook without browning for 10 minutes, stirring, shimmying, and thrusting your body forward for no real reason as often as is possible.

2. Add the tomatoes, parsley stems, peppercorns, and bay leaf; cover with the cold water and bring to a boil.

3. Once the stock reaches a rapid boil, reduce the heat and simmer uncovered anywhere from 45 minutes to an hour (a longer cooking time yields a more highly flavored stock). Strain the stock into a saucepan, bring to a boil, and reduce the liquid to no more than 4 to 5 cups in volume. Add the dried mushrooms to the reduced stock, and simmer over a very low, yet deeply intense and seething heat. After 10 minutes, remove mushrooms with a slotted spoon, slice, and set aside.

4. Combine the butter, olive oil, salt, and chopped onion in a large, thick-bottomed skillet over medium heat. Sweat the onion without browning for about 3 minutes, stirring often with a flat-edged wooden spoon or spatula until the onion becomes translucent.

5. Add the Arborio rice to the onion mixture and stir well to moisten the rice grains with the oil in the pan.

6. Begin adding the hot vegetable stock to the rice one-half cup at a time, all the while stirring and scraping the bottom of the pan with the wooden spoon. Allow each addition of stock to be absorbed by the rice before adding more stock. (The entire process of adding stock while stirring will take more than 20 minutes, so it may be wise to have a partner spot you in case you lose your balance or forget the routine.)

7. After 15 minutes, add the yellow squash and sliced mushrooms. Continue stirring and adding stock a little at a time until all of it has been absorbed by the rice, about 10 more minutes. At this point, the rice should be getting tender.

8. Add and stir in the champagne and half of the scallions, remove from the heat, and stir in the grated Parmesan. Season with a grinding of fresh black pepper, and sprinkle the remaining scallions over the top. Serve at once, making sure to eat with a certain anger and intensity.

9. Celebrate your victorious risotto debut by cinching up your dance belt and executing a proud strut right out past the dirty dishes and on into the spotlight of certain culinary stardom. (Tip: If you really want to make it big, double the recipe.)

Yield: 4 servings

Art Imitates Life?

When Tony's dejected walk back to Brooklyn takes him past the disco he frequented in *Saturday Night Fever*, we see on the marquee that it has become a gay bar. And that's exactly what happened in real life to the 2001 Odyssey club where the club scenes in *Saturday Night Fever* were filmed.

Inside Scoop

In addition to directing, co-producing and co-writing this film, Sylvester Stallone also supervised the rigorous physical training that transformed John Travolta from an amateur disco dancer into a buff Broadway dancing machine. Watch for Stallone's tasteful, understated, Hitchcockian cameo in the opening scene.

CHEW ON THIS

In Northern Italy, pasta takes a back seat to rice. And the rice from the village of Arborio is most often the rice of choice. It contains a special form of starch that becomes deliciously creamy when stirred constantly while cooking.

U.S. Marshals

1998

2 whole heads garlic

3 tablespoons extra-virgin olive oil

1 pound whole-milk ricotta cheese

1 ounce dried wild mushrooms

1 medium onion, chopped fine

1 ½ cups cooked and chopped spinach

1/2 cup coarsely grated mozzarella

1/2 cup grated Pecorino Romano
  cheese plus more for garnish

1 large egg, beaten

Salt, pepper, and freshly grated
  nutmeg to taste

8 manicotti shells

3 cups of your favorite tomato sauce

1 warrant for an arresting meal

We Always Get Our Manicotti

Gentlemen, looks like we've got ourselves a stuffed pasta recipe here. I want to set a perimeter from the stovetop, extending down to the counter and over to the fridge. I want you to search out every ripe roma tomato, every onion, and every drop of extra-virgin olive oil in the vicinity. I want to know what brand of pasta you're using—is it fresh or is it dry? Has it been around since J. Edgar Hoover or was it extruded Tuesday? I want to know the village where the pasta was made, the shoe size of the farmer who harvested the semolina, and the genus and phylum of the grain. I want to know the plate presentation and the garnish you plan to use and most important of all . . . I want to know what time dinner is served.

1. Preheat oven to 375°F. Slice 1/2-inch from the pointy end of the garlic heads. Drizzle heads with olive oil and wrap in foil. Bake 45 minutes to an hour, until golden and soft. Cool, and squeeze into a small bowl and set aside.

2. Meanwhile, place ricotta in a large strainer set over a mixing bowl. Transfer to the refrigerator and let stand 45 minutes to drain excess water. Soak the wild mushrooms in 1 cup of warm water for 20 minutes. Drain, reserving soaking liquid for later; chop fine.

3. Heat remaining olive oil in a medium sauté pan over medium heat. Add the onion, and sauté until fragrant and softened (about

FOOD FOR THOUGHT

In a hurry to bring a stockpot of water to boil for pasta? Pour half of the water into a second pot and heat it on another burner. When both come to a boil, combine them in the larger pot. Should be twice as quick.

3 minutes), then add the chopped reserved mushrooms and spinach; continue cooking another 2 minutes.

4. Transfer the warm mixture to a large mixing bowl and add the ricotta, mozzarella, Romano, mushroom liquid, and roasted garlic. Season to taste with salt, white pepper, and nutmeg.

5. Cook manicotti in lightly salted boiling water until al dente (usually a few minutes less than package instructions) and immediately transfer to a bowl of ice water. Pat dry with a clean cloth.

6. Using a pastry bag, stuff pasta with filling and arrange in an oiled baking dish. Smother with tomato sauce, cover loosely with foil and bake 30 minutes.

7. After everyone has eaten, instruct your guests to make a perimeter around the sink and not give up until every dish has been apprehended, washed, and put away.

Yield: Serves 4

CHEW ON THIS

Although *U.S. Marshals* lacks a key ingredient of the original—namely, Harrison Ford—it IS considered a sequel to his immensely popular film, *The Fugitive*. The trailer was almost identical to that of the first film because the marketers wanted audiences to understand that this was a sequel. And, of course, Tommy Lee Jones reprises his Oscar®-winning performance as U.S. Marshal Sam Gerard.

Inside Scoop

Despite his rough-and-tumble screen image, Tommy Lee Jones graduated cum laude from Harvard where he was former Vice President Al Gore's roommate. *Love Story* **author Erich Segal, who met Gore and Jones while teaching at Harvard, has said the lead character in the story— wealthy athlete Oliver Barrett—was an amalgam of the two young men. Ironically, Jones' film debut was as one of Oliver's friends in the classic movie based on Segal's book.**

Chapter 4

Poultry

A Christmas Carol 1938

Scrooge's Turkey Legs with Crispy Gruel Stuffing

For scrooge's turkey legs:

3 large onions, peeled and sliced in
   1/2-inch rings
1 tablespoon minced garlic
4 tablespoons olive oil
6 turkey drumsticks, on sale if possible
Salt and pepper

For the crispy gruel stuffing:

1/2 cup golden raisins
1/4 cup vermouth
8 ounces pork sausage
1 onion, chopped
1 cup chopped celery
2 Granny Smith apples, peeled, cored,
   and chopped
1 ½ cups gruel (dry oatmeal)
3 cups dried bread cubes
1 cup walnut pieces
1/2 cup chicken broth
1 egg, beaten
1 teaspoon ground sage
1/4 cup chopped fresh parsley
1/2 teaspoon freshly ground black
   pepper
2 ounces (1/2 stick) melted butter
1 set of chains, forged in life, to be
   worn eternally

Here at "Dinner & a Movie" we have certain traditions. When we watch A Christmas Carol, we need to be sliding the turkey legs into the oven the moment we hear, "Marley was dead. Dead as a doornail"; basting at "Bah, humbug!"; and, if all goes well, dining with the Cratchits when we hear Tiny Tim utter, "God bless us, every one!" Hey, it's just something we do. This year, why not start the tradition at your house?

1. Roast the legs: Preheat oven to 350°F. Brush the onion slices with a little olive oil and lay side by side in a shallow roasting pan. Combine the garlic with the remaining olive oil and rub onto the drumsticks. Season with salt and pepper.

2. Arrange the turkey legs over the onion slices and place pan in the lower third of the preheated oven. Roast for a total of 90 minutes. (The stuffing goes in the oven for the last 45 minutes of cooking.) Occasionally baste both the stuffing and the legs with any accumulated pan juices.

3. Make the stuffing: Put the golden raisins into a small saucepan, cover with vermouth, and bring to a simmer. Remove from the heat and set aside.

4. In a large skillet over medium heat, lightly brown the sausage, breaking it up as it cooks. Use a slotted spoon to transfer sausage to a large mixing bowl and set aside. Add the onion and celery to the skillet and cook until softened. Stir in the chopped apples and cook 15 minutes, stirring often. Add the raisins and vermouth, increase the heat to high, and cook until most of the liquid has evaporated. Scrape the hot mixture into the mixing bowl containing the sausage, stir together, and cool to room temperature.

5. Fold in 1 cup oatmeal, 2 cups bread cubes, 1/2 cup walnuts, chicken broth, and the beaten egg. Season with sage, parsley, and black pepper, and mix together well. Turn the mixture into a well-buttered shallow casserole or baking dish, sprinkle the remaining gruel, bread cubes, and walnuts evenly over the top, and drizzle with melted butter. Bake for 45 minutes.

6. On a single dinner plate, balance all six turkey legs atop the pile of now caramelized onions, surrounded by a ring of crispy gruel stuffing. Eat every bite yourself. Don your nightcap, climb into bed, and see which shows up first: The Ghost of Christmas Past or the Pain of Heartburn Present.

Yield: 4–6 servings (or 1 miser)

CHEW ON THIS

"I have endeavored in this ghostly little book, to raise the ghost of an idea, which shall not put my readers out of humor with themselves, with each other, with the season, or with me. May it haunt their homes pleasantly."
—Charles Dickens, December 1843

FOOD FOR THOUGHT

When preparing turkey for a large crowd, avoid all stress by roasting the legs and thighs in one pan and the breast in another. Pull the breast out when it's ready and let the legs cook until they're done. You'll never, ever end up with white meat that dries out before the dark finishes cooking.

City Slickers II
1994

Home on the (Free) Range Chicken Wings with Dude Ranch Dressing

For the dressing:

3 tablespoons finely chopped
   yellow onion

1 large clove garlic, minced

2 tablespoons minced fresh parsley

1/2 teaspoon each: celery salt,
   fresh dill, salt, white pepper, and sugar

1/4 cup buttermilk

1 cup sour cream

2 teaspoons Worcestershire sauce

2 teaspoons cider vinegar

For the chicken:

1 teaspoon coriander

2 teaspoons paprika

1 tablespoon New Mexico chili powder

2 teaspoons brown sugar

1 teaspoon kosher salt

1 ½ teaspoons freshly ground black pepper

2 teaspoons garlic powder

2 dozen chicken wings, free range if you
   can get them

1 cup (2 sticks) butter

3 cloves garlic, minced

3 tablespoons Tabasco® sauce

3 tablespoons fresh lemon juice

1/2 teaspoon each: dried basil, oregano,
   and thyme

Your lucky saddle, spurs, and cell phone

Thar's gold in them thar hills . . . golden chicken wings, that is.

1. Combine the dressing ingredients in a food processor or blender and blend well. Cover and refrigerate.

2. Combine the coriander, paprika, chili powder, brown sugar, kosher salt, black pepper and garlic powder.

3. Rinse the chicken wings in cold water and cut in half at the joint, discarding the tips of the wings.

4. Rub the dry spice mixture well into the wings, cover, and refrigerate. Preheat the oven to 400°F.

5. Melt the butter in a small saucepan. Add the garlic, Tabasco, lemon juice and dried herbs; simmer for 15 minutes.

6. Arrange the chicken on a roasting pan or baking dish and bake 20 minutes, turning once.

7. Remove wings from oven and baste generously with the sauce. Return to the oven, reduce the heat to 350°F, and continue cooking another 20 minutes, or until crisp and brown.

8. Saddle up and start snacking your way through your next male mid-life crisis. Yee-haw.

Yield: Serves 4

Spill The Beans

We have been vocal proponents of naturally raised meats and poultry for years. We believe the combination of superior flavor and texture; health benefits and ecological sustainability are worth the added cost. However, the sometimes seemingly contradictory labeling of these products can be confusing to even the most well informed consumer. Allow us to attempt to translate:

Natural or Naturally Raised must be free of artificial colors, flavors and preservatives.

Free Range or Free Roaming requires that birds have been given access to the outdoors for an undetermined period each day.

Organic prohibits the use of genetic engineering, hormones, pesticides, antibiotics, irradiation, and a host of artificial ingredients.

Pampered designates poultry raised in spas on imported bottled water and watercress sandwiches.

Big House Bred poultry is forced to dress in striped clothing but allowed the use of the prison library to appeal their convictions.

But Are Their Brights Brighter?

You probably know that French dressing is really an American concoction. However, did you know that ranch dressing did in fact originate at the Hidden Valley dude ranch near Santa Barbara, California? We're told the house dressing was so popular that guests requested jars of it to take home. A wholesale business was launched and eventually became so successful that the entire ranch was converted into a packing center. The business was sold in 1972 and now the good people at Clorox make the most popular ranch dressing in the world. No word on whether they've made it any whiter...

Cliffhanger

1 double chicken breast, bone in, skin on

2 onions, 1 peeled and quartered,
the other finely diced

2 cups chicken broth

1½ pound tomatillos or ripe tomatoes

4 cloves garlic, peeled

1–2 jalapeño peppers

1/4 teaspoon salt

1/2 cup safflower or corn oil

1 cup queso fresco

1/2 cup sour cream

1/4 cup chopped cilantro (plus more
for garnish)

1 dozen fresh corn tortillas

1 high-impact, safety-rated cheese helmet

Inside Scoop

Although *Cliffhanger* is set in Colorado, it was actually filmed in Italy. The American Environmental Protection Agency wouldn't allow filming in Colorado for fear of the damage that might be done by the shoot. Italy was chosen as the stand-in because its majestic mountains could easily double for the Rockies but the production still had to pay a large deposit in case any damage was done. No word on whether they got their money back.

Avalanchiladas

Grab your cheese rappelling ropes, tortilla ax and chile pitons—this classic Mexican dish will have your tastebuds yelling to your stomach, "Look out below!"

1. Place the chicken breast and the quartered onion in a medium saucepan. Add the broth and just enough water to cover. Bring to a boil; reduce heat to a simmer and cook, uncovered, for 20 minutes. Remove from heat and allow the chicken to cool in the broth. Strain and reserve the broth and the onion. Shred the meat, cover, and refrigerate.

2. Heat an ungreased griddle or cast iron skillet over medium-high heat. Place the tomatillos, garlic, and jalapeño on the griddle and roast for about 10 minutes, until the tomatillo skins begin to blister and brown. Transfer mixture to a blender and add the salt, reserved broth, and onion; blend until smooth.

3. Heat 1 tablespoon of the oil in a medium skillet over medium heat until hot, but not smoking. Add the pureed sauce and cook for 10 minutes, stirring often. Continue cooking and stirring until the sauce reduces in volume to about 2 cups. Stir in the chopped cilantro and keep warm. Preheat oven to 425°F.

4. Heat the remaining oil in a skillet until the oil begins to simmer. Hold one of the tortillas down flat into the oil with a spatula and fry for 10 seconds. Flip and fry the reverse side for 10 seconds; don't let the tortillas get crispy.

5. Drain on paper towels and immediately dredge through the warm sauce. Place some chicken, onion, and sour cream across the center and roll up. Transfer the enchilada to a baking dish and repeat with the remaining tortillas and filling; top with remaining sauce, cover with foil and bake for 15 minutes.

6. On a large serving platter, pile the Avalanchiladas as high as humanly possible and don't stop building upward until the air becomes so thin that oxygen masks are required. Garnish with a liberal blizzard of queso fresco, sour cream, onions, and cilantro.

7. When it's time to tackle the mountain of dishes in the sink, signal for a rescue team.

Yield: Serves 4

CHEW ON THIS

Preview audiences were responsible for two substantial changes to this movie. First, audiences laughed so hard at an impossible forty-foot jump made from cliff-to-cliff by Stallone's character that the footage was replaced in the final film with a more plausible jump. Second, though unfazed by the amount of human carnage featured in the film, audience members reacted so strongly to a scene in which a rabbit gets killed by gunfire, Stallone invested $100,000 of his own money to re-shoot it so the rabbit escapes. Hope nobody tells them what we cooked for *Roger Rabbit*.

Say Queso!

As authentic, regional Mexican cuisine has gained popularity in the U.S., so too has Mexican cheese. Long  underrated, we're happy to see these versatile quesos finally making their way to supermarkets. Allow us to introduce you to some favorites of ours:

Queso Asadero: This mild cheese melts beautifully, somewhat similar to Provolone.

Queso Blanco: Made from fresh curds like a farmer's cheese, mild and crumbly. Melts without losing its shape.

Queso Cotija: An aged dry cheese. Firm and salty, use like Parmesan or Romano.

Queso Oaxaca: Stringy like mozzarella, great on pizza.

Queso Requeson: Mild, fresh and spreadable, use like Ricotta.

Crema Mexicana: A sweet, thick cream. Use like sour cream.

The Cutting Edge

Edge 1992

Triple Axel Rotisserie Chicken

One (3 ½ to 4 pounds) roasting chicken
1 cup kosher salt
1/2 cup sugar
3 quarts cold water
1 cup black olives
1 lemon, quartered
10–15 cloves garlic, crushed and peeled
1 sprig fresh thyme
3 tablespoons butter
Salt, freshly ground black pepper,
    and paprika
1/2 cup white wine
1/2 cup chicken stock
1 toe pick

Just as every skater must master a basic axel, every cook should master a simple, elegant roasted chicken. We call it "rotisserie" chicken but you don't really need a rotisserie to make it. Just treat your bird like a skating partner, deftly flipping it three times while it roasts to a golden brown. Once you get this in your repertoire, you can move on to a "Slow-Roasted Flying Camel" but, at 20 minutes per pound, you'll be roasting it forever.

1. Combine the kosher salt, sugar, and water and mix together in a bowl large enough for the chicken.

2. Submerge the chicken in the salt brine solution and refrigerate for anywhere from 30 minutes to 2 hours (depending on how much time you have, the longer, the juicier).

3. While the chicken soaks in the brine, prepare the remaining ingredients.

4. Preheat the oven to 475°F. Rinse the chicken inside and out with hot water and dry well with paper towels.

5. Season the cavity liberally with freshly ground black pepper, then stuff with the olives, lemon, and crushed garlic. Tie the ends of the drumsticks together very loosely with kitchen twine to partially seal the cavity.

6. Coarsely chop the thyme and combine with the butter in a small saucepan over low heat. When the butter has melted, remove the pan from the heat.

7. Brush the skin all over with the melted thyme-butter mixture, and season with salt, black pepper, and paprika.

8. Place a rack over a roasting pan larger than the chicken to be roasted. Arrange the chicken on one side of the rack and place in the preheated oven. Set a timer for 20 minutes.

9. When the timer sounds, turn the bird onto its other side, (don't drop it or you'll lose points); brush with melted butter and reduce the oven temperature to 350°F. Set the timer again for 20 minutes.

10. This time when the timer goes off, turn the chicken breast-side up, brush with the remaining melted butter and roast for an additional 15 minutes. Check the internal temperature with an instant-read thermometer inserted in the thickest part of the thigh. It should register from 165–170°F; if not, continue roasting another 10 minutes and check again. When the chicken is fully cooked, transfer to a cutting board or platter and let rest 10–15 minutes before carving.

11. Spoon off and discard most of the rendered fat from the roasting pan. Add the white wine and chicken stock and place over a medium-high heat, scraping the bottom of the pan with a wooden spoon or Zamboni to loosen any tasty browned bits. Cook down until syrupy, and spoon over the portions, along with the olives and garlic from inside the bird.

12. After dinner, give yourself a "10" and bribe the nearest French judge to do the dishes.

Yield: 4 servings

Worth its Salt

Although we know we're often guilty of overstatement, we just can't say enough good things about brining. Adding this simple step adds an extraordinary amount of moisture and tenderness to all types of meat, poultry, and even shellfish. Here's how it works: prior to cooking, just submerge the food to be cooked in a cold, salt-water solution anywhere from 20 minutes for shrimp to 24 hours for a large turkey. We recommend using 1 cup of salt and 1/2 cup of sugar to 1 gallon of water, with a brining time of 30 minutes per each pound of meat.

CHEW ON THIS

Four out of five comics agree, the word "Zamboni"—used in any context—is a sure-fire laugh-getter. Bring it up in conversation and let the guffaws begin.

Ingredients

1 gallon water

3 ounces ginger root, sliced 1/8-inch thick

4 ½ cup soy sauce

1 cup Chinese black vinegar

1 cup blackstrap molasses

3 whole star anise

One four- to five-pound duck

1 bunch scallions, thinly sliced

2 teaspoons kosher salt

1 teaspoon Chinese five-spice powder

1 jar hoisin sauce

1 tablespoon toasted chopped peanuts

1 tablespoon lime juice

1 package fresh flour tortillas

1 egg

1 very small pair of crutches

Special equipment:

1 bicycle pump

Half Baked

That's director and professional conspiracy theorist Oliver Stone doing a cameo as the man trying to convince a reporter that the president has been switched.

$\mathcal{D}$ave

1993

$\mathcal{L}$ame $\mathcal{D}$uck

What would happen if a complete imposter took over the presidency? We don't know (or do we)? One thing's certain: our duck may sound lame—when was the last time you saw a bicycle pump as a main ingredient in a recipe—but its crispy skin and moist meat will have you singing "Hail to the Chef!"

1. Trim duck of excess fat, then rinse inside and out with cold water, massaging and loosening the skin as you do so.

2. (This next step can be omitted if desired. However, if followed, the result is an exceptionally crisp skin.) Starting with the front of the neck, carefully pierce the skin of the duck, inserting the needle of the bicycle pump into the area between the skin and the layer of fat just beneath the skin. Pump until the skin puffs and inflates over the breasts and hopefully down into the thighs and legs. Repeat this until most of the skin has been inflated and thus separated from the fat layer. Note: The skin need not remain inflated.

3. In a pot large enough to lay the duck in, combine the water, half of the ginger, soy, vinegar, molasses, and star anise. Bring to a rapid boil. Place the duck on its side in the boiling mixture for 2 minutes, then turn over and repeat on the other side. Remove from the pot and blot dry with paper towels

4. Combine half of the scallions, kosher salt, five-spice, and the

remaining ginger in the work bowl of a food processor and pulse 2 or 3 times. Rub duck inside and out with the ginger-scallion mixture. Place on a rack in the refrigerator and refrigerate, uncovered, at least 20 minutes and up to 12 hours. Preheat oven to 400°F.

5. Fill a roasting pan with an inch of water (the water keeps the grease from smoking as it hits the hot pan). Place the duck breast-side-up on a rack over the pan and roast for 20 minutes, turning the duck over after 10 minutes.

6. Remove from oven and pierce the skin all over with the tines of a fork. (This causes the fat to cook out.) Reduce heat to 325°F and continue roasting breast-side-up until the leg meat juices run clear when pierced, about 90 minutes.

7. Combine the hoisin sauce, peanuts, and lime juice, and set aside. Brush tortillas with beaten egg, and sprinkle some of the remaining scallions over the top. Pile the prepared tortillas, place in a covered steamer and steam for approximately four minutes, remove tortillas and serve alongside the duck and hoisin sauce.

8. After dinner, convene the Cabinet; have them do the dishes and then stick them in your cabinet.

Yield: Serves 4

Although duck has the reputation of being fatty, it needn't be. In our adaptation of the celebrated Peking duck (or is it *Beijing* now?), we use a bike pump to create space between the skin and the fat. This allows the fat layer to cook off, leaving crisp, flavorful skin. Hey, it may seem lame, but we think the results are worth the ridicule.

In China, Peking duck restaurants always cut the duck into exactly 120 pieces.

CHEW ON THIS

The term "lame duck," first used in 1761, was stock exchange slang for a person who could not fulfill his contracts. These days the term usually refers to an elected official who will not be running for reelection due to term limits or personal choice.

Inside Scoop

In 2002, the ZDF public television network in Germany, working in conjunction with a forensic scientist and specialist in facial recognition, announced after a scientific study of 140 photographs, they believed there were at least three different doubles posing as Iraqi President Saddam Hussein. In the "Dinner & a Movie" test kitchen, we've stared at 140 photographs of Alfred E. Neuman and we swear, in at least twelve of them, the *Mad Magazine* coverboy is being played by a prominent world leader.

The Game

1 ½ pounds duck breast meat

1 ½ pounds duck leg and thigh meat

1/4 pound duck or chicken fat, chopped fine

1 tablespoon kosher salt

2 teaspoons sugar

2 teaspoons orange zest

1 tablespoon finely chopped garlic

2 teaspoons freshly ground black pepper

2 teaspoons sweet paprika

1/4 teaspoon cayenne pepper

1/2 teaspoon ground sage

1/2 teaspoon dried thyme

1 pinch allspice

1 pinch cinnamon

1/4 cup orange liqueur

2 tablespoons chopped fresh basil

3 tablespoons toasted pine nuts

3 tablespoons golden raisins

1/4 cup finely diced green apple

2–3 feet of sausage casings (ask your butcher)

1 large onion, sliced

1 bunch green onions, sliced

2 tablespoons olive oil

1 "get out of jail free" card

Wiener Takes All

It's not whether you win or lose, it's how you eat your game.

1. Begin the game: Trim meat of sinew and cut into 1-inch cubes. Combine with the next 12 ingredients (salt—orange liqueur) and mix together well. Cover and place in freezer for 20–30 minutes until very cold, but not quite fully frozen.

2. Using a meat grinder or food processor, grind the ice cold seasoned meat. Transfer the mixture to a cold mixing bowl and mix in the basil, pine nuts, raisins, and apples. To check seasonings, heat a small sauté pan and fry up a small patty of the sausage mixture. Adjust seasonings as needed, then transfer the mixture into a large pastry bag.

3. Rinse out the sausage casing in cold water and tie a knot in one end. Slide the unknotted end of the sausage casing over the tip of the pastry bag then slowly and carefully squeeze the mixture into the casing.

4. Tie the open end closed with a piece of butcher's twine. Then begin creating links by twisting every 6–7 inches and tying into links with small pieces of kitchen twine.

5. Brown the onions in olive oil and set aside.

6. Bring a large pot of water to boil. Add the sausage all at once, then immediately remove from heat and cover. After 10 minutes, remove and separate the links. Finish cooking on the grill or in a skillet and serve on warm French rolls with plenty of spicy mustard and sautéed onions.

7. When your guests begin to head for home, gently remind them that the game ain't over until someone does the dishes.

Yield: 8 winning wieners

Don't Be A Weenie!

Enthusiastic Austrians cite the name "wiener"—derived from the German word for Austria's capital city of Vienna—as proof positive that the hot dog was born in their country. According to legend, the Austrian inventor of this classic sausage got his early training in Frankfurt and called his brainchild a "wiener-frank-furter." It eventually became known as a "wienerwurst" throughout Europe and was later shortened to "weenie" by fast-talking Yanks.

Alternate Ingredients

Jodie Foster was originally supposed to play the role of Michael Douglas' sibling, eventually played by Sean Penn.

Time On Their Hands

Word has it there's a real life "Game" supported by wealthy benefactors including Microsoft honcho Bill Gates. Basically a high-level scavenger hunt, it's a team event with each group consisting of a van full of players who decipher clues, usually in the form of puzzles, to find their way to the next clue until they make it through all the clues to the finish. Many of the clues are acted out by performers in small theatrical productions. There is no prize money and each team's entry fee is $25,000 with all the money going to charity.

Inside Scoop

That's Linda Manz, the long-lost child star from Terrence Malick's *Days of Heaven* playing Christine's roomate, Amy, early in the film. Later, when Michael Douglas goes into a Chinese restaurant, you can see Manz in an autographed *Days of Heaven* still on the wall.

Harry and the Hendersons 1987

3/4 pound chicken thigh meat, skinless and boneless

3/4 pound chicken breast meat, skinless and boneless

1 teaspoon soy sauce

1 teaspoon garlic, minced

1 egg white

1/2 teaspoon onion powder

2 tablespoons paprika

1 ½ teaspoon salt

1/4 teaspoon celery seed

1/4 teaspoon ground sage

1/2 teaspoon white pepper

1 ½ teaspoon sugar

1 cup ice cubes

1 very large flea collar

Big Hoax

Though, according to bigfootencounters.com, there were Sasquatch sightings in the U.S. as early as 1840, the Bigfoot we all know and love entered popular consciousness in 1958 when giant footprints were found on the grounds of a construction company in Humboldt County, California. In 2002, the construction company's owner, Ed Wallace, died and his children revealed the 16-inch-long wooden feet he'd used to make the footprints and fool the world.

Bigfoot Longs

During our search for the elusive "healthful-yet-tasty hot dog," there were times when we felt we had a better chance of finding Sasquatch at a swap meet. It seems we "misunderestimated" ourselves. This very low-fat, all-chicken foot-long is loaded with flavor, while the only Yeti sightings we've witnessed so far have been in this 1987 comedy starring John Lithgow. (Although a friend of ours thought she saw a chupacabra at the car wash once.)

1. Cut the chicken up into 1/2-inch pieces and place in a medium mixing bowl. Add and stir in the soy sauce, garlic and egg white. In a small bowl, combine the onion powder, paprika, salt, celery seed, sage, white pepper, and sugar. Pour the spice mixture over the chicken and mix in well. Place the bowl in the freezer and chill for 30 minutes.

2. Put the ice cubes in the bowl of a food processor fitted with a metal cutting blade. Process for 30 seconds until well pulverized; scrape the ice into a bowl and set aside. Add the chicken to the processor bowl and grind in 2 15-second pulses, scraping the sides of the bowl with a rubber spatula between pulses. Add the crushed ice and grind for a final 20 seconds.

3. Transfer the ground chicken to a pastry bag with a 3/4-inch opening. Oil a 15-inch length of aluminum foil and pipe out 6 nice bigfoot longs side-by-side. Bring 1 inch of water to a boil in a large skillet or saucepan; carefully transfer the foil and the foot-longs into the pan. Cover and reduce the heat to medium. Steam for 8-10 minutes. Remove the dogs and either serve hot from the pan with garnishes of choice or plunge in ice water to cool quickly before wrapping and refrigerating.

4. WARNING: When serving your foot longs, beware of the oft sighted North American Drop-In Dinner Guests, a slow-moving, bloated creature spotted loping through areas where sumptuous meals have been prepared. This behemoth shouldn't be confused with the elusive North American Dishdoin' Dinner Guest, the only apparition with fewer reported sightings than Bigfoot.

Yield: 6 bigfoot longs

FOOD FOR THOUGHT

The hot dog was given its current name in 1901. Until that time, the product had been sold under the name "red-hot dachshund sausages."

Inside Scoop

A darling of critics and his fellow actors, John Lithgow has been nominated for and won some major awards for his acting work:
- ★ **3 Emmy Awards®** ("Third Rock from the Sun")
- ★ **1 Tony Award®** ("The Changing Room")
- ★ **2 Academy Award® nominations for Best Supporting Actor** (*The World According to Garp* and *Terms of Endearment*)

The Jerk

For the jerk seasoning:
1/3 cup cider vinegar
1 tablespoon molasses
1 tablespoon soy sauce
1 tablespoon Worcestershire sauce
Juice and zest of 1 lime
1 teaspoon light brown sugar
4 tablespoons softened butter
4 scallions, chopped
3 cloves garlic, peeled
1/4 teaspoon black pepper
1 teaspoon salt
2 teaspoons ground cinnamon
2 teaspoons ground allspice
1 tablespoon peeled and thinly
   sliced fresh ginger
1 habanero pepper (aka Scotch bonnet),
   or 2–3 jalapeños, seeded

For the chicken:
One 4–5 pound chicken
1 thumb-sized piece of ginger,
   sliced thinly
1 whole head garlic, cut in half
1 lime, cut in quarters
1 habanero or jalapeño, halved
   lengthwise
1 pair opti-grabs

What a Jerk Chicken!

We're picking out a chicken for you
No ordinary chicken will do
But the extra best chicken that you can cook
With real jerk spices and flavor built right in . . .

1. Prepare the jerk: Measure out and combine all jerk seasoning ingredients in the work bowl of a food processor or blender. Blend until smooth.

2. Prepare the chicken: Adjust oven rack to the center of the oven and preheat to 450°F. Rinse and dry the chicken; massage 1/2 of the jerk seasoning all over the chicken, under the breast skin, and inside the cavity. Place the ginger, garlic, lime, and habanero inside the cavity and close by tying the ends of the drumsticks together loosely.

3. Set the chicken with the breast-side down on an oiled rack in a roasting pan. Roast uncovered for 30 minutes, brushing with pan juices and jerk seasoning every 10 minutes or so. If the pan juices sizzle too loudly or begin to smoke, add 1/2 cup of water to the pan.

4. Flip the chicken breast-side up and reduce the oven temperature to 350°F. Continue roasting an additional hour, basting frequently. The chicken is done when the skin is crisp and brown and the drumsticks feel loose in their sockets. A meat thermometer inserted into the thick part of the thigh nearest the body should register 165°–175°F. Transfer chicken to a platter or carving board and let rest for 15–20 minutes before serving.

5. While the chicken rests, transfer the pan juices to a small saucepan and skim off the fat. Remove the garlic and habanero from the cavity, chop finely, and combine with the pan juices. Heat to a simmer and serve alongside the chicken.

Yield: 4 servings

FOOD
FOR THOUGHT

Believed to have come from the Spanish word "chaqui" which referred to barbecued meat and later evolved into "jerky," "jerk" dishes can be traced back to the early 17th century when Jamaican natives—in order to avoid capture by British slave traders—hid in the mountains and cooked meals beneath the earth.

CHEW ON THIS

If you're trying to find out someone's age but don't want to come out and ask it, we suggest the more subtle approach of asking whether they remember Steve Martin's hilarious arrow-through-the-head stand-up act. If they never knew Steve Martin did stand-up, assume an authoritative, elder-statesmanish attitude and dispatch them at once to purchase his classic comedy albums, "Let's Get Small," "A Wild and Crazy Guy" and "Comedy is Not Pretty!"

Inside Scoop

The practice of breaking the wishbone to see who gets the larger half dates back more than 2,000 years. It also is most likely the origin of the term "a lucky break."

The New Guidebooks Are Here!
The New Guidebooks Are Here!

Steve Martin got his start by selling 25-cent guidebooks and entertaining at Disneyland. In addition to his acting career, Martin is also a successful playwright ("Picasso at the Lapin Agile"), author (*Shopgirl, Pure Drivel*) and frequent contributor to *The New Yorker* magazine.

Lethal Weapon 4

1998

4 tablespoons kosher salt

8-10 garlic cloves, peeled and smashed

1 pinch ground bay leaf

1 tablespoon hot pepper sauce

1 tablespoon peanut butter

4 cups buttermilk

1 organic chicken, cut into 12 parts
   for frying

3 ½ cups self-rising flour

1 teaspoon freshly ground black pepper

2 teaspoons paprika

Peanut oil, for frying

Plus the same wacky cast as
   "Fried Chicken 4"

FOOD FOR THOUGHT

We feel frying has gotten a bad rap. We say, just use clean oil with a high smoke point, make sure it's hot enough and don't fry too much at one time. Following these rules may in fact produce fried foods that absorb less oil than a sauté.

Fried Chicken 5

Whenever there's a hit in Hollywood, you can be sure of one thing: they're going to make it again and again and again. But with a twist! This fourth installment of the Lethal Weapon franchise features our lovable regulars—Mel and Danny—teamed up with an interesting new character played by Chris Rock. On "Dinner & a Movie," we like to follow the sequel philosophy as it applies to cooking, giving a successful recipe an exciting new spin. Case in point: Fried Chicken 5! We've taken our already successful fried chicken recipe and made it more moist, more tender and more explosively delicious than all the previous fried chickens! Our twist? We've added an unconventional ingredient—peanut butter (that's our Chris Rock, you see how we play the game)—to bring a new flavor and nutty crunch.

1. Combine the salt, garlic, ground bay leaf, hot pepper sauce, peanut butter, and buttermilk in a large glass bowl. Stir until the peanut butter and salt dissolve.

2. Submerge the chicken in the buttermilk mixture; cover and refrigerate at least 30 minutes and up to 2 hours.

3. Remove chicken from the marinade, pat dry and transfer to a wire rack. Refrigerate uncovered another 20–30 minutes. (Although this step helps ensure a crisp skin, it may be omitted.)

4. Combine the flour, pepper, and paprika in a large baking dish and set aside. Preheat oven to 200°F.

5. In a large cast-iron Dutch oven or heavy skillet, heat 2 ½ to 3 inches of peanut oil over medium-high heat to 350°F. If you don't have a deep-fry thermometer, check the temperature by dropping a small piece of bread in the hot oil; it should take just under 30 seconds to brown.

6. Dredge both sides of each piece of chicken in the flour mixture, shake off excess flour, and dip into the buttermilk mixture again, then once again into the flour. Shake off excess flour and transfer to a wire rack.

7. Lay the chicken in the hot oil without crowding or touching (frying too many pieces at one time will cause the oil to cool down and you'll end up with greasy chicken). Once the pan is full, gently lift each piece once with tongs to prevent the coating from sticking. Fry 5-8 minutes on each side, turning when golden. Reduce heat to medium if the chicken browns too quickly.

8. Using tongs, carefully remove chicken from oil and drain on large paper bags or a few layers of paper towel. When cooking more than one batch, keep chicken warm on a rack or baking sheet in the preheated oven. Add peanut oil to the frying pan as needed, always making certain the oil has returned to 350°F before frying.

9. If anyone asks for seconds, explain that there will be no sequel in the works until the cast and crew have been chosen for "Doing the Dishes, Part 1."

Yield: Serves 4

Inside Scoop

Discovered by Eddie Murphy while doing stand-up, Chris Rock languished in the cast of "Saturday Night Live" for three years before hitting stride (and winning two Emmy Awards®) with his HBO comedy special "Bring The Pain."

CHEW ON THIS

Some film franchises don't know when to quit and some, in our opinion, stopped too soon. Here are a few sequels we'd love to see (but we're not holding our breath):

★ *Three Octogenarians & A Caregiver.*
★ *Look Who's Drooling.*
★ *Malcolm XII* .
★ *Babe At 350 Degrees.*
★ *My Old Lady* (*My Girl*'s Anna Chlumsky can't stay young forever).
★ *Problem Trustee* (taking the *Problem Child* series to its logical conclusion).
★ *Star Truss* (empowered by supportive new undergarments, the *Star Trek* team goes boldly into a new galaxy).

Life

1999

1 cup kosher salt

1/2 cup sugar

4-5 quarts cold water

4 Cornish game hens

4 tablespoons maple syrup

2 tablespoons Dijon mustard

2 tablespoons minced garlic

4 tablespoons cider vinegar

1/3 cup olive oil

2 lemons, quartered

4 rosemary sprigs

3-4 cups vermouth

1 friendly cellmate, preferably smaller
   than oneself

Jailbirds

With a movie called Life *we could have made "Just a Bowl of Cherries" but for a film depicting lifetime in a Southern prison, it didn't seem quite appropriate. "Jailbirds" may not sound much better, but despite the ominous name, we promise these Cornish game hens are tastier than a conjugal visit.*

1. Combine the salt, sugar, and water in a large stockpot and stir until dissolved. Submerge the hens in the sugar-salt solution and soak, refrigerated 45 minutes to an hour.

2. In a small saucepan, combine the maple syrup, mustard, garlic, vinegar, and olive oil. Simmer 10 minutes.

3. Remove birds from brine; rinse thoroughly and pat dry. (Steps 1 and 2 may be omitted but salt brining will yield a much more succulent product.)

4. Preheat oven to 400°F. Place oven rack in the center of the oven. Place a rosemary sprig and 2 lemon quarters in each bird and arrange breast side down on a rack over a large roasting pan. Pour half of the vermouth in the pan to prevent smoking. Brush hens well with the maple glaze and roast for 30 minutes, adding more vermouth as needed.

5. Flip hens over, brush with glaze and add remaining vermouth to the drip pan. Continue roasting an additional 30-35 minutes or

Spill The Beans

With two million American citizens now in prison—a 300 percent increase since the '70s—America is now considered the largest jailer on Earth.

until the thickest part of the thigh registers 165°-170°F on an instant-read thermometer.

6. Remove hens from oven and let them rest 10 minutes before serving.

7. Pour collected juices from the drip pan and any remaining glaze into a small saucepan. Skim off excess fat, bring to a boil, and simmer 5 minutes. Serve hens whole, 1 per person, and pass the warm sauce around the table.

8. Sentence any guest found guilty of poor table manners to 45 minutes hard labor . . . a.k.a. the dishes.

Yield: Serves 4

Inside Scoop

Though *Life* got off to a great start at the box office on its opening weekend (it grossed $20.7 million, setting a record for highest three-day debut in April and knocking *The Matrix* out of its number one seat) it quickly lost momentum. This was reportedly due to the unfortunate marketing decision to promote the film as a wacky prison comedy when in reality it was a moving period drama with poignant and compelling performances by Eddie Murphy and Martin Lawrence (plus a memorable turn by comedian Bernie Mac).

Contrary to popular belief, Cornish game hen isn't an underage chicken but rather the proprietary name for a crossbreed between White Rock and Cornish hens. Usually weighing in at about a pound and a half, these birds are ideal for entertaining with each hen presenting just one elegant serving. They take substantially less time to cook than chicken so you can pop them in the oven just before cocktails are served and if things don't get out of hand, be eating in under an hour. If things do get out of hand, make sure to turn off the oven before you pass out.

FOOD FOR THOUGHT

Ted Demme, We'll Miss You!

This was one of director Ted Demme's last movies. The director of such acclaimed movies as *Blow*, *The Ref*, and *Beautiful Girls*, he died in 2002.

*S*traight *T*alk

3 cups low-sodium chicken broth

2–3 carrots, peeled and cut into
1/4-inch slices

1 basket pearl onions

2 pounds boneless, skinless turkey thigh
or breast meat

1 cup quartered mushrooms

5 tablespoons butter

2 stalks celery, cut into 1/4-inch slices

6 tablespoons all-purpose flour

2 tablespoons whole grain mustard

1 cup half & half or milk

2 tablespoon dry sherry

1 cup frozen green peas

2 tablespoons fresh, chopped parsley

1 pound biscuit dough to cover
a 9-inch x 13-inch pan or two sheets
frozen puff pastry, thawed

1 egg yolk, beaten with 1 teaspoon water

Salt and pepper to taste

1 heapin' helpin' of ol' fashioned
common sense

CHEW ON THIS

The first cloned sheep was named "Dolly" after Dolly Parton because it was cloned from breast tissue. Dolly reportedly insures her famous chest for $600,000.

*T*alkin' *T*urkey *P*ot *P*ie

If you've been complaining about pot pie, quit your belly-achin' and shut your pie hole. This is our version of the American classic and it's a truth-tellin', straight-talkin', shoot-from-the-hip pie that won't lie.

1. Bring the chicken broth to a boil in a large saucepan. Blanch the carrots and onions in batches until not quite tender. Remove vegetables with a slotted spoon and set aside. Slip the onions from their skins when no longer hot as blue blazes.

2. Return the broth to a boil and add the turkey and mushrooms. Reduce heat and simmer, covered, for 20 minutes or until the turkey is firm to the touch. Remove pan from heat, allow turkey to cool in the broth before chopping into bite-size pieces. Chop mushrooms and reserve broth.

3. Melt the butter in a medium saucepan over medium heat. Add the chopped celery and sauté 1 minute. Add the flour and cook for about 2 minutes, stirring constantly. Do not brown. Remove mixture from heat and slowly pour in the broth while whisking rapidly. Return to the heat and continue whisking until the sauce comes to a boil. Let the sauce boil for another minute, then remove from heat and add the mustard, half & half, and sherry. Season to taste with salt and pepper and keep warm over a low heat.

4. Preheat oven to 400°F. Add the turkey, blanched vegetables, peas, and parsley to the sauce and pour the mixture into a greased 10-inch pie plate or baking dish. If a bottom crust is desired, line with pastry before adding the mixture.

5. Lay the pastry over the filling, trim to a 1-inch overhang and tuck the edges down into the sides of the pan. Don't worry about being overly neat. (Remember that a nod's as good as a wink to a blind horse.)

6. Cut a few well-placed vents for steam to escape and brush the pastry top with the egg mixture. Bake for 25 to 30 minutes or until the pastry is golden brown and the filling begins to bubble. Remove from the oven and allow to cool a few minutes before serving, but not too much. (Remember, revenge is the only dish served cold.)

7. At this point, you'd be dumber than ditch water if you didn't remind your guests you've been busier than a one-armed paper-hanger and now that they're as full as Alabama ticks, you'd be happier than a dog with two tails if they did the dishes. If they refuse, tell them you're madder than a bear with a sore throat and that they're about as useless as a bunch of chocolate teapots.

Yield: Serves 6

FOOD FOR THOUGHT

Although our recipe calls for drumsticks, most turkeys are raised for maximum production of white meat. It's not uncommon for their breasts to get so big that they can't get near enough to reach each other to mate.

"Hey man, I can stop any time I want"

The Union of Concerned Scientists report that an estimated seventy percent of all the antibiotics produced in the United States are administered to farm animals, which in turn may contribute to antibiotic resistance in humans, thus potentially altering life as we know it on the planet. Why all the antibiotics? Our theory is that too many intrepid farmers are actually at the mercy of coddled hypochondriac chickens using any lame excuse for their next penicillin fix. Did we mention it's just a theory?

Tin Cup

1996

1 whole (3 ½–to–4 pound) free-range
  chicken
3 large garlic cloves, minced fine
Juice and zest of 1 lemon
2 tablespoons chopped fresh herbs of
  choice, or a mixture (sage, parsley,
  tarragon, rosemary, etc.)
1 teaspoon sea salt
1 teaspoon freshly ground black pepper
1 teaspoon red pepper flakes
4 tablespoons olive oil
18 holes and a free afternoon

Birdie!

We call it Birdie! Your tastebuds will call this a hole-in-one!

1. Place the chicken breast-side down on a cutting board. Using a pair of poultry shears or a large cook's knife, cut completely through the bones on either side of the backbone.

2. Remove the backbone and turn the birdie over breast-side up. Place a second cutting board on top of the chicken and press down with all your might. If friends are over, have someone else press as well. Sit on it if you need to.

3. In a small bowl, combine the garlic, lemon juice, zest, herbs, salt, pepper, pepper flakes, and half the olive oil.

4. Turn the now flattened chicken over once more and slather with the seasoning mixture, anywhere you can get to, including under the skin. Cover with plastic wrap and refrigerate anywhere from 45 minutes to 24 hours. (A longer marinating time will yield a more strongly seasoned chicken.)

5. Wrap 4 bricks with aluminum foil. Don't ask why. Preheat the oven to 500°F.

6. Place a large cast iron skillet over medium-high heat for 5 minutes. Add the remaining olive oil (swirl to coat the pan) and place the chicken in skin-side down. Place a cookie sheet over the chicken then place the bricks on the cookie sheet to further flatten the bird.

7. Cook for 5–7 minutes on the stovetop, then place the whole works in the preheated oven and roast for 10 minutes. Remove from the oven, take off the bricks and cookie sheet and turn the chicken over (being careful not to tear the skin) and roast an additional 20 minutes. An instant-read thermometer inserted in the thickest part of the thigh should read 170°F.

8. Remember the credo of the golfer and, if the recipe goes well, take all the credit. If not, blame your caddy. In any case, make him do the dishes while you belly up to the 19th hole.

Yield: Serves 4

FOOD
FOR THOUGHT

This recipe is a variation of an ancient Etruscan dish called pollo al mattone, translating as "with brick." This early technique of flattening out a whole chicken and pressing it between heavy stones over an open fire allowed the bird to cook evenly without burning or drying out. Our contemporary version is geared for the home kitchen using a cast iron skillet and a couple of bricks. If you shoot par, the meat will be moist and flavorful...the skin unbelievably crisp.

CHEW ON THIS

Did you know the film world was almost deprived of Kevin Costner? Apparently, a discouraged Costner had given up acting for a career in marketing when a chance meeting with Richard Burton on a flight back from Mexico convinced him to pursue his dream. There's no truth to the rumor that, after a few complimentary cocktails, Sir Richard gave the same advice to the skycap, the stewardess and the farm-equipment salesman in the seat next to him.

Please allow me to introduce myself...

Rene Russo was discovered by a talent scout at a Rolling Stones concert when she was 18 years old.

Chapter **5**

Seafood

Arachnophobia

For the crab legs:
6–8 frozen king crab legs, defrosted

For the curry sauce:
2 medium tomatoes
2 tablespoons olive oil
1 teaspoon grated ginger
1 tablespoon mild curry powder
1/2 cup dry sherry

For the lemon-butter:
1 stick butter
2 tablespoons finely chopped parsley
2 tablespoons grated onion
1-2 teaspoons hot pepper sauce
2 tablespoons fresh lemon juice
1 copy of *Charlotte's Web*

CHEW ON THIS
Although a significant percentage of the world's population happily includes insects as an important part of their diet, you probably think you've never eaten them. Think again. It's estimated the average person inadvertently consumes over a pound of insects in his lifetime.

Creepy Crawly Crab Legs

We couldn't see wolfing down spider legs dipped in butter (can you imagine our test kitchen crawling with spiders?) So we chose a fellow member of the phylum Arthropoda—crabs. Proof that you can't judge a crustacean by its cover, these crab legs may look creepy but their delicious taste will leave you screaming with delight.

1. Search kitchen cupboards, cracks, and corners for any lurking, malevolent presence waiting to suck the life out of you, your loved ones, or dining companions. If you survive, proceed to step 2.

2. Make the curry sauce: Peel, seed, and finely chop the tomatoes. Heat the olive oil in a small saucepan over medium heat. Add the ginger and curry powder and sauté until fragrant, about 45 seconds. Add the tomatoes and sherry and simmer 20 minutes or until thickened. Season to taste with salt and pepper.

3. Make the lemon-butter: Combine the butter, parsley, onion, pepper sauce, and lemon juice in a small saucepan over low heat. Cook until melted; keep warm until use.

4. Prepare the crab: Split the shells lengthwise and cut into manageable pieces. Brush each piece with your choice of sauce.

5. Place the crab legs cut-side up on a broiler pan and broil until lightly browned and heated through, about 4 minutes.

6. Serve with plenty of extra sauce and a semi-dry anti-venom serum of a good vintage.

7. Spin a web of deceit all your own: Tell your guests a spider sighting left you too scared to leave your seat so obviously someone else will have to do the dishes.

Yield: 4 servings

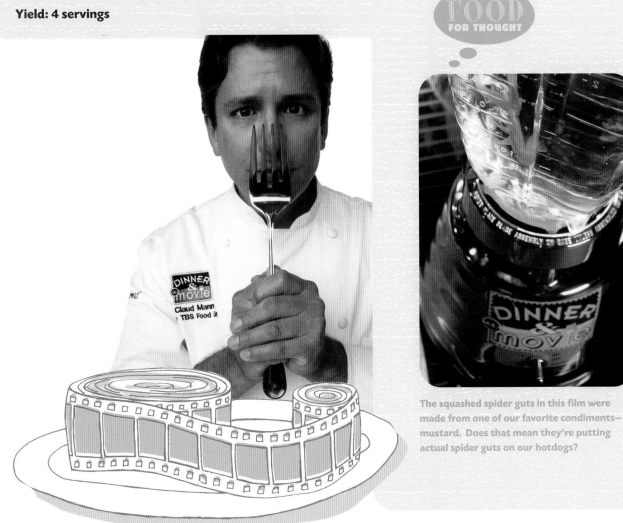

Inside Scoop

King Crabs can measure 10 feet across from claw to claw.

The squashed spider guts in this film were made from one of our favorite condiments—mustard. Does that mean they're putting actual spider guts on our hotdogs?

$\mathcal{B}$asic $\mathcal{I}$nstinct

1992

For the cakes:

4 tablespoons peanut oil

1 each red and yellow bell pepper,
   cut into 1/4-inch dice

1 or 2 jalapeños, seeded and
   chopped fine

1 egg

3 tablespoons mayonnaise

1 teaspoon dry English mustard

1 tablespoon Old Bay® seasoning

1/4 cup minced scallions

3 slices white bread, crusts trimmed,
   chopped fine

1 ½ pounds stone or lump crabmeat

1 cup crushed saltine cracker crumbs

For the sauce:

1/2 cup mayonnaise

2 teaspoons lemon or lime juice

2 tablespoons fresh herbs of choice,
   dill, cilantro, basil, etc.

1 ice pick (used for good and not evil)

Alternate Ingredients

Geena Davis and Ellen Barkin passed on
Basic Instinct because of the nudity.

$\mathcal{S}$tone-$\mathcal{C}$old $\mathcal{K}$iller $\mathcal{C}$rab $\mathcal{C}$akes

FADE IN: An icy siren from the ocean depths beckons you with her delicate claws. The attraction is powerful, the draw irresistible. You know she's trouble but you can't help yourself. You have to touch her . . . taste her . . . eat her up. We recommend doing it with some herbed mayonnaise.

1. Heat one tablespoon peanut oil over moderately high heat and sauté bell peppers and jalapeño until softened and fragrant, about 5 minutes.

2. After peppers have cooled, combine them with the egg, mayonnaise, dry mustard, Old Bay, scallions and chopped bread. Stir until well blended and carefully mix in the crabmeat without breaking apart. Cover and chill at least 20 minutes.

3. Depending on the size desired, divide crab mixture into either four or eight equal portions and pat each into a plump disk.

4. Spread crushed saltines out in a pie dish and press the crab patties gently into the crumbs, coating all sides evenly. Carefully place on a cookie sheet; cover with plastic wrap and refrigerate at least 20 minutes and up to 12 hours.

5. Combine sauce ingredients and refrigerate.

6. Heat remaining peanut oil in a cast iron skillet over medium-high heat until very hot, but not smoking, and sauté crab cakes until golden brown and crisp, about 4 minutes. Gently turn and cook another 3 to 4 minutes. Transfer to heated plates and eat immediately or place carefully on a baking sheet and keep warm in a 325°F oven.

7. Follow your most basic instinct and eat as many as possible.

Yield: Makes 4 large or 8 small crab cakes

Give 'Em A Hand

Relax, you don't have to be a killer to enjoy stone crabs. Since only the claw is eaten, fisherman remove one claw, leaving the other for self-defense. The crabs are then returned to the water and regenerate a replacement claw in about 18 months. Then just when they start feeling good about themselves, the process starts all over again.

Inside Scoop

When Sharon Stone saw the infamous interrogation scene in the finished film, she was shocked and threatened to take legal action to block distribution of the film. She reconsidered when director Paul Verhoeven convinced her that the movie was going to make her a star. The film was released on schedule and the rest is history.

Beetlejuice

For the beet sauce:
5-6 medium beets, greens intact
3 cloves garlic, peeled
3 tablespoons lemon juice
1 tablespoon rice wine vinegar
Salt and pepper to taste

For the sole:
4 large sole fillets
2 tablespoons softened butter
Salt and freshly ground black pepper
   to taste
Zest of 1 lemon and 1 orange
1 cup bone dry white wine
1 "Handbook for the Recently Deceased"

Inside Scoop

Tim Burton's first big project, the half-hour cartoon, "Frankenweenie," was shelved by Disney because it was considered too violent for children. Luckily, Warner Bros. was looking for someone to direct real-life cartoon Pee-Wee Herman and hired Burton to helm *Pee-Wee's Big Adventure*. Burton has gone on to direct some of our favorite films, including *Edward Scissorhands* and *Ed Wood*.

Dearly Departed Sole

Does death scare you? Calm down, there's nothing to be afraid of. In Beetlejuice we learn that the dead can be cute and friendly and even kind of sexy—as long as they're played by Geena Davis and Alec Baldwin. It's our mission with this recipe to show you that fish and beets don't have to be scary either. Prepared our way they can be savory and delicious and, like Geena and Alec, kind of sexy. So dive in, and if you feel afraid, just repeat three times: Beets are delicious, beets are delicious, beets are delicious . . .

1. "Has being dead got you down? Well friends, you've come to the right recipe!" Wash the beets well, then cut off the beet greens about 2 inches from the base. Reserve greens.

2. Place the beets and garlic cloves in a pot; cover with cold water and bring to a boil. Reduce the heat and simmer, uncovered, for 30-45 minutes, or until tender.

3. Dip the beet greens one by one in the boiling water until limp (about 15 seconds). Trim off any thick stems and lay the wilted greens out flat on a towel.

4. Beetsauce! Beetsauce! Beetsauce! When the beets can be easily pierced with a fork, peel under running water and cut into quarters. Then place the beets, garlic cloves, 1/2 cup of the cooking liquid and the lemon juice in a blender and process until smooth.

Transfer the mixture to a small saucepan and place over low heat; season to taste with rice wine vinegar, salt and pepper.

5. Preheat oven to 425°F.

6. Search your sole: Lightly spread the tops of each sole fillet with butter, then season with salt, black pepper and citrus zest.

7. Wrap the fillets individually in beet greens (to resemble cozy little mummies), then transfer to an oiled baking dish and moisten with white wine. Cover loosely with foil and bake anywhere from 10 minutes to an eternity, whichever comes first.

8. It's ShowTime! Serve over a ghastly but tasty pool of beet sauce, garnish with freshly manifested ectoplasm (or a little lemon zest) and eat as though it's your last meal.

9. Summon help with the dishes from beyond. Lure any guests—living or dead—into the kitchen with a rousing chorus of "Day-O," and hope someone offers to release you from the torment of "dirty dish purgatory."

Yield: 4 servings

We had to do some "sole" searching for this one, but, after haunting our local fish market, we found that true sole is about as rare as being raised from the dead. Presumably, most of what is sold as sole in the U.S. is actually Cousin Flounder, not just a sole substitute but a flavorful fish in its own right.

CHEW ON THIS

Although "Betelgeuse"—which means "armpit of the giant" in Arabic—is the name of a celestial body, it has nothing to do with Michael Keaton's character in *Beetlejuice*. Apparently the studio was so confused by the title *Beetlejuice* they wanted to change the name of the film to *House Ghosts*. As a joke, Tim Burton suggested the name *Scared Sheetless* and was horrified when the studio actually considered it.

Beet the Odds!

Wanna live longer? Eat beets—our idea of a wonder food. They're loaded with vitamins A and C, potassium, iron, folacin, protein, fiber, calcium, and beta carotene.

Days of Thunder

1990

Four 8-ounce flatfish fillets (turbot, flounder, halibut, sole, etc.)
1/2 cup mild white miso paste
1 cup chopped cilantro
1/2 cup poppy seeds
3 tablespoons chili powder combined with 3 tablespoons crushed chili flakes
1 cup sake or dry white wine
1 thumb-sized piece ginger, cut into coin-sized pieces
2 scallions, cut into 2-inch pieces
2 fresh jalapeño, serrano, or habenero chiles, cut in half lengthwise, seeds removed
3 cups clam juice
6 ounces coiled fideo noodles or angel hair pasta
3 tablespoons vegetable oil
8 baby bok choy
Plenty of guts, nerves of steel, and a pair of tight black jeans

"Well, I can wear heels now."
—Nicole Kidman, discussing her split with Tom Cruise on "The Late Show With David Letterman"

"Cruise Control" Turbot

Gentlemen . . . start your ovens!

1. Gentlemen, start your burners: Cut each fillet in 3 equal pieces and rub each piece with a light coating of miso paste.

2. Coat 4 of the pieces with chopped cilantro, 4 pieces with poppy seeds and 4 pieces with the chili mixture. Refrigerate until use.

3. Pit stop: Combine the wine, ginger, scallions, chiles, and clam juice in a saucepan or wok with a fitted steamer top and bring to a boil. Reduce heat to low and simmer 10 minutes.

4. While the broth simmers; heat the vegetable oil in a medium saucepan over medium heat. Add the uncooked pasta and fry until golden brown.

5. Pull the pasta from the oil, drain briefly, and set aside.

6. Return the clam juice mixture to a rapid boil and place the coated fish and bok choy in steamer compartments. Steam for 10 to 12 minutes, adding the fried pasta to the broth 5 minutes before the fish is done.

7. Checkered flag: Pile some pasta in the center of each bowl; top with turbot and chili broth and don't stop eating until you see the checkered flag. Claim your trophy and leave the dishes to your pit crew.

Yield: Serves 4

Spill The Beans

Tom Cruise's real name is Thomas Cruise Mapother IV. His cousin, William Mapother—who stuck with his original surname—played Marissa Tomei's abusive ex-husband in the 2001 indy hit, *In The Bedroom*.

We get steamed just thinking about it . . .

We think steaming is a cooking method too often overlooked. All right, so it may not offer the spectacle of a sauté or be as dramatically macho as roasting, but what steaming lacks in sizzle, it makes up for in substance. Steamed vegetables retain their color and vitamin content while meat and fish emerge plump, moist, and tender.

The Distinguished Gentleman

1992

The sauce:

2 tablespoons olive oil

1/3 cup dry red wine

1 tablespoon tomato paste

1 pound plum tomatoes, split
lengthwise, seeds removed

1 yellow onion, diced

4 cloves garlic, peeled and crushed

1 teaspoon kosher salt

1 teaspoon black pepper

The squid:

2-3 pounds whole squid, cleaned

3 cups self-rising flour

1 tablespoon salt

2 teaspoons *each* black pepper, paprika,
and baking soda

1 ½ quarts peanut oil, for frying

3 lemons, cut into wedges

1 highly paid Squid P.A.C. lobbyist

CHEW ON THIS

A latin phrase meaning "something
for something," quid pro quo is most
commonly used to describe campaign
contributions made to candidates in
return for political favors.

Squid Pro Quo

Under very shady circumstances, a likable but laughably under-qualified candidate with a famous last name claims one of the highest offices in the land. Great plot for a comedy but it could never happen in real life. . . .

1. Preheat oven to 375°F.

2. Combine olive oil, red wine, and tomato paste. Arrange tomatoes, onion, and garlic on a cookie sheet and drizzle with the olive oil mixture. Roast for 45 minutes until lightly browned and fragrant.

3. Transfer the tomato mixture to a blender; puree, season to taste, and set aside.

4. First, cut any large tentacles in half lengthwise, then slice into 1/4-inch to 1/2-inch rings. Rinse with cold water and dry well with paper towels or in a salad spinner.

5. Heat at least 4 inches of oil in a heavy saucepan or fryer to 350°–360°F.

6. In a large bowl combine the flour, salt, pepper, paprika, and baking soda. Add a handful of squid and toss until evenly coated, transfer the floured squid to a colander and shake excess back into the bowl of seasoned flour.

7. Working in small batches, add the squid to the hot oil. Cook for 2 minutes until crisp and golden. Drain on paper towels; serve hot with marinara sauce and a squeeze of lemon.

8. Create a "Dirty Dish Political Action Committee" to raise funds for your campaign to clean up the kitchen. When elected, explain that the problem is really too complex to do anything about without further studies and substantially more donations.

Yield: Serves 4–5

Kitchen Quid Pro Quo
You scratch our back, we'll scratch yours, and we'll both wash our hands before touching the squid.

FOOD FOR THOUGHT
Squid are proud members of the cephalopod family (literally meaning "head-foot"). The largest of these feisty invertebrates is known to have the biggest eyeball in the world—about the size of a soccer ball.

Inside Scoop
Producer-screenwriter Marty Kaplan was a speechwriter for former Vice President Walter Mondale before turning to a career in show business. He based many of the events in the film—including the ethically questionable ones—on actual congressional happenings.

The Goonies

4 tablespoons butter

1 tablespoon chopped cilantro

Juice and zest of 2 lemons

1 small cedar plank, about 16-inches long (make certain it is untreated)

Peanut oil, for brushing the plank and for frying

One 3 pound salmon fillet, skin on

1 teaspoon each: salt, freshly ground black pepper, ground coriander

2 bunches scallions, washed and trimmed

1 Culinary Institute of America-approved floatation device

Walk the Plank Salmon

Treasure Map

AAARRGH, Maties! 1) Walk ten paces down the hall to the cave (a.k.a. kitchen). 2) Turn right (or left as the case may be) and open the big rusty door of the ancient vault (a.k.a. refrigerator). 3) Dig down to secret ingredient (a.k.a. salmon fillets). When the sun meets the horizon (a.k.a. dinner time), cook up some culinary treasure (a.k.a. Walk The Plank Salmon).

1. Combine the butter, cilantro, and lemon in the work bowl of a food processor and pulse until the mixture is smooth. Transfer to a piece of plastic wrap, roll into a cylinder, and refrigerate until use.

2. Preheat oven to 400°F.

3. Scrub the plank well with a scrub brush under running water. Blot dry and brush both sides lightly with peanut oil.

4. Place the plank on a rack in the preheated oven for 15 minutes.

5. While the plank heats, brush the salmon with olive oil and season with salt, black pepper, and coriander.

6. Remove the plank from the oven (careful, it's hot!) and reduce the temperature to 325°F. Spread the scallions on the plank in a single layer, then place the salmon fillet skin-side-down on top of the scallions. Place the planked salmon on a rack in the center of

Inside Scoop

Three *Goonies* cast members have famous parents. Martha Plimpton's father is actor Keith Carradine. Sean Astin's parents are actors Patty Duke and John Astin. Josh Brolin's dad is actor James Brolin and his stepmother is showbiz legend Barbra Streisand.

the oven and bake 20-30 minutes, until the thickest section is still slightly opaque.

7. Divide salmon into 6 pieces, garnish with a thin slice of lemon butter.

8. After dinner, play a rousing game of treasure hunt! First bury all the dirty dishes and then issue authentic-looking maps and soapy sponges to all of your guests.

Yield: Serves 6

Board with Cooking?

Salmon cooked on cedar is unparalleled and you needn't bother with purchasing an expensive cedar-cooking plank for this recipe. An untreated 1-inch x 10-inch cedar board from any lumberyard should cost about five dollars and do just fine.

It Could Happen to You 1994

3 live, 1 ½ pound lobsters
6 tablespoons olive oil
1 medium onion, chopped
1 stalk celery, chopped
1 carrot, chopped
1 head garlic, sliced crosswise
2 bay leaves
1/3 cup cognac or brandy
1 cup good champagne
2 cups clam juice
2 tablespoons tomato paste
4 tablespoons flour
4 tablespoons softened butter
1/2 cup cream
2 tablespoons chopped shallots
1/2 cup thinly sliced morels or
**   chanterelles**
2 cups diced fennel
As much freshly shaved truffle as you
**   can afford**
1 tablespoon chopped tarragon
1 package frozen puff pastry
1 egg, beaten with 1 tablespoon water
1 teeny-tiny chance in a million

Jackpot Pie

So what would YOU do if you won the lottery? We answered that burning question with a recipe that just may become the gold standard against which all other potpies are measured. Take one bite of this pastry-encrusted, creamy lobster and truffle celebration and your taste buds will think they hit the jackpot. Sure, the ingredients may be a little pricey, but this pie will make you FEEL like a winner even when your numbers don't come up.

1. Bring a large, lightly salted pot of water to a boil. Place the lobsters in the water headfirst and cook, covered, for 8-10 minutes. Dunk the lobsters in cold water to stop the cooking process. Reserve 3 cups of the cooking liquid.

2. When cool enough to handle, place each lobster on its back and cut in half, lengthwise, from head to tail. Remove tail meat; twist off claws, then crack and remove claw meat. Chop meat into large bite-sized pieces and refrigerate. Rinse the shells under running water and chop.

3. Heat half of the olive oil in a large, heavy saucepan, on a medium-high heat, until shimmering. Add the chopped lobster shells, onion, celery, carrot, garlic, and bay leaf; sauté 5 minutes.

4. Add the cognac and ignite, shaking the pan to burn off the alcohol. Add champagne and reduce until syrupy, then add the clam juice and the reserved lobster cooking liquid. Bring to a boil and simmer 30 minutes. Preheat oven to 400°F. In a small bowl cream together the tomato paste, flour, and softened butter and set aside.

5. Strain the simmered mixture into a saucepan, bring to a boil and reduce until about 2 cups remain. Add the cream and whisk in the flour-butter-tomato paste mixture until smooth. Return to a boil, whisking often. When the mixture thickens, reduce heat to low and keep warm until use.

6. In a large sauce pan over medium heat, sauté the shallots, morels, and fennel in remaining olive oil until fragrant. Add chopped reserved lobster meat, truffle shavings, chopped tarragon, and warm lobster-cream sauce; season to taste with salt and pepper and simmer for 5 minutes.

7. Ladle the lobster mixture into four 10-ounce ovenproof ramekins and seal the top of each with a piece of puff pastry. Cut a few vents for steam to escape and brush the pastry top with egg wash; bake for 30 minutes or until the pastry is golden brown and the filling bubbles around the edges.

8. Fun dinner game idea: Hold your very own after-dinner lottery, with one lucky winner taking home not only all the leftovers, but all your dirty dishes as well!

Yield: Serves 4

FOOD
FOR THOUGHT

Lobsters must be purchased either live or fully cooked. Never buy one that is recently deceased or swimming at death's door. The moment a lobster dies, both bacterial growth and its own natural enzymes begin breaking down the meat, making it unhealthful for consumption. People who swear they've heard lobsters screaming during cooking are most likely referring to the sound of steam escaping from the shell. (The other hideous screaming sound most often heard around lobsters is when the waiter presents the check.)

Inside Scoop

Actress Bridget Fonda is the daughter of actor Peter Fonda, the granddaughter of actor Henry Fonda and the niece of actress Jane Fonda who once won the marriage lottery with our TBS founder, Ted Turner. Over the past 60 years, the acting Fondas have collectively starred in over 250 films.

CHEW ON THIS

Here's a reassuring thought: Your odds of winning the lottery actually ARE better than your odds of getting struck by lightning. According to one study, here's what lottery winners did with their newfound riches:

- 80 percent buy a new vehicle
- 70 percent seek financial counseling
- 60 percent take a vacation
- 60 percent pay off debt
- 60 percent give to charity
- 50 percent buy a new house
- 50 percent retire or quit their jobs
- 30 percent keep their jobs
- 15 percent find new jobs

Gilded Cage

A longtime comic book enthusiast, Nicolas Cage—who appropriated his name from Marvel Comic hero Luke Cage—surprised fellow comic fans by auctioning off his collection of 400 Golden Age issues in 2002, earning $1.6 million from the sale.

Jaws

1 ½–2 pounds shark steak or fillet
2 tablespoons chopped garlic
5 tablespoons olive oil
1 teaspoon chili flakes
1 teaspoon ground cumin
1 teaspoon oregano
Flour, for dusting
1 yellow onion, sliced
1/2 cup white wine
2 tablespoons capers
1/4 cup olives
3 cups chopped tomatoes (or one 28-ounce can chopped Italian tomatoes)
One 12-ounce bottle clam juice
2 bunches chard, washed and cut into 2-inch strips
Salt and pepper to taste
1 copy "Mack the Knife"

Man Eating Shark... and Loving It!

Just when you thought it was safe to go back in the kitchen . . .

1. In a large mixing bowl, combine and stir together the garlic, 3 tablespoons of the olive oil, chili flakes, cumin, and oregano.

2. Cut the shark into 2-inch chunks and toss with the garlic and olive oil mixture. Set aside.

3. Heat a large skillet over medium-high heat until quite hot. Add the remaining olive oil and swirl the pan to coat the bottom evenly.

4. Dust the shark with a small amount of flour, season with salt and pepper, and quickly sear the shark in batches until lightly browned, but not fully cooked.

5. Transfer the browned fish to a warm platter.

6. Reduce the heat under the skillet to medium, add the sliced onions, and sauté about 5 minutes.

7. When the onion becomes translucent, add the white wine. Using a wooden spoon, scrape the bottom of the pan to loosen any tasty brown bits stuck to its surface.

8. Add the capers, olives, and tomatoes and sauté a moment before adding the clam juice. Reduce the heat to low and simmer, uncovered, for 15 minutes.

Inside Scoop

When Roy Scheider was trapped in the sinking Orca, it took 75 takes to get the shot right. Scheider reportedly did not trust the special effects team to rescue him in case of an emergency so he hid axes and hatches around the cabin just in case.

9. Add and stir in the chard, cover and cook for 2 minutes.

10. Return the browned shark back to the skillet and cook no more than 5 minutes, until just heated through.

11. Season to taste with salt and pepper, ladle into bowls, and serve with chunks of hot garlic bread.

12. No need to worry about cleanup! Cooked properly, this dish should start a feeding frenzy that won't stop until your guests have frantically devoured everything in front of them: dishes, silverware, placemats, napkins . . . .

Yield: 4 servings

That's A Lot of Clams

This was the first movie in history to make over $100 million.

Truly fresh fish should not smell "fishy" at all; ask the clerk for a sniff (of the fish, that is) and inspect it. If the fish is whole, the gills should be pink and the eyes clear. Pressed lightly with a fingertip, the flesh should be supple enough to spring back. Also, it's not a bad idea to establish a relationship with your butcher or fishmonger. No, you don't have to go on long drives together; just get to know them well enough to trust their information about what's fresh and what isn't.

CHEW ON THIS

Director Steven Spielberg and editing great Verna Fields kept the audience in suspense for 80 minutes into this 124-minute film before revealing the monster shark. Just 26 when he directed *Jaws*, Spielberg nicknamed the shark "Bruce" after his lawyer.

Private Benjamin

Ingredients

- 2 cups water
- 2 cups kosher salt
- 3 cups ice
- 1 cup dry white wine
- 1/2 cup extra-virgin olive oil
- 6–12 whole, peeled cloves garlic, sliced very thinly
- 1 pinch salt, plus more to taste
- 2 pounds large peeled prawns or shrimp, shells reserved
- Juice of 1 lemon or lime
- 2 tablespoons freshly chopped Italian parsley, tarragon, or chervil
- 1 pinch cayenne pepper
- 2 tablespoons cold butter
- 1 olive drab, government issue lipstick

Goldie Prawns

Okay, we know that shrimp and prawns fall under different biological classifications as crustaceans but for all practical purposes, the terms are used interchangeably in the U.S. From what we can tell, most markets and restaurants describe small and medium size shrimp as "shrimp" and large and jumbo shrimp as "prawns." We describe our take on the classic scampi as "delicious" and, for our practical purposes, "Goldie Shrimp" just didn't work.

1. Bring water to boil in a large saucepan, add salt and stir until dissolved. Remove from heat and set aside to cool for 2–3 minutes.

2. Add the ice to the salt-water mixture and stir until melted. Stir the raw shrimp into this salty slush and set aside for 20 minutes. Remove shrimp from salt brine and rinse well in cold water and peel. Devein if desired.

3. In a medium saucepan, combine shrimp shells with white wine; cover with cold water and bring to a boil. Boil for 5 minutes. Transfer all the shells and 2 cups of the hot liquid to a blender and puree for 30 seconds. Strain the mixture back into the saucepan and reduce to one cup in volume.

4. Pour the oil into a large skillet over a low heat. Add sliced garlic and a pinch of salt; cook very slowly until garlic begins to hint at turning golden, stirring often.

Inside Scoop

Goldie Hawn received an Oscar® nomination for Best Actress for her role as Private Judy Benjamin. In 1969, she won the Oscar® for Best Supporting Actress for her role in *Cactus Flower*.

5. Add shrimp in one even layer and increase the heat to medium. When the shrimp just begin to turn pink, turn them over and continue cooking another 2 minutes or so. Don't overcook.

6. Remove from heat and stir in the hot shrimp shell broth, lime juice, a small handful of fresh minced parsley, tarragon or chervil, and a pinch of cayenne. If you like butter in this dish, add it now off the heat, and swirl the pan until butter is incorporated in the sauce.

7. Garnish with fresh herbs and serve with chunks of hot, crusty bread. Then assemble all troops for top secret underwater maneuvers, a.k.a. The Dishes.

Yield: Serves 4

FOOD FOR THOUGHT

Some or our favorite oxymorons: Jumbo shrimp, military intelligence, freezer burn, plastic silverwear, airline food, deafening silence, original copies, old news, accordion music.

Look That Up in Your Funk & Wagnalls!

Dubbed by *Look* magazine "television's dumbest and most delectable bonbon" when she was 24 years old, Goldie Hawn first gained attention as a go-go dancing comedienne on the classic '60s comedy show, "Rowan & Martin's Laugh-In."

Twins

Mussels and Shrimp

2 pounds large shrimp

2 pounds mussels

1 cup dry white wine

1/4 teaspoon saffron threads

1/2 cup olive oil

2 bell peppers, diced

1 onion, diced

2 tablespoons chopped garlic

1 cup quartered artichoke hearts

1 bay leaf

1 teaspoon paprika

2 cups short grain or Arborio rice

4 cups chicken stock

1 ½ cups chopped, canned plum
  tomatoes

1/2 cup frozen tiny peas

1 cup sliced Spanish olives

1 genetically engineered egg, divided in
  two (half beaten, the other half
  coddled)

Arnold Schwarzenegger and Danny DeVito play improbable twins in this 1988 comedy about genetic engineering's efforts to create the perfect man. In the "Dinner & a Movie" test kitchen, we've used culinary engineering to create the perfect recipe, Mussels & Shrimp.

1. Peel and devein shrimp, clean and scrub mussels.

2. In a small saucepan, bring wine to a boil, add the saffron and remove from heat.

3. Heat olive oil over medium heat in the largest, heaviest skillet or saucepan you've got. Add the bell peppers and onion until the onion softens, about 3 minutes.

4. Add the garlic, artichokes, bay leaf, and paprika and sauté a minute more. Add the rice and stir to coat.

5. Add chicken stock and tomatoes, increase heat and bring to a boil. Reduce heat to medium and cook uncovered for about 15 minutes.

Who's That Girl?

That's Heather Graham as the twin's mother Mary Ann Benedict.

6. Add the saffron infused wine, shrimp, and mussels; cover and continue cooking another 15 minutes until the rice is tender and the mussels pop open.

7. Season to taste with salt and pepper. Five minutes before serving mix in the green peas and olives.

8. Be sure to save some room for some "Separated at Birthday Cake."

Yield: 4 servings

CHEW ON THIS

Word has it two real life twins were reunited with their father after spotting him playing an extra in *Twins*.

We think the maxim about shellfish being safe in any month ending in the letter "r" should be put to rest. "Red Tides" can and do occur throughout the year, creating hot spots where shellfish are indeed unsafe to eat. When purchasing shellfish it's best to shop in a reputable store, one that buys fish from a licensed USDA-inspected vendor. If digging for shellfish yourself, use that big muscle between your ears and check with the health department for a local shellfish update.

Inside Scoop

The six-foot-two-inch Arnold Schwarzenegger was called by the *Guinness Book of World Records*, "the most perfectly developed man in the history of the world." The five-foot-tall Danny DeVito was once a hairdresser, whose clients affectionately called him "Mr. Danny."

Chapter **6**

Meat & Flesh

9 to 5

Male Chauvinist Pig

This glass-ceiling favorite is popular with pork lovers everywhere, regardless of gender.

For the pork roast:

One 2–3 pound boneless center loin pork roast
1/4 teaspoon ground bay leaf
1/2 teaspoon ground clove
1/2 teaspoon ground cinnamon
2 teaspoons freshly ground black pepper
2 teaspoons kosher salt
1 tablespoon finely chopped fresh rosemary
8 cloves garlic, cut into slivers

For the cabbage:

2 tablespoons butter
1 yellow onion, thinly sliced
6 cups shredded red cabbage
3 tablespoons cider vinegar
3 tablespoons honey (feel free to substitute Skinny & Sweet)
1/2 cup dark beer
1/2 cup chicken stock
1/4 teaspoon celery seed
Salt and pepper to taste
4 tablespoons chopped Italian parsley
1 bottle window cleaner (for glass ceiling)

1. Adjust oven rack position to the upper middle of the oven and preheat to 475°F.

2. Tie 'em up: Cut a length of twine about 6 times the length of the rascal you're about to lasso. Make a slip knot and drop it over the end that's not kicking. Continue by making a series of half hitches until you've used up your slack. (By this time he may have stopped struggling and will listen to reason . . . Nah.)

3. Rub it in: In a small bowl, combine the bay leaf, clove, cinnamon, pepper, salt, and rosemary. Rub spice mixture into meat. If your chauvinist gets suspicious, tell him it's a new blend of Old Spice®.

4. Stud the stud with garlic: Pierce the pork in 15-20 spots with a paring knife or skewer and insert the garlic slivers into each opening.

5. Roast 'em up: Place the roast on a rack in a roasting pan. Slide the pan into the oven for 30 minutes. After 30 minutes, remove the roast from the oven and reduce the oven temperature to 325°F. Allow the oven to cool before returning the meat to the oven (about 20 minutes). Cook for a final 20-30 minutes, to an internal temperature of 150°F. Let rest for 15 minutes before carving into slices.

6. Make the bed: Melt the butter in a medium saucepan over medium heat. Add the onions and sauté until limp, about 3 minutes. Add the remaining ingredients, cover, and cook for 15-20 minutes. Toss with chopped parsley just before serving. Arrange slices of roast over a bed of cabbage.

7. Savor the moment: Now you've got your male chauvinist pig just the way you want him: tasteful, submissive, and served on a bed of your own choosing (in this case, cabbage).

Yield: 6 servings

FOOD FOR THOUGHT

Most popular politically incorrect food names:
honeybun, sugarpie, peaches, peanut, pumpkin, bundt cake, head cheese, pork butt, java drawers.

Bringing Home the Bacon

In 1820, women's average earnings were one third of men's. In 1980 (the year this film was made) women earned approximately 60 percent of what their male counterparts did. By 2001, that figure rose to close to 75 percent. That figure may never equalize; the 80% of American women who do bear children invariably do so during the same time frame in which their male co-workers advance steadily through the ranks.

Inside Scoop

All three of *9 to 5*'s leading ladies are big award show winners. Jane Fonda has won two Academy Awards®, for 1971's *Klute* and 1978's *Coming Home*. Lily Tomlin has won two Tony Awards, including one for her one-woman show "The Search for Signs of Intelligent Life in the Universe." Dolly Parton has won seven Grammy Awards, including two for the *9 to 5* title song.

Pork & Jelly Sandwich, Anyone?

Because contemporary pork is no longer bred for lard, it's much more healthful than its plump predecessor. One ounce of lean pork contains about two grams of fat as compared to 16 grams for the same amount of peanut butter.

Angus

Outcast-Iron Skillet Steak

A movie named after a delicious variety of meat? The choice was obvious.

For the bleu cheese butter:

6 tablespoons unsalted butter, softened

6 tablespoons bleu cheese; i.e., Stilton, Roquefort, or Gorgonzola

2 tablespoons chopped Italian parsley

2 teaspoons finely chopped shallots

1 teaspoon brandy or cognac

For the steak fries:

2 pounds baking potatoes or Yukon Gold potatoes

3 to 4 cups vegetable oil for frying

Salt to taste

For the steaks:

4 boneless rib-eye steaks, 1 ¼–to– 1 ½ inch thick

1 clove garlic, peeled and sliced in half

Kosher salt and freshly ground black pepper

2 tablespoons peanut oil

1 "Drain Dawson's Creek" bumper sticker

CHEW ON THIS

Throughout the film, the band Green Day is referenced many times. Perhaps that's because Rob Cavallo, the band's then-producer, was one of the film's executive producers.

1. Make the blue cheese butter: In a mixing bowl, combine the butter, cheese, parsley, shallots, and cognac; mash together with a fork until thoroughly combined.

2. Place the mixture on a sheet of plastic wrap and roll up tightly into a narrow cylinder and refrigerate.

3. Start the fries: Cut potatoes into strips 3-inch long and 3/8-inch square. Cover with cold water and let stand 10-20 minutes. Drain and dry very well with paper towels.

4. Fill deep fat fryer or large saucepan with oil to a depth of 5-6 inches. Using a frying thermometer, slowly heat to a temperature of 325°F.

5. Fry potatoes in 1-cup batches until they just begin to turn a very pale gold (about 6 minutes). Remove fries with slotted spoon and drain on paper towels in a single layer until cool to the touch. Raise oil temperature to 360°F.

6. Heat the pans: While the fries cool, place two cast iron skillets over medium heat. Season the steaks by rubbing with the cut side of the garlic clove and sprinkling with salt and pepper.

7. Add 1 tablespoon peanut oil to each skillet and swirl or brush lightly to evenly coat the pan. Place 2 steaks in each pan and cook for 4-5 minutes until nicely browned on one side. Turn steaks and cook 2-3 minutes for rare, 3-4 minutes for medium-rare and 4-5 minutes for medium. Transfer to a warm platter and allow meat to rest while finishing the fries.

8. Finish the fries: Refry the potatoes a second time in small batches, moving them constantly until crisp and golden, about 2 minutes. Drain; transfer to paper to drain again. Toss with salt and serve.

9. Ask the nearest person to prove the Bethune theory of elemental relationships by deftly dipping one small greasy dish into one large soapy body of water. If they don't understand the concept, just tell them to repeat the process until it becomes clear.

Yield: Serves 4

FOOD
FOR THOUGHT

Inside Scoop

The "Angus" story has gone through more changes than an adolescent boy. In the original short story about a teenage outcast, Angus' dad was alive and both his mom and dad were gay. When Hollywood got a hold of it, the controversial gay theme was gradually whittled away. First Angus' mom was straight and his dad was gay. After the final cut, the filmmakers decided to abandon the gay parent idea altogether, kill off the dad and add a new beginning and other key scenes with George C. Scott playing Angus' grandfather.

Are you suffering from cast iron guilt? You aren't alone—a lot of people have a neglected, rusty, cast iron skillet stashed away in a cabinet and don't know what to do about it. Fortunately, this embarrassing condition is nothing to be ashamed of and responds well to a little therapy. Simply scrub away the rust with steel wool, wash and rinse well, then dry and coat liberally with peanut oil inside and out. Place the pan in a preheated 350° oven for one hour then turn the oven off and allow the pan to cool before removing. Your pan is now "seasoned" and you should never wash it with soap or put it in the dishwasher. Just rinse and wipe with a little oil after each use.

3 tablespoons corn oil
2 pounds skirt steak, cut into
 2-inch cubes
2 pounds pork sausage
10 cloves garlic, minced
2 medium onions, coarsely chopped
4 jalapeño peppers, seeded and
 finely diced
2 tablespoons ground cumin seed
2 bay leaves
1 tablespoon ground coriander seed
5 tablespoons chili powder
1 tablespoon paprika
2 teaspoons oregano
1 teaspoon sage
1 bell pepper, diced
2 stalks celery, diced
One 28-ounce can crushed tomatoes
One 6-ounce can roasted chiles,
 finely chopped
2 cups each: fully cooked black,
 pinto and kidney beans
Two 12-ounce cans of beer
2 cups beef stock
2 tablespoons fine corn meal or
 masa harina
1 jar Beano®

Blazing Saddles 1974

Wilder West Chile with Madeline Con Carne

Is it twue what they say about this chile being gifted?

1. *Gather round the campfire, boys.* Place a large cast iron skillet over a small campfire (or a medium-high heat) until hot, but not smoking. Add the oil and lightly brown the meat. (To avoid over-crowding the skillet, brown the meat in three or four batches.) Transfer the browned meat to a large Dutch oven or heavy casserole. Discard all but 3 tablespoons of fat from the skillet.

2. Reduce the heat under the skillet to medium, and add the garlic, onion, and diced jalapeño pepper. Sauté for 2 minutes, stirring often.

3. Add the cumin, bay leaf, coriander, chili powder, paprika, oregano, and sage to the skillet, stirring well to coat the onions, garlic, and jalapeño with the spices. Continue cooking the spice mixture for another minute, stirring frequently to avoid scorching.

4. Add the bell peppers, celery, crushed tomatoes, and roasted chiles. Stir well with a wooden spoon, scraping the bottom and sides to loosen any tasty bits stuck to the skillet. Transfer contents of the skillet to the Dutch oven and place over medium high heat.

5. *Hey, where are all the white beans at?* Add the beans, beer, and beef stock, stir well and bring to a boil. Reduce the heat to low and simmer anywhere from 20 minutes to 2 hours (depending on how desperate your desperados are to eat). If desired, thicken the chili by stirring in 2 tablespoons of the corn meal or masa harina (While the chili simmers, feel free to pass the time by attempting to diagram the town of Rockridge's Johnson family tree.)

6. *Oh, it's twue, it's twue!* Serve your bubbling masterpiece with a few thoughtfully appropriate side dishes like Pull My Finger Sandwiches and freshly baked Who Cut the Cheese Puffs, then evacuate the vicinity immediately.

Yield: Serves 6–8

Full Of Beans

Mel Brooks' character, "Le Petomane" takes his name from a popular Moulin Rouge performer who sang and did impressions through flatulence.

Oh, Madeline!

The world lost one of its funniest women when Madeline Kahn passed away in 1999. A Tony® Award-winner and recipient of two Oscar® nominations (one for *Paper Moon* and one for *Blazing Saddles*), Kahn was perhaps best known for her hilarious collaborations with writer/director Mel Brooks. In addition to *Blazing Saddles*, the two worked together on the monster movie spoof, *Young Frankenstein*, and the Hitchcock take-off, *High Anxiety*. In her later years, Kahn focused mostly on stage work including her Tony-winning turn in Wendy Wasserstein's "The Sisters Rosensweig."

Bean Counting

Blazing Saddles is one of the highest grossing Westerns ever made. It grossed $47 million on initial release and has made an additional $60 million since then.

"Mongo only pawn in game of life."
— *Mongo*

FOOD FOR THOUGHT

Contrary to popular opinion, we feel it's best NOT to soak your beans before cooking. In our experience, the beans retain more of their flavor and nutrients without soaking and we consider the audible gastrointestinal turbulence—which soaking is supposed to eliminate—to be an added bonus to the bean-eating experience.

CHEW ON THIS

In the famous scene in which Lili von Schtupp seduces Sheriff Bart in her dressing room and questions him about the size of his endowments, Bart followed up with a witty rejoinder that was cut from final film. Originally, he answered her query, "Pardon me, miss, but you're sucking on my elbow."

Conspiracy Theory *1997*

It's All in Your Headcheese

1 pig's head, brains removed
4 pig's feet
(If you can't get your hands on feet and head, feel free to substitute 1 bone-in pork butt)
2 tablespoons salt
1 handful parsley
2 onions, quartered
2 heads garlic, halved
2 bay leaves
2 carrots, chopped
3 stalks celery, chopped
15 black peppercorns
5 whole cloves
10 juniper berries
3 tablespoons plain gelatin
1/2 cup water
2 teaspoon each: cayenne pepper, chopped fresh sage, and nutmeg
1 grassy knoll

Travelers Headcheese Advisory

Paranoid you won't be able to order headcheese in foreign lands? An international favorite, headcheese is called "brawn" in England and "fromage de tete" in France.

Headcheese. Deliciously gelatinous variety sausage or sinister conspiracy? You've heard about it all your life. But have you ever seen it made? Have you ever seen it eaten? Is it head or is it cheese? We at "Dinner & a Movie" are kicking off our own top secret conspiracy. Our mission: to tempt people into eating intimidating foods. We're concerned that too many Americans are missing delicious dishes simply because the ingredients are unfamiliar. The recipe below is the first step in our plan. We'd tell you the second step but then we'd have to kill you.

1. Scrub head and feet well, place in large stock pot, and cover with cold water. Add the salt, parsley, onions, garlic, bay leaves, carrots, celery, peppercorns, cloves, and juniper berries.

2. Bring the mixture to a boil, reduce heat, and simmer until the meat falls from the bones, about 2 hours, skimming occasionally.

3. Remove head (or butt) from the broth and allow to cool; then pull off as much meat as possible, chop, and set aside. Combine the gelatin and 1/2-cup cold water; stir until no lumps remain.

4. Strain the broth into a saucepan; skim off fat and add the gelatin mixture, cayenne, sage, and nutmeg. Bring the mixture to a boil and reduce to about 3 cups in volume.

5. Transfer the chopped meat to a loaf pan lined with plastic wrap. Pour the broth over the top and refrigerate until firm.

6. When firm, slice thinly and serve on *Catcher in the Rye* bread with plenty of mustard and onion.

7. Admonish guests that not only are "they" watching you at this very moment, but "they" also maintain a precise list of people who don't eat all their headcheese. (Of course, everyone knows that the only way to be removed from the dreaded "list" is to offer to do the dishes.)

Yield: 4 servings

Donner, Party of One

Director Richard Donner makes a cameo in the film as one of Jerry's passengers in the opening credits.

Inside Scoop

Don't let that Australian accent fool you. Mel Gibson was born in the U.S. and didn't move to Australia until he was 11 years old. His dad used winnings from a successful run on "Jeopardy" to move the family to Australia.

Dragnet

1 gallon water

1 cup brown sugar

Three 12-ounce bottles stout beer

4 to 6 pound smoked ham, fully cooked

1/2 cup each: chopped onion, carrots, and celery

1 teaspoon ground sage

3 tablespoons orange marmalade

1/2 cup Marsala or sherry

1 tablespoon dry mustard

6 tablespoons honey or pure maple syrup

Whole cloves

1/2 cup cream (optional)

The will to serve (hot) and to protect (your reputation in the kitchen)

FOOD
FOR THOUGHT

Novelist James Ellroy (*L.A. Confidential*) credits Jack Webb's nonfiction book *Badge of Honor* for helping to inspire his early interest in crime.

Just the Facts, Ham

Your name is chef. You carry a spatula. Your mission is to protect and serve . . . dinner. You have the right to remain in the kitchen. You have the right to an apron. If you don't have an apron, we can provide you with one. Anything you burn can and will be used against you at the dinner table. The recipe you're about to make is true. The ingredients have been named to make them easier to cook.

1. Scrub the ham well under cold, running water and place in a large stock pot. Add the water, brown sugar, and two of the beers and bring to a boil over high heat. Once the mixture comes to a boil, reduce the heat to low and cover.

2. Simmer covered for 20 minutes, then remove the pot from the heat and allow the ham to sit in the hot cooking liquid an additional 15 minutes. Preheat oven to 375°F.

3. Place ham fat side-up (or cut side-down if using a half ham) in a rack in a roasting pan, toss the vegetables and sage around it and pour the third beer over the top.

4. Set the roasting pan over medium-high heat on the range top until the stout begins to boil; then cover, transfer to the oven and bake for one hour.

5. Meanwhile, whisk together the orange marmalade, Marsala, dry mustard, and maple syrup; set aside.

6. Remove ham from the oven and increase the oven temperature to 400°F.

7. Slice off the rind (if it has one) and lightly score the fat in a latticework design, a pinwheel or the shape of an LAPD badge. Stud decoratively with cloves if desired.

8. Brush the Marsala mixture over the surface of the ham and bake uncovered for 15 to 20 minutes or until nicely glazed and golden brown.

9. During these last few minutes of cooking, baste every five minutes or so, taking care not to let the glaze burn.

10. Strain and degrease the pan juices to serve alongside the ham as-is, or combine with a little cream and reduce till thickened.

11. You've finished your work, what do you see . . . just a ham? . . . Well, that's not all I see. Mister—I see the good people of this city lined up with arms akimbo waiting to try an honest piece of pork grown by thousands of proud hog farmers working hard to produce a leaner, more healthful pork product . . .

Yield: 12-16 servings

Inside Scoop

"Dragnet" began as a radio show in 1949 and in 1952 it moved to television, spawning several successful runs of the series. Highly influential on the police show genre, "Dragnet" is considered by many to be the model for Dick Wolf's successful "Law and Order" television franchise. Just like "Dragnet," "Law and Order" features fictionalized accounts of actual police stories, focuses on the details of one case instead of on character development and uses a dramatic voice-over at the show's beginning. Wolf's franchise currently includes four different "Law & Order" series and not surprisingly, an updated version of "Dragnet."

CHEW ON THIS

Did you know . . . a good country ham is often smoked for more than a month.

Fame

I Want Liver Forever, I Wanna Learn How to Fry!

For the marinade and liver:

1 ½ pounds calves' liver, sliced
 1/4-inch thick, or as thinly as possible
2 cups cold milk
2 tablespoons finely chopped shallots
5 tablespoons extra-virgin olive oil
4 tablespoons balsamic or sherry vinegar
1 tablespoon Dijon mustard

For the flour mixture:

1/2 cup all-purpose flour
3/4 cup bread crumbs
1/2 teaspoon salt
1/4 teaspoon freshly ground black
 pepper

For the sauce:

Pure olive oil for sautéing
3 tablespoons capers
1 tablespoon chopped shallots
1/4 cup balsamic or sherry vinegar
1 cup beef stock
3 tablespoons cold butter, cut into
 pieces
2 tablespoons minced fresh parsley
1 subscription to Daily Variety Meats

LOCATION: *The Streets of New York City*
FADE IN: *Groups of promising young cooking students wildly dancing through the streets with whisks, paring knifes, and slotted spoons. Two have leapt onto a taxi cab and are air-sautéing . . . CUT TO:*

1. The liver prepares: Rinse the liver well in cold water; place in a bowl and cover with cold milk while assembling the next few ingredients.

2. In a small mixing bowl, combine the shallots, olive oil, vinegar, and mustard. Drain the milk well from the liver and coat with the shallot marinade. Cover and refrigerate for 20 minutes.

3. Combine the flour, bread crumbs, salt, and pepper on a large plate and stir together with a fork.

4. Learn how to fry: Heat a large frying pan over high heat with just enough oil to cover the bottom of the skillet. When the oil is very hot, dredge pieces of liver in the flour mixture and shake off the excess. Fry for no more than a minute on each side. The liver should be crisp and golden brown on the outside and a little pink in the middle. Cook in batches, transferring the cooked liver to a warm platter loosely covered with aluminum foil.

5. Sauce, "The Method": Reduce the heat under the frying pan and allow it to cool a minute before adding capers, chopped shallots, and vinegar. Boil and reduce the vinegar until syrupy; then add the beef stock and reduce by half. Remove the pan from the heat and add the cold butter piece by piece, while whisking vigorously and shaking the pan. Stir in the chopped parsley.

6. Arrange the liver on serving plates and spoon some sauce over each portion.

Yield: 4 servings

CHEW ON THIS

As you can imagine, we were excited to know that *Hot Lunch* was the original title for this film.

FOOD FOR THOUGHT

When buying liver, choose lighter-colored calves' liver over beef liver whenever possible. Calves' liver is milder and more tender and doesn't have the bitterness often associated with mature beef liver.

Inside Scoop

Many of the teachers featured in this film were actual drama, music and dance teachers from the Fiorello LaGuardia High School for the Performing Arts at the time the film was shot. Famous real life graduates of the school include Ellen Barkin, Wesley Snipes, Helen Slater, Al Pacino, and Adrien Brody.

A Flintstones Christmas Carol 1994

For the standing rib roast:
6 pounds prime rib (2–3 ribs, ask for "first cut")
1 tablespoon kosher salt
1 tablespoon freshly ground black pepper
2 tablespoons olive oil

For the vegetables:
1/2 pound brussels sprouts, trimmed
1/2 pound small white onions, whole, peeled
1 pound small red potatoes, cut in half

For the rockshire pudding:
2 eggs
1 teaspoon salt
1 pinch nutmeg
1/4 teaspoon minced fresh thyme
1 cup milk
1 cup all-purpose flour
3 tablespoons ice water
3 tablespoons fat (rendered from the roast)

For the horseradish sauce:
4 tablespoons freshly grated horseradish, mixed with 2 tablespoons white-wine vinegar, or 4 tablespoons prepared horseradish
1 cup sour cream
1/4 teaspoon white pepper
1/2 teaspoon salt
1 teaspoon sugar
1 stocking-full quarry rocks, freshly cracked

Standing Rib Roast with Rockshire Pudding

It was the best of times, it was the worst of times, it was the beginning of time, it was the Stone Age. If you've been afraid to make a standing rib roast, don't be. This recipe is easy to yabba-dabba-do.

1. Prepare the rib roast: After you've discovered fire, adjust rack to the lower third of the oven and preheat oven to 450°F. Rinse and dry meat. In a small bowl, combine the salt, pepper, and olive oil. Rub oil into roast, and arrange fat side up in a shallow roasting pan. Place in the preheated oven and roast for 20 minutes.

2. Reduce oven temperature to 325°F. Continue roasting for another hour, or until a meat thermometer inserted in the larger end of the roast reads about 120°F for rare, 130° for medium rare, or 140°F for medium. (If not using a meat thermometer, calculate 13-18 minutes total cooking time per pound of meat.)

3. Prepare the veggies: Add the prepared vegetables to the roasting pan during the last 45 minutes of cooking.

4. Prepare the Rockshire pudding: Combine the eggs, salt, nutmeg, and thyme; beat until fluffy. Alternately add the milk and flour and continue beating until smooth. Refrigerate until use.

5. Prepare the horseradish sauce:
Squeeze excess vinegar from the grated horseradish (omit this step if using prepared horseradish.) Combine with remaining ingredients and whisk until creamy. Set aside for flavors to blend.

6. Remove the roast to a platter and allow to rest at room temperature for 30 minutes before carving. This allows the roast to finish cooking evenly and gives the juices time to be reabsorbed into the meat. While the roast rests, raise the oven temperature to 400°F for the Rockshire pudding.

7. Heat rendered fat from the roasting pan in a large cast-iron skillet over medium-high heat until it begins to sizzle. Whisk the ice water into the Rockshire batter and pour all at once into the hot skillet. Bake in the 400°F oven until puffy, crisp, and golden brown. Cool and cut into wedges.

Yields: 4 servings

FOOD FOR THOUGHT

If Dickens had been alive in the Stone Age, would he have been Charles Dickrock?

CHEW ON THIS

Don't ask the butcher to remove the bones on your roast. They keep the roast moist and help conduct heat evenly, allowing the meat to cook in less time.

"The Flintstones" cartoon was based on the television classic "The Honeymooners," starring Jackie Gleason and Art Carney.

Inside Scoop

Few people know that this masterful epic almost didn't make it to the big screen. According to *The Hollyrock Reporter*, it was rumored that during the filming of this movie, Fred and Wilma had creative differences. Wilma was weary of the network television grind and wanted to return to her first love—the theater—but Fred wanted to break into feature films. He felt he was being typecast as a big Stone Age guy. At one point, Fred's confidence was so shattered he had trouble remembering his dialogue. "Yabba da ba...line please!" The production was halted for three days while the lawyers hammered out a compromise. Luckily for us they did. The work speaks for itself.

Guarding Tess

For reincarne asada:

Four 6-ounce pieces beef fillet

1/4 cup fresh lime juice

1 tablespoon olive oil

Salt and pepper

For rajas:

5 large pasilla peppers, thinly sliced

1 medium onion, thinly sliced

4 cloves garlic, peeled and sliced thinly

1 bay leaf

6 black peppercorns

Pinch of salt

1/2 cup cold water

1/4 cup white vinegar

1/2 cup cream

For guacamole:

1 teaspoon salt

1/4 cup chopped cilantro

1 small onion, very finely diced

1 tablespoon finely chopped jalapeño
  or serrano peppers

2 ripe avocados, cut into chunks

1 teaspoon fresh lime juice

1/2 pound panela cheese, cut in 1/2-
  inch slices (panela available in
  Mexican markets)

1 past-life insurance policy naming
  your next incarnation as the sole
  beneficiary

Shirley's Reincarne Asada

TBS Food Guy Claud Mann came up with this recipe during one of his past lives. It was back in the 1800s when he was a lowly lady chuckwagon cook for a ragtag bunch of vaqueros down in Southern Chihuahua. Ever a visionary, Claudia would spend nights around the campfire entertaining her compadres with stories about a magic box that would bring cooking shows and movies to people of every age and socioeconomic status. The vaqueros thought she was loco but never said a thing. When the carne is this sabroso, you leave well enough alone.

1. Butterfly each piece of meat by slicing horizontally through the middle without cutting all the way through. Open up and pound a few times to end up with long, thin pieces.

2. Place the meat in a bowl and toss with the lime juice, olive oil, salt and pepper. Cover and refrigerate at least 20 minutes and up to 4 hours.

3. Heat oil in a large skillet over a medium heat. Add the sliced pasilla peppers, onion, garlic, bay leaf, peppercorns, and salt. Cook until the onions begin to turn translucent, then add the water and vinegar and cook 15 minutes. Once most of the liquid has evaporated, add the cream and continue cooking at a low heat for 15 minutes.

4. Combine the salt and half of the cilantro, onion, and jalapeño pepper in a bowl and crush with the back of a wooden spoon. (Or better yet, use a mortar and pestle.)

5. Add the avocado and lime juice and mash roughly, then add the remaining cilantro, onion, and jalapeño and stir together. Adjust seasonings, cover with plastic, and refrigerate until use.

6. Heat a lightly greased cast-iron skillet or charcoal grill until very hot. Season the fillet with salt and pepper; sear 45 seconds on each side for rare, a minute and a half for medium rare, and 2 minutes for well done. Once the meat is finished, grill the fresh Mexican cheese for 30 seconds on each side.

7. Serve everything immediately with hot tortillas and cold beer. Then attempt to persuade your bloated guests to work off their past-life Karma by doing the dishes while you go into a very deep trance that may indeed resemble sleep. (If they don't fall for it then convene all your past lives and force them to do the dishes.)

Yield: Serves 4 people (or 1 person over 4 lifetimes)

FOOD
FOR THOUGHT

This recipe explores the age-old question: What would carne asada want to be reincarnated as? Fillet, of course! Instead of flank steak, our lime-marinated reincarne asada calls for tender beef fillet. As always, may we remind you it is better to have marinated for as little as 5 or 10 minutes than never to have marinated at all.

Inside Scoop

Though she made her film debut in Alfred Hitchcock's *The Trouble with Harry*, Shirley MacLaine's most memorable early work was with acclaimed director Billy Wilder in the funny, poignant, and socially relevant films, *The Apartment* and *Irma La Douce*. MacLaine has been nominated for five Best Actress Oscars® and won one, for 1983's *Terms of Endearment*.

Look Who's Talking Too 1990

Bite Your Tongue Tacos

For the tongue:
1 pound beef tongue
1 head garlic, cut in half
2 white onions, peeled and quartered
2 carrots, coarsely chopped
2 stalks celery
1 tablespoon salt
3 bay leaves
5 black peppercorns
Cold water to cover
4 tablespoons peanut oil

For the salsa:
1/2 pound tomatillos, husked
1/2 pound tomatoes
4 cloves garlic, peeled
2 jalapeño peppers
1/2 cup cilantro, chopped
1/4 teaspoon salt

For service:
1 dozen corn tortillas
Plenty of garnishes; i.e., limes, chopped
    cabbage, tomatoes, onion, cilantro,
    sour cream, etc.
1 box of tongue depressors

CHEW ON THIS
One of the crew members on this movie is
listed as "Sperm Wrangler."

*If you think this is gross, wait'll you see what we're making for
Alive. We call it . . . Bob.*

1. Prepare the tongue: Scrub the tongue under running water and
place in a large pot.

2. Add the garlic, onion, carrots, celery, salt, bay leaves and peppercorns. Cover with water and set over high heat.

3. When the water comes to a boil, reduce the heat, half cover and
simmer for 45 minutes.

4. While the tongue simmers, make the salsa. Heat a dry cast-iron
griddle or skillet over medium-high heat. Place the tomatillos,
tomatoes, garlic, and jalapeños on the griddle and pan roast for
about 10 minutes, until their skins began to blister.

5. Transfer the roasted ingredients to a blender or food processor
along with the salt and half of the cilantro. Puree for about 30
seconds, transfer to a bowl and stir in the remaining cilantro.

6. Remove the tongue from the pot and rinse with cold water to
cool a little before slicing in half lengthwise.

7. Peel and discard the skin, return the trimmed meat to the simmering pot and continue cooking for 45 minutes.

8. Heat the peanut oil in a heavy skillet over medium heat. Retrieve the onions and garlic from the stock and add to the hot oil. (You should be able to squeeze the garlic right from its skin into the oil.) Cook for 5 minutes, stirring often.

9. Remove the tongue from the stock, chop into very small pieces and add to the hot skillet along with the garlic and onion. Add a cup of the cooking liquid and cook down until the stock has evaporated, about 30 minutes. At this point, the tongue should be rich, tender and flavorful.

10. Keep warm over a low heat while heating tortillas and arranging the garnishes artfully around the table, then eat with gusto.

11. Once dinner is over, strut around the dining room like a proud parent making speeches and passing out cigars. If anyone mentions the dishes, bite your tongue.

Yield: 6 servings

Out Of The Mouths Of Babes

The voice of Mickey is Bruce Willis, the voice of baby Julie is Roseanne and the voice of Mr. Toilet Man is Mel Brooks.

FOOD FOR THOUGHT

Be Honest With Your Food

What is it about Americans that prevents us from enjoying foods that honestly look like what they are? While the world around us happily asks for seconds of tongue and other tasty organ meats, many folks here avert their eyes when at the butcher. Ironically this is often when they're on the way to the sausages, some of which may be chocked full of pork tongues and snouts.

Inside Scoop

Kirstie Alley and John Travolta are both active members of the Church of Scientology, founded by science fiction author L. Ron Hubbard. The Church reportedly seeks out celebrity members.

Money Talks

3/4 pound beef fillet

2 tablespoons dry sherry

1 teaspoon sugar

2 tablespoons soy sauce

1/4 pound mushrooms

1/4 pound asparagus

2 scallions, chopped

2 tablespoons minced ginger

1 ½ tablespoons minced garlic

2 tablespoons Chinese fermented
black beans (available in the Asian
foods section of most supermarkets)

3–4 tablespoons peanut oil

1/2 cup chicken stock

1 tablespoon cornstarch

1 Vic Damone box set

Stir Fry Woks

C'mon, you know the saying . . . but who'd want to serve ambulatory fertilizer to their guests?

1. Place beef in the freezer for 45 minutes. Remove when firm, but not frozen solid.

2. Slice the beef fillet as thinly as possible against the grain and place in a mixing bowl. In a small bowl, combine the sherry, sugar, and soy sauce; pour over the sliced beef and toss to coat evenly with the mixture.

3. While the beef marinates, quarter the mushrooms and cut asparagus on the bias into 2-inch pieces. Combine the scallions, ginger, garlic, and black beans in a small bowl and place within reach of the stove.

4. Take batteries out of smoke alarms. Heat a wok over high heat until very hot, about 2 minutes. Pour a thin line of peanut oil around the circumference of the wok. Let the oil run down the side and pool in the middle. If the wok is hot enough, the oil will begin to shimmer and smoke.

5. Immediately add half of the garlic-scallion mixture; stir fry just long enough to flavor the oil, then scatter half of the meat around the lower half of the wok. Allow the wok to regain heat by not stir-

Double Dipping

Making her television debut in 1981, Heather Locklear made history by starring in two different primetime shows at the same time. She played a beleaguered wife on "Dynasty" and a police woman on "T. J. Hooker."

ring the meat for 15-20 seconds, then stir-fry until it just begins to lose its redness, another 45 seconds or so.

6. Shovel the meat onto a plate and wipe the wok clean with a wad of paper towel. Reheat wok and stir fry remaining meat as above; transfer to the plate and wipe the wok again.

7. Reheat wok and drizzle with oil as above. Add mushrooms and asparagus and stir-fry until the colors are bright, about 45 seconds. Combine the chicken stock and cornstarch in a small bowl and stir into the asparagus and mushrooms. Return the meat to the pan and stir fry to blend flavors. Continue cooking until the sauce is shiny and thick enough to coat the meat and vegetables, but not gloppy. If the sauce seems too thick, add a splash of water or chicken stock.

8. Return batteries to smoke alarm and serve at once with steamed rice.

Yield: Serves 4

As far as we're concerned, stir-fry rocks. Done right, you've got a one-dish meal that is delicious, healthful, economical, and takes just minutes to cook. There are some pitfalls, but keep a few things in mind and you'll do fine:

- Have all preparation complete before you begin cooking.
- Get the wok or skillet as hot as possible by preheating a few minutes before adding oil.
- Stir-fry in small amounts, otherwise foods will stew and toughen.
- Marinate poultry, meats, or seafood for added flavor and to avoid sticking.

Inside Scoop

Capping off a run of small but memorable parts—including our favorite, Beaumont Livingston, in *Jackie Brown*—Chris Tucker got his first starring role in this film. He also served as executive producer.

CHEW ON THIS

The son of actor Martin Sheen and brother of actor Emilio Estevez, Charlie Sheen discovered an interest in filmmaking while in high school and started making Super-8 films starring his buddies Rob Lowe and Sean Penn.

For the stew:

2 pounds lamb shoulder, cut into
   1–to–2-inch cubes
1 tablespoon olive oil
2 cups chicken stock, beef stock or water
2 each: bay leaf, thyme sprig, garlic clove
4 medium potatoes, peeled and sliced
2 yellow onions, peeled and sliced
1 carrot, sliced
One 10-ounce can cannelini beans
Salt and pepper
3 tablespoons chopped parsley

For the soda bread:

2 cups flour
1 teaspoon salt
1/2 teaspoon baking soda
1 teaspoon chopped rosemary
2 tablespoons tomato paste
1 cup buttermilk
1 copy "How to Be Your Own Best Friend"

Only the Lonely

1991

Irish Stew for One

Mom hate your girlfriend? Girlfriend hate your mom? Do they both hate you? Take the high road: curl up with a cup of Irish Stew for One, and ponder the joys of the single serving. You'll never sit by the phone waiting for YOU to call. You'll never have to dress for dinner to please YOU, and when YOU ask yourself that age-old question, "Will you respect me in the morning?", only YOU will know the answer. To paraphrase our infamous former surgeon general, Joycelyn Elders, "Help yourself!"

1. Take a quick peek at your date book. Anything on for tonight? If not, proceed to step 2.

2. Preheat oven to 250°F.

3. Prepare the stew: Heat the oil in a large, heavy pot over medium-high heat.

4. Brown the meat in 3 batches, then return all the meat to the pot and add the stock, bay leaf, thyme, and garlic. Season with salt and pepper.

5. Bring to a simmer, cover, and transfer to the preheated oven. Cook 45 minutes.

6. Meanwhile, cut the vegetables. (You obviously have nothing else to do, loser.)

7. Add the potatoes, onions, carrot, cannelini beans and chopped parsley. Cover and continue cooking until the vegetables are tender, about 20 minutes.

8. Prepare the soda bread: Meanwhile, make some Irish soda bread. (Unless you've got plans for later? . . . didn't think so.) Preheat the oven to 375°F.

9. Combine the flour, salt, baking soda and rosemary in a mixing bowl.

10. In a small bowl, mix together the tomato paste and the buttermilk.

11. Add the buttermilk mixture to the flour mixture and knead just until the dough holds together.

12. Shape the dough into small, depressing, 1 person loaves and brush with a little olive oil. Bake about 15–20 minutes, or until done.

13. Set the table and get ready to party.

Yield: MAKES ONE LARGE, LONELY SERVING

FOOD FOR THOUGHT

This recipe, like most long-cooked stews, is best if cooked the day before you want to eat it.

CHEW ON THIS

The world lost a great comedic presence when John Candy passed away in 1994. The winner of two Emmy® awards for his writing on the influential comedy show "SCTV," Candy created such memorable characters as accordion whiz Yosh Schmenge of the polka duo The Schmenge Brothers and Dr. Tongue, the hulking star of the late-night "Monster Chiller Horror Theater." In film, Candy left an equally entertaining legacy with *Planes, Trains & Automobiles, Uncle Buck, Cool Runnings* and, of course, *Only The Lonely.*

Inside Scoop

This movie is actually based on two older movies. The plot was loosely based on the 1955 classic, *Marty*, which won Academy Awards® for Best Picture and Best Actor for star Ernest Borgnine. The character of John Candy's cantankerous mother was written especially for Maureen O'Hara as a continuation of her role in the 1952 classic *The Quiet Man*. O'Hara had retired from acting but returned to star in this film because of these special circumstances.

Road House

1989

Swayze's Cracked Ribs and Black-Eyed Peas

In this 1989 classic—and we do mean classic—Patrick Swayze plays that rarest of triple hyphenates: Zen Master-Philosopher-Bar Room Bouncer. His favorite dish may be a knuckle sandwich, but we'll take cracked ribs and black-eyed peas any day.

Pain Don't Hurt

Speaking of cracked ribs . . . in the course of his various athletic pursuits—football, gymnastics, ice skating and dancing—Patrick Swayze has broken his ankle and all ten fingers and had five operations on his left knee.

Ribs and rub:

5 pounds pork ribs, cracked

2 quarts beer

2 cups cider vinegar

1 tablespoon each: fresh ground black pepper, ground oregano, ground cumin

2 tablespoons each: celery salt, brown sugar, chili powder

3 tablespoons each: garlic powder, paprika

BBQ sauce:

2 tablespoons butter

1 medium onion, diced

4 cloves garlic, finely chopped

1 teaspoon dry mustard

4 tablespoons brown sugar

1 teaspoon instant coffee

1–3 tablespoons hot pepper sauce

2 cups tomato sauce

1/2 cup cider vinegar

Salt and pepper to taste

Black-eyed peas:

I yellow onion, diced

2 cloves garlic

1 carrot, diced

1 celery stalk, diced

One 10-ounce package frozen black-eyed peas (or use fresh if available)

1 bay leaf

2 cups chicken stock

Salt and pepper to taste

A good health plan

1. Preheat oven to 425°F. Place the ribs in a large pot over high heat and cover with the beer, vinegar, and just enough water to completely submerge the ribs. As soon as the water begins to boil, remove the pot from the heat, cover and set aside for 20 minutes.

2. The BBQ sauce: In a medium saucepan, over medium heat, melt the butter and sauté the onions and garlic until soft and golden.

3. Add the mustard, brown sugar, and instant coffee to the saucepan and cook for one minute, stirring constantly.

4. Stir in the hot sauce, tomato sauce, and vinegar. When the mixture comes to a boil, reduce the heat and simmer 30–45 minutes. Season to taste with salt and black pepper.

5. The rub: Mix the dry rub ingredients. Remove the ribs from the pot and rub well with the dry rub mixture.

6. Place the ribs fat-side up in a foil-lined pan and bake for 40 minutes, turning once halfway through cooking.

7. Reduce the heat to 350°F. Pour the grease from the pan, reserving 2 tablespoons, and cover the ribs with hot sauce. Wrap well in foil and bake until tender, about 45 minutes.

8. The black-eyed peas: In a medium saucepan, sauté the onion and garlic in the reserved rib drippings until lightly golden.

9. Add the carrot, celery, peas, bay leaf and chicken stock; bring to a boil. Reduce heat and cook until the beans are tender, about 30 minutes. Season to taste with salt and pepper

10. Macho Zen observation: Cracked ribs may not hurt, but they sure do taste good.

Yield: 4 servings

Inside Scoop

Sam Elliott's film debut was in the quintessential modern western *Butch Cassidy & the Sundance Kid*. Though he had only a bit part, he managed to snag the leading lady—he and actress Katharine Ross have been together ever since.

FOOD FOR THOUGHT

We know of at least two key theories on the origin of the word Barbecue. The French (as usual) claim it as their own, huffily insisting that it's derived from *"de barbe et queue"* meaning "from beard to tail." As fond as we are of the pulled pork at "Pierre et Genevieve Du Maurier's Hickory Pit #2," we have to go with the second theory. As early as the 1500's, the Taino Indians of the Carribbean slow cooked meats on wooden frames over a fire pit. Their word for the pit...barabicu.

CHEW ON THIS

Keep your eyes peeled for the real life musicians in this movie. John Doe, founder and bass player of the seminal punk rock band X, plays road house regular, Pat McGurn, and blind bluesman Jeff Healy of the Jeff Healy Band plays the Double Deuce's resident singer, Cody.

Stripes

For the beef:

2 pounds beef tenderloin, trimmed
and cut into 1-inch slices

1 bay leaf, crushed

1/2 onion, thinly sliced

1/4 cup dry vermouth

Salt and pepper to taste

For the mushrooms and onions:

3 tablespoons butter

3 tablespoons olive oil

1/2 pound mushrooms, quartered

3/4 cup pearl onions, peeled

For the sauce:

2 tablespoons shallots, finely chopped

1/2 cup beef broth

1/3 cup dry vermouth

1/4 cup heavy cream

1/8 teaspoon nutmeg

1 cup sour cream

2 tablespoons chopped parsley

1 shingle (optional)

Kudos to Bill Murray for finding a new
use for the spatula. How many can you
think of?

Be All That You Can Beef Stroganoff

Listen up, troops! The mission on which you are about to embark is not child's play. Some of you will spill stuff on your pants. Some of you, sadly, may opt to use low fat sour cream. And some of you, God forbid, may even mis-measure the amount of nutmeg in the sauce. But at the end of the day, you'll be able to look at yourself in the mirror and say "I'm a lean, mean cooking machine." Dismissed!

1. Marinate the meat, SIR: In a large mixing bowl, combine the bay leaf, onion, and vermouth. Add beef, stir to coat, cover, and set aside for 20 minutes.

2. Sauté the mushrooms and onions, SIR: In a large, heavy skillet over medium-high heat, add 1 tablespoon each of the butter and olive oil. Add the mushrooms and sauté until light brown, about 3 minutes. Add the pearl onions to the pan with the mushrooms and continue sautéing 2 more minutes. Transfer the mushrooms and onions to a warm dish. Wipe the pan out, add the remaining butter and olive oil, and return to the heat.

3. Sauté the beef, SIR: Remove the meat from the marinade and dry well with a paper towel. Season lightly with salt and pepper. Sauté in batches until nicely browned, but still rare inside.

Remove the browned meat and transfer to the dish with the mushrooms and onions.

4. Make the sauce, SIR: Add the shallots to the pan and sauté for 1 minute. Then add the beef stock, vermouth, cream and nutmeg. Boil and reduce the liquid until only 1/4 cup remains. Lower heat, stir in the sour cream, and bring to a low simmer. (From this point on, do not allow the sauce to come to a full boil. It will separate.)

5. Construct the stroganoff, SIR: Fold the beef, mushrooms, and onions into the sauce and simmer for 5 minutes, until heated through.

6. Thank you, SIR, may I have another: Taste and adjust seasonings as desired. Serve over buttered noodles, rice, or a shingle. Garnish with chopped parsley.

7. News from the front, SIR: Inform your dining companions that you've suddenly been called off to engage in secret nighttime training maneuvers, and will most regrettably, be unavailable for KP duty. At ease, soldier.

Yield: 6 servings

Mushrooms are tricky. When being sauteed, they initially absorb the oil in the pan. Keep cooking and watch for the oil to reappear. When it does, they're done.

FOOD FOR THOUGHT

Inside Scoop

Producer/director Ivan Reitman, writer Harold Ramis and actor Bill Murray made four very successful films together: *Meatballs, Stripes* and *Ghostbusters I & II.*

Worth Their Salt

Beef Stroganoff is credited to the noble Stroganoff family of Russia who, among other things, developed Siberia. Much of the family's vast wealth came from salt—as valuable as gold in the 15th century. We're sorry to say that, as usual, the brilliant chef and true creator of this dish has been forgotten while his affluent employer remains immortalized in meat.

The Mask
1994

Smokin' Jim Curry

1/2 cup cumin seed

1/2 cup coriander seed

1 tablespoon whole cloves

3 cinnamon sticks

1/4 cup whole black peppercorns

2 tablespoons cardamom

2 tablespoons clarified butter

2 medium yellow onions, thinly sliced

1 tablespoon minced garlic

2 tablespoons freshly grated ginger

1 teaspoon chili powder

1 teaspoon ground turmeric

1 or 2 serrano chiles, halved and seeded

2 teaspoons salt

2 pounds boneless lamb leg, trimmed
   and cut into 1–2 inch cubes

2 ripe tomatoes, roughly chopped

1 pound chopped spinach

1 ½ cups yogurt

6 medium red potatoes, quartered

1 smoke alarm

Inside Scoop

1994 was a banner year for Jim Carrey. In addition to *The Mask*, he starred in *Dumb & Dumber* and *Ace Ventura: Pet Detective*, three hugely successful films that were all released that year.

This authentic lamb curry may not give you superhuman powers but, like Cameron Diaz, it's an all-righty dish!

1. In a small saucepan, over medium heat, dry roast the cumin, coriander, cloves, cinnamon, black peppercorns, and cardamom for 8-10 minutes, stirring and shaking the pan often. The spices should become brown and fragrant, but not blackened. Transfer the toasted mixture to a cookie sheet to cool, then pulverize with a coffee grinder in batches.

2. Heat the butter in a large skillet and cook the sliced onion over medium heat about 10 minutes, until the onions are a deep golden brown. Stir often to avoid burning.

3. Add the garlic, ginger, chili powder, turmeric, chiles, salt, 2 tablespoons of the roasted and ground spice mixture, and fry for a minute longer. Transfer remaining spice mixture to air-tight container.

4. Add the lamb cubes and stir well to distribute with the spice mixture. Cook 5 minutes, stirring often, then add the tomatoes and continue cooking until the liquid evaporates and the spices begin to fry, about five more minutes.

5. Stir in the spinach, yogurt, and potatoes; bring to a boil and reduce heat to simmer. Cook, uncovered, until the lamb is tender, about 45 minutes. Add a little water or cream if the sauce begins to cook off too quickly. Serve with basmati rice.

6. After dinner, instruct guests to look deep within themselves to reveal their own true natures. With any luck someone will discover a dishwasher.

Yield: Serves 6

FOOD FOR THOUGHT

Curry is not a spice but a combination of a number of herbs and spices.

CHEW ON THIS

Based on a Dark Horse comic, *The Mask* features visual effects created by Industrial Light and Magic. The company reportedly had 90 people working over the course of a year to create the 10 minutes of effects used in the final film.

This is your brain . . . This is your brain on chiles

When you eat hot peppers or extremely spicy food, pain impulses are sent to the brain. The brain, thinking the body is being attacked, responds by releasing a dose of natural painkillers called endorphins. The endorphins in turn activate the brain's opiate receptors thus producing feelings of well-being and a temporary tolerance to pain. Studies at the University of Pennsylvania have concluded this so-called euphoria cycle can be clinically addictive. As if the streets aren't treacherous enough already, now we have to worry about desperate chile heads combing through ethnic restaurant dumpsters looking for their next fiery fix.

Ingredients

2 large russet potatoes

2-3 pounds skirt steak, cut into 4 equal pieces

2 tablespoons chopped garlic

1 teaspoon chopped, fresh thyme

2 teaspoons cracked black pepper

1 bay leaf, chopped

1 tablespoon red wine vinegar

1/2 cup olive oil

8 ounces Gorgonzola cheese

2 cups thinly sliced leeks

1 jar industrial strength bikini wax

Inside Scoop

Dustin Hoffman sued *Los Angeles Magazine* for running a 1997 fashion story featuring a computer-generated image of him, in *Tootsie* drag, wearing a Richard Tyler dress and Ralph Lauren shoes. He testified that he did not want his image being used to sell women's clothes. He won a judgement of $3 million which was later overturned.

Tootsie

1982

What's Under Your Skirt Steak?

Only your hairdresser knows for sure . . .

1. Cut the potatoes in half and cover with cold water in a saucepan. Bring to a boil, reduce the heat to a simmer and cook about 15-20 minutes.

2. The potatoes should still be firm and slightly underdone. Cool under cold running water.

3. Trim the skirt steak of excess fat and membrane, then set aside.

4. Combine the garlic, thyme, black pepper, bay leaf, vinegar, and 3 tablespoons of the olive oil.

5. Rub the marinade well into the skirt steak, and then spread a thin layer of Gorgonzola onto 1 side of each piece.

6. Roll each piece of steak into a pinwheel and secure each pinwheel with 2 small wooden skewers, 1 at the top and 1 at the bottom. (At this point it should resemble a sensible wraparound skirt.)

7. Cut each pinwheel in half at the midway point between the skewers and season with a little salt and pepper. Set aside.

8. Peel the potatoes and grate through the large side of a cheese grater, season with salt and pepper, and set aside.

9. Heat a nonstick pan or well-seasoned cast-iron skillet with a little olive oil. When it is quite hot, spread about 1 cup of grated potatos and a small handful of sliced leeks. Cover the leeks with another half-cup of potatos and sauté over medium heat until crisp and light brown. Flip and brown the other side, then transfer to a cookie sheet and keep warm.

10. Wipe the hot pan with a paper towel to remove any remaining potato. Increase the heat to medium-high and open the windows. (It might get a little smoky.)

11. Sear the skirt steak about 2-3 minutes on each side for medium-rare, 4-5 minutes for medium, 6-7 minutes for well done, and 12-14 hours for jerky.

12. Place each steak on a potato bed, then peel off your lashes, pull off your falsies, sit down and eat like a man.

Yield: 4 servings

FOOD FOR THOUGHT

Skirt steak is actually the diaphragm muscle of the cow. In recent years, this once obscure "butcher's cut" has become more popular (and more expensive) as the meat of choice for fajitas.

CHEW ON THIS

Two-time Oscar®-winner Dustin Hoffman had a clause in his *Tootsie* contract guaranteeing him the right to pull out of the picture if he didn't like his character's make-up.

Chapter 7

Sweets

Carrie

1976

For the fruit filling:

5–6 Fuji or Granny Smith apples (about 6 cups when sliced)

2 tablespoons fresh lemon juice

1 ½ pints strawberries, hulled and quartered

1 teaspoon vanilla

2–3 tablespoons sugar, depending on sweetness of the fruit

1 tablespoon all-purpose flour

For the crisp topping:

1 cup walnuts

1 cup all-purpose flour

1/2 cup light brown sugar

2 tablespoons white sugar

1/3 cup oatmeal

1 ½ teaspoons cinnamon

1/2 cup cold butter, cut into 1/4-inch pieces

15 gallons pig blood, well aged

CHEW ON THIS

Carrie was Stephen King's first published novel and provided him with the means to finally quit his job as a high school English teacher and write full-time.

Carrie's Prom Crisp

They're not "all gonna laugh at you!" They're not "all gonna laugh at you!" And you can bet they'll ask for seconds.

1. Sit perfectly still in a comfortable chair. Using only the untapped power of your impassioned Epicurean mind, will the razor-sharp knife to peel, core, and thinly slice the fleshy fruit of the apples in a macabre dance of flashing steel and flying peel. Preheat the oven to 350°F and grease a 10- to 12-inch cast-iron skillet with butter.

2. For the filling: Toss fruit slices with lemon juice to prevent darkening. In a large mixing bowl, combine the vanilla, sugars, and flour. Add the apples and strawberries and toss gently to mix, being careful not to break apart the apple slices.

3. For the crisp topping: Lay walnut pieces on a cookie sheet and toast for 10 minutes in the 350°F oven. Cool and chop viciously into small pieces.

4. In a medium mixing bowl combine the flour, sugars, oatmeal, and cinnamon. Add the walnuts and stir together. Work the butter pieces into the topping mixture a little at a time with your fingers or a pastry blender. Continue blending until the topping holds together and crumbles to the size of small peas.

5. Assembly: Pour the fruit filling evenly into the buttered skillet. Distribute the topping over the filling, pressing down lightly.

6. Fire drill: Put the skillet in the hot oven. Slam and lock the oven door. Walk slowly out into the night. (Make sure to return in 40-45 minutes to find the topping brown and crunchy and the glistening crimson juices beginning to bubble up and ooze from the surface.) Eat without mercy.

Yield: 6–8 servings

FOOD
FOR THOUGHT

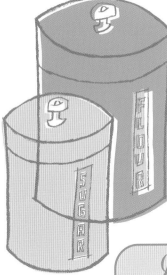

Fruit crisps are easy to make and hard to ruin. Although we used apples, strawberries and walnuts, try experimenting with seasonal fruits and other types of nuts. And, hey, as long as you're experimenting, you could also make some fake pig's blood using Karo syrup and food coloring just like the filmmakers did.

Don't Know Your Buckle from Your Betty?

Betty—Fruit baked with buttered bread
Buckle—Fruit folded with cake batter and baked
Cobbler—Fruit topped with a biscuit topping or cookie dough
Crisp—Fruit topped with a mixture of butter, sugar, flour and nuts or grains
Grunt (Also called a slump)—Fruit topped with biscuit dough, covered and steamed
Pandowdy—Fruit covered with pastry dough and baked

Inside Scoop

Homecoming queen of her high school in Quitman, Texas, Sissy Spacek reportedly conjured up the sense memories necessary for her *Carrie* audition by wearing a dress her mother had forced her to wear to a seventh grade party.

A Christmas Story

1983

For the "fruit" part:

1 ½ cups dried, diced apricots
(1/2-inch chunks)
1 ½ cups dried cranberries
1 ½ cups golden raisins
1 cup diced pineapple (1/2-inch chunks)
1/4 cup Gran Marnier

For the "cake" part:

2 ½ cups all-purpose flour
1/2 teaspoon salt
1 teaspoon baking powder
2 teaspoons ground cinnamon
1/2 teaspoon ground nutmeg
1/4 teaspoon ground ginger
1 cup coarsely chopped pecans
1 cup coarsely chopped blanched almonds
1/2 cup light brown sugar
1 cup confectioner's sugar
6 eggs, separated
2 sticks butter, softened
Zest of 1 lemon, grated
Zest of 2 oranges or tangerines, grated
2 teaspoons vanilla extract
1/2 teaspoon almond extract
1 leg of lamp

Edible Fruit Cake ... No, Really!

Hey, hey, hey, wait a minute, before you turn the page . . . you should know that this fruitcake has been designed to be less dense than the traditional, family heirloom, brandy-soaked, half-life of plutonium, door-stopper kind of fruit cake. It actually can be enjoyed warm, out of the oven if desired.

1. Preheat oven to 250°F. Butter two 9-inch x 5-inch loaf pans and line with parchment paper or aluminum foil. Butter the paper or foil and set aside.

2. In a medium mixing bowl, combine the apricots, cranberries, golden raisins, pineapple, and Gran Marnier; stir well and set aside. In another mixing bowl, sift together the flour, salt, baking powder, cinnamon, nutmeg, and ginger. Add the chopped nuts and toss a few times.

3. In a large mixing bowl, cream together the brown sugar, confectioner's sugar, and butter until fluffy and smooth. Blend in the egg yolks, one at a time, allowing each to incorporate before adding the next. Stir in the vanilla, almond extract, lemon zest, and orange zest.

4. To the butter mixture, alternately fold in the flour mixture and the fruit mixture; stir until well blended. Beat the egg whites until salt peaks begin to form. A third at a time, fold the beaten egg whites into the batter.

5. Pour half of the batter into each of the prepared pans, filling them no more than 1 inch from the top. Smooth out the tops and bake about 2 hours. To see if the fruitcake is cooked through, insert a knife or skewer in the center. If the knife emerges clean, you might as well put in all the rest of your silver and clean it while you've got the chance. Cool in the pans for 30 minutes, turn out, and brush the tops and sides with a little Gran Marnier. Eat warm, or wrap tightly in plastic wrap and refrigerate.

6. Note: If what you want is a fruitcake that can withstand the ravages of time better than yourself, double the Gran Marnier and add at least two cups of brandy or rum to the dried fruit. Soak for 24 hours before proceeding with recipe. (The next thing to do is decide who in the family is worthy of inheriting these durable, fruity monoliths in years to come.)

Yield: Two 9-inch loaves or one 18-inch doorstopper

Harpers Index once listed the density of the average fruitcake as that of mahogany.

FOOD FOR THOUGHT

Fruitcake Confidential
We must admit that prior to tracing the roots of the modern, joke-butted fruitcake, we were all too ready to place the blame squarely on the stiff shoulders of the English. We apologize. It seems for centuries these festive depth charges have existed simultaneously and been thrust annually upon the unsuspecting citizens of Germany, Italy, Mexico, Ireland . . . and of course . . . England.

Want to turn your next ill-advised winter pole-licking dare into a party? Try our version (but only with adult supervision): the refreshing "Fruity Frozen Flagpole." Just pour your favorite fruit juice on a frozen outdoor pole and watch the fun. We feel that since your tongue will be painfully stuck to the pole for a long while, it should at least taste good. Your guests will never want to leave! . . . Well, they can't.

Diamonds Are Forever 1971

6 egg whites

1/8 teaspoon cream of tartar

1/4 teaspoon salt

2 teaspoons vanilla

1 ¾ cup sugar

1/4 cup finely ground saltine crackers

1 cup finely ground pecans

1/2 cup chopped unsweetened chocolate

1/2 pound bittersweet chocolate

1/2 pound white chocolate

Cocoa powder, for dusting

Powdered sugar

1 license to spill

Inside Scoop

This marked Sean Connery's return to the Bond role after a one-film hiatus in which the ill-fated George Lazenby tried to fill Bond's shoes in *On Her Majesty's Secret Service.* **Connery was lured back to the series with a then-unprecedented $1.25 million fee and 12.5 percent of the film's gross profits.**

Bon Bons . . . Chocolate Bon Bons

They're called Bon Bons . . . Chocolate Bon Bons . . .

1. Preheat the oven to 300°F. Line 2 baking sheets with foil.

2. In a large metal or ceramic mixing bowl, combine the egg whites, cream of tartar, salt, and vanilla. Beat rapidly until the whites begin to stand at soft peaks. (Although for Bond, soft peaks may not be possible.)

3. Continue beating while adding the sugar a little at a time until the mixture reaches stiff peaks (much more Bond-like).

4. Using a rubber spatula, fold in the ground saltines, pecans, and unsweetened chocolate.

5. Transfer the mixture to a pastry bag fitted with a plain tip and pipe 1-inch mounds, about 1 inch apart onto the lined baking sheets. (You can also just drop the batter from a teaspoon in globs.)

6. Bake for about 20 minutes. Turn off the oven and continue baking another 10 minutes until firm, then cool and shape into diamonds or traditional bon bons.

7. Melt the bittersweet and the white chocolate separately in bowls over a hot water bath.

8. Using a toothpick, dip the diamonds into your chocolate of choice and dust with powdered sugar and cocoa.

9. Employ your best Bond impersonation and explain to your waiting cadre of guests and intruders that these are not just bon bons—they're chocolate bon bons. (Don't forget to save a few for yourself. Unlike the real thing, diamonds this tasty can't possibly last forever.)

Yield: Makes about 2 dozen chocolate bon bons

Things You Would Never Hear James Bond Say

1. "Oops! That's never happened to me before."
2. "Do you validate parking?"
3. "This thing is going too fast for me!"
4. "No martinis for me. I'm on antibiotics."
5. "Do these pants make my butt look big?"

CHEW ON THIS

In addition to providing inspiration for the character of eccentric millionaire Willard Whyte, real life eccentric millionaire Howard Hughes allowed the Bond team to film in his Las Vegas casinos and other properties. Not exactly hurting for cash, he only asked for a 16 mm print of the film in return.

FOOD FOR THOUGHT

Like so many things, the melting of chocolate is a breeze if done properly, a nightmare if not. Just remember three rules:
—Cut into small pieces before melting.
—Use the lowest heat possible.
—Beware of water! One drop can cause melted chocolate to suddenly stiffen. Oh, James!

# Fargo

1996

Green syrup:

2-3 cups fresh mint leaves, chopped

1 cup cold water

1 ½ cups sugar

1 tablespoon mint extract

Green food coloring (optional)

Red and blue syrup:

1 cup water

1 ½ cups sugar

2 cups fresh or frozen raspberries,
blueberries, strawberries, etc.

1/2 teaspoon vanilla extract

1 combination wood chipper-ice crusher

Yellow syrup:

1 cup water

1 ½ cups sugar

Zest of 1 lemon

1 ½ cups fresh-squeezed lemon juice

Yellow food coloring (optional)

1 copy *Mastering Dakota Dialects in
3 Easy Lessons*

CHEW ON THIS

Frances McDormand worked with
Larissa Kokernot (Fargo's "Hooker
#1") to perfect the now legendary
accent and mannerisms she used in
Fargo. McDormand referred to these
affectations as "Minnesota Nice."

Snow Coens

Is that your snow cone in the ice chipper?

Green syrup:

1. Place chopped mint leaves in a saucepan and cover with cold water.

2. Bring to a boil; immediately remove from heat and strain through a fine mesh sieve.

3. Return mixture to the saucepan over medium-high heat; add the sugar and bring to a boil.

4. As soon as the mixture begins to thicken, remove from heat and add the mint extract and the food coloring (if desired).

Red and blue syrup:

1. Combine the sugar and water in a heavy saucepan over medium-high heat. Boil the sugar and water together for 15 to 20 minutes.

2. Add the berries; return to a low boil and cook another 20 to 30 minutes or until the syrup starts to thicken.

3. Strain the liquid through cheesecloth into a mixing bowl, squeezing the fruit to press out all the liquid.

4. Stir in the vanilla extract and refrigerate until use.

Yellow syrup:

1. Combine the water, sugar and lemon zest; bring to a boil and simmer 10 minutes.

2. Add lemon juice, strain and refrigerate.

Snow Coens:

1. Grind ice in food processor or ice crusher.

2. Scoop into paper cups and bathe ice in syrup.

3. Get ready to get what you deserve.

Yield: Makes enough to kill for.

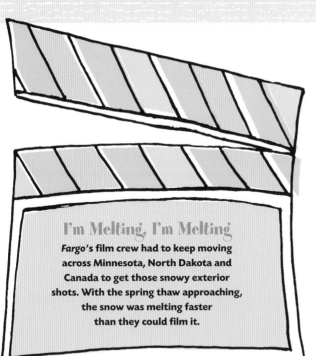

I'm Melting, I'm Melting

Fargo's film crew had to keep moving across Minnesota, North Dakota and Canada to get those snowy exterior shots. With the spring thaw approaching, the snow was melting faster than they could film it.

Who Says You Shouldn't Eat Yellow Snow

To celebrate his bloody conquest of Egypt in 345 B.C., Alexander the Great treated his troops to what may have been the largest snow cone in the history of mankind. After ordering fifteen immense trenches filled with snow from afar, he had vats of fruit syrups poured over the top and told the men to dig in. We're told the troops loved the light, fruity treat and agreed it didn't leave them bloated for the pillaging to follow.

Moving

This Side Upside-Down Cake

For the topping:

1/2 cup butter

1/4 cup sugar

1/2 cup brown sugar

1/4 teaspoon ground cinnamon

About four cups of your favorite fruit
sliced thinly: papaya, apricot, peach,
pear, mango, cranberries, figs or any
combination thereof. (If feeling
adventurous, one might even
try . . . pineapple!)

For the spongecake:

2 cups flour

2 teaspoons baking powder

1/2 teaspoon salt

1 ½ sticks butter, softened

1 cup granulated sugar

Grated zest of 1 lemon

2 teaspoons vanilla extract

4 eggs

1 cup milk

1 change-of-address form

*Psychologists tell us that moving is one of the most stressful events
a person can experience. Other stressful events include: Christmas,
pregnancy, jail time, and outstanding achievement. If you're looking
for an outstanding achievement that's not a bit stressful, try this
upside-down cake. Its comforting richness makes it a great dessert
for Christmas revelers, pregnant women, or your favorite ex-con.*

1. Preheat oven to 350°F. Arrange rack in the center of the oven.

2. Prepare the topping: Melt the butter in a 9 to 10-inch cast iron
skillet over medium heat.

3. Add the sugar and brown sugar and cook until dissolved, stirring
constantly. Stir in the cinnamon and remove from heat.

4. Arrange all but one cup of the fruit artfully into the hot syrup in
a single layer and set aside.

5. Prepare the spongecake: Sift together the flour, baking powder,
and salt into a small bowl or on a piece of wax paper and set aside.

6. In the work bowl of an electric mixer, cream together the sugar,
butter, and lemon zest until fluffy.

7. Beat in the vanilla and then the eggs, one at a time.

8. Add the flour mixture in 3 batches, alternating with the milk,
beating after each addition until the batter is well blended.

9. Chop the remaining fruit into small chunks and add to the batter.

10. Scrape the batter over the fruit into the skillet and smooth out the top.

11. Bake in the preheated oven for 45-60 minutes, until the top is golden and springy. The juices should be bubbling around the sides of the pan.

12. Allow the cake to cool 5 minutes before running a knife around the edges and inverting onto a serving platter. Serve warm with whipped cream.

13. Eat quickly before the welcome wagon smells something yummy and decides to make an appearance.

Yield: One 9 to10-inch cake

Inside Scoop

One of the co-screenwriters of *Blazing Saddles*, Richard Pryor also was supposed to star in the film but he was ultimately replaced by Cleavon Little because he was considered too controversial.

CHEW ON THIS

A comedic inspiration to almost any stand-up you can name, Richard Pryor stopped performing due to multiple sclerosis. Luckily, his greatest work is as close as your local video store. Check out "Richard Pryor Live on the Sunset Strip" and his other stand-up shows to see the master at work.

FOOD FOR THOUGHT

Usually believed to be a Hawaiian treat, pineapples are deliciously indigenous to the Americas. An early symbol of hospitality in the West Indies, pineapples were hung over doorways to declare the availability of food and drink. Taking the tradition a step further, at "Dinner & a Movie," we hang a pineapple upside-down cake over our doorway. Of course we hang it right-side up.

My Girl 2

Girls Just Wanna Have Flan

"They just wanna. They just wanna . . ."
—Cyndi Lauper, 1984

You'll wanna have:

3 tablespoons citrus zest (i.e. lime, lemon, tangerine)

1/2 cup orange juice

2 ½ cups sugar

2 ½ cups half & half

1 ½ cups whole milk

1 vanilla bean, split in half lengthwise

1/2 teaspoon salt

6 large egg yolks

4 large whole eggs

Trimmed tangerine segments, for garnish

1 cup laughter

1 cup tears

1. Lay out eight 6-ounce custard cups or ramekins and sprinkle a little zest in the bottom of each.

2. Combine the orange juice and 1 ½ cups of the sugar; swirl the pan over medium heat until the sugar dissolves.

3. Once the sugar has dissolved, increase the heat to high and cook without stirring until the syrup first comes to a boil, then begins to turn to a rich amber color, around 6 to 8 minutes. Work quickly, the syrup will harden.

4. Divide the hot mixture evenly between the custard cups. Tilt and swirl each ramekin (or cup) to evenly coat the sides and bottom with caramel. (Use an oven mitt to do this so you don't burn the you-know-what out of your fingers.)

5. Place oven rack in the center of the oven and preheat to 325°F.

6. Combine the half & half, whole milk, vanilla bean and salt in a medium size, heavy saucepan over medium heat. Bring to a simmer and remove from the heat.

7. Combine the eggs, egg yolks and the remaining 1-cup sugar in a large mixing bowl and whisk together until just blended.

Question: What's the difference between crème caramel, créme renversee, flan and créma caramella?

Answer: The spelling. Whether in French, Spanish or Italian, all these names refer to the same thing: sweetened custard, baked slowly in a caramel-coated mold.

8. Remove the vanilla bean from the hot mixture, scraping the edges to release any remaining seeds into the milk. Whisk the hot milk mixture into the egg mixture slowly and gently. Try to create as little foam as possible.

9. Transfer the mixture to a large measuring cup and divide evenly among the zest and caramel-lined ramekins.

10. Place the ramekins in a large roasting pan or baking dish and set in the preheated oven. Immediately pour enough scalding hot tap water into the pan to come two-thirds of the way up the sides of the ramekins.

11. Bake anywhere from 45 to 55 minutes until set, but still a little quivery in the center. Cool on a rack and refrigerate at least 2 hours before serving.

12. To serve, dip the bottoms of the ramekins in hot water, slip a paring knife around the sides to loosen and invert ramekins onto plates. Garnish with tangerine segments and zest.

13. After eating your flan, embark on a search for your own mother and when you find her, make her do the dishes.

Yield: 8 servings

Inside Scoop

The first *My Girl* was quite successful, grossing over $87 million. At the end of that movie, Macauley Culkin dies from a bee sting. If the producers of the movie had known how popular he would become, maybe they would have given him a can of bug spray and let him live for the sequel.

That's Lady Jamie Lee To You

Born to Hollywood royalty Janet Leigh and Tony Curtis, Jamie Lee Curtis is married to actual British royalty. Her husband, film director and certified genius Christopher Guest, inherited the title of Lord from his father. In addition to her acting career, Jamie Lee Curtis is also the author of several best-selling children's books.

CHEW ON THIS

Could the *My Girl* films have been the inspiration for HBO's ground-breaking series, "Six Feet Under"? We choose to think so. Where else have you seen the story of a slightly eccentric family who lives above their own funeral parlor?

Outrageous Fortune 1987

1/2 cup flour

2 tablespoons very finely ground toasted almonds

1/4 cup sugar

1 pinch salt

5 tablespoons soybean oil

3 egg whites

1/4 teaspoon very finely grated orange rind

2 teaspoons vanilla extract or your choice of flavored extracts (lemon, orange, coffee, etc.)

16 outrageous fortunes, typed, scrawled, or cut out ransom-style (consider using non-toxic ink . . . nah)

Misfortune Cookies

You will find great happiness if you follow the recipe instructions below.

1. Preheat oven to 325°F.

2. While the oven is heating, write out the fortunes. Be creative. Be clever. Be cruel. (And don't forget that any well-written fortune will invariably benefit by adding the words "in bed" at the end.)

3. In a large bowl, sift together the flour, ground almonds, sugar, and salt. Add oil and beat until smooth.

4. Beat egg whites into the mixture. Add and beat in the orange rind and vanilla.

5. Using a tablespoon, drop the mixture onto a well-greased cookie sheet. Leave 2 to 3 inches between each cookie.

6. Carefully spread the batter out into thin, 3 to 4-inch rounds using the back of an oiled tablespoon.

7. Bake for 10-12 minutes until very lightly golden around the edges, but not brown. Now you have to work fast . . . and, unless your hands are impervious to heat, put on a pair of cotton gloves.

8. Remove one hot cookie with a spatula and transfer to your gloved hand. Place a fortune in the center and fold the cookie in half away from you, but do not flatten it. Now grasp the pointed ends and bend them together toward you, leaving the seam on the outside.

Inside Scoop

A native Hawaiian, Bette Midler worked at the Dole® pineapple processing plant during her youth.

9. Nestle the warm cookies in muffin tins or ramekins to hold their shape while cooling.

10. Your Fortune: Confucius says, "the man who serves fresh, warm cookies to his friends should never have to do dishes . . . in bed!"

Yield: Makes 12–14

Party Tip

Next time you're finishing up a Chinese meal, try playing the Fortune Cookie Game. Have all your guests take a turn reading their fortunes aloud, adding the words "in bed" to the end of the messages. Sure, it sounds lame now but this old chestnut never fails to get laughs and, anytime we can combine food and laughter, we feel we've done our job.

CHEW ON THIS

Although she's a big star today, Bette Midler began her career performing in a bathhouse with another unknown musician, Barry Manilow. Gaining national exposure—and an Emmy® Award—from her early appearances on "The Tonight Show," Midler repaid the favor by appearing as exiting host Johnny Carson's legendary final guest, singing a much-talked about, tear-jerking rendition of "One for My Baby."

The Way The Cookie Crumbles

As early as the 12th century, Chinese monks secretly passed battle strategies baked into moon cakes. The fortune cookie as we know it didn't make its appearance until 1907 . . . in San Francisco, California.

The Pelican Brief

1993

The Supreme Torte

Though an actual legal tort involves wrongful acts, injury or damage, we promise eating our Supreme Torte will be a righteous act that causes no injury. It may, however, cause damage to your waistline.

1. Preheat oven to 375°F. Cut a piece of parchment paper to fit the bottom of a 9-inch springform pan. Butter the pan bottom and line with parchment, then butter the paper and the insides of the pan. Sprinkle a couple of tablespoons of flour in the buttered pan and rotate a few times to distribute the flour. Tap out excess flour and set aside.

2. Break chocolate into pieces, combine with the honey and butter and melt over a double boiler. (If you don't have a double boiler, fit a ceramic mixing bowl over a saucepan filled with 2 inches of water.) Bring the water to a simmer and melt slowly, stirring occasionally. (The low heat is important; if the chocolate gets too hot it may become grainy.)

3. Once the chocolate mixture is completely melted and the mixture is smooth, set aside to cool a few minutes.

4. While the chocolate cools, separate the eggs into two large mixing bowls. Add vanilla to the yolks and beat until smooth. Slowly stir the cooled chocolate mixture into the egg yolk mixture, then stir in the ground almonds and flour; set the mixture aside.

For the torte:

1 ½ sticks butter, plus more for greasing the pan

2/3 cup honey

8 ounces high quality bittersweet chocolate

4 large eggs

1 teaspoon vanilla

1/4 cup toasted and ground almonds

2 tablespoons all-purpose flour plus more for dusting

1/8 teaspoon cream of tartar

1 pinch salt

For the frosting:

6 ounces cream

6 ounces bittersweet chocolate

4 ounces toasted sliced almonds

1 pint strawberries

1 double culinary-law degree

Torte Reform

Think of a torte as a reformed cake. Swearing off flour and relying instead on ground nuts or breadcrumbs, tortes can be single or multi-layered, filled with jam or buttercream or like ours, slathered in warm chocolate.

5. Beat whites until foamy, add the cream of tartar and salt; whisk until soft peaks form. Stir a few tablespoons of the beaten whites into the chocolate to loosen, and then gently fold the remaining whites into the chocolate mixture until combined. Spread the batter evenly into the prepared springform pan and bake in the center of the preheated oven for about 30 minutes. The cake will still be slightly soft at the center and fully set around the edges.

6. Allow to cool before inverting onto a serving platter and removing the parchment from what is now the top of the cake.

7. In a small saucepan, bring the cream to a boil. Remove from heat, add chocolate and stir until smooth. Pour the warm chocolate mixture over torte and spread with a spatula. Garnish with nuts and strawberries.

8. If asked to help clean up, cite the controversial legal precedent of Chef v. Slacker, 1892. Then rest your case (and anything else that needs a rest.)

Yield: Makes one 9-inch torte

Inside Scoop

Denzel Washington became only the second African American to win the Oscar® for Best Actor when he won in 2002 for *Training Day*. The first, Sidney Poitier, was given his second Oscar®— this one for lifetime achievement—on the same night Washington won.

CHEW ON THIS

John Grisham sold the movie rights to *The Pelican Brief* from a writing sample long before the actual book was ever written. However, there's no truth to the rumor that a subsequent project was sold on the basis of one particularly boisterous belch following a bowl of chili at Chasens.

For the pie shell:

1 egg

2 teaspoons cold milk

1 ½ cups all purpose flour

2 tablespoons finely ground pecans

1/2 teaspoon salt

2 tablespoons sugar

4 tablespoons cold shortening, cut into pieces

6 tablespoons butter, cut into pieces

For the filling:

3 eggs, at room temperature

6 tablespoons melted butter

1 cup packed dark brown sugar

1/2 cup dark corn syrup

1/2 cup light corn syrup

2 tablespoons maple syrup

1 tablespoon vanilla extract

1/2 teaspoon salt

2 cups toasted , chopped pecans

1 cup pecan halves

1 number of a good divorce lawyer

Sleeping with the Enemy *1991*

Pecan Someone Your Own Size Pie

Those eyes, that mouth, that utter defenselessness . . . when you see Julia Roberts there's just one thing you wanna do. Feed her pie. That's right, our favorite Southern dish . . . for our favorite Southern dish.

Maybe pie can't solve all the world's problems, but, doggonit, it's a good place to start. "Dinner & a Movie", Healing the World One Pie at a Time.

1. The pie shell: Preheat oven to 425°F. Separate egg and reserve yolk. In a small bowl whisk the egg white and milk together, set aside. Combine flour, ground pecans, salt, and sugar in the work bowl of a food processor. Add the shortening and butter over the top and pulse a few times until the mixture has the texture of breadcrumbs. Transfer mixture to a mixing bowl.

2. Sprinkle the egg white-cold milk mixture a little at a time over the dry ingredients and mix with a wooden spoon until the dough begins to hold together. Form the dough into a disk, cover with plastic wrap and refrigerate at least half an hour.

3. Roll dough out into a 12-inch round and transfer to a 9-inch pie pan. Trim edges to leave a 1-inch overhang and fold the edges under. Prick the bottom of the dough with the tines of a fork, brush with egg yolk and cover loosely with foil. Bake in the center of the preheated oven for 15 minutes.

4. The filling: Beat the eggs and set aside. In a mixing bowl, combine the melted butter and brown sugar and beat until smooth. Beat in the eggs, corn syrup, maple syrup, vanilla, and salt. Fold in the chopped pecans and scrape mixture into the pie shell.

5. Carefully arrange the pecan halves over the top of the pie with a creepy, yet strangely attractive, anal-retentive intensity and bake exactly in the dead center of the preheated oven for 10 minutes. Reduce the oven temperature to 350°F and continue baking about 45 minutes until done. Cool before serving.

6. Quickly and cleverly fake your own death before someone asks you to do the dishes.

Yield: One 9-inch pie

CHEW ON THIS

Sleeping with the Enemy features music from Hector Berlioz' "Symphonie Fantastique" which was used in another movie about an abusive husband, Stanley Kubrick's *The Shining*.

FOOD FOR THOUGHT

If you've ever wondered why pecans are so great, there's a simple answer: they have the highest fat content of any nut—over 70 percent. North America's only native nut gets its name from the Algonquin Indian word *paccan*, meaning something like, "nuts with hard shell" (sorry, our high school Algonquin is a little rusty).

Inside Scoop

Like our recipe, Julia Roberts is authentically Southern. She hails from Smyrna, Georgia where her parents ran an acting school.

Sleepless in Seattle 1993

1 cup water
1 tablespoon sugar
1/4 cup butter cut in small pieces
1/4 teaspoon salt
1 ¼ cup flour
3 eggs, plus 1 for egg wash
1/2 teaspoon vanilla extract
8 ounces semi-sweet chocolate, melted
1 cup whipped cream
1 cup of your favorite homemade
    pudding
3,000 letters from desperate women

An Éclair to Remember

We remember it like it was yesterday. We saw you across a crowded kitchen and our hearts skipped a beat. You were wearing that tasteful chocolate overcoat we love. We knew right then there was no other pastry for us. Just saying your name makes our mouths water . . . Éclair, Éclair, Éclair.

1. In a medium saucepan, combine water, sugar, butter, and salt. Bring to a boil and reduce heat to low.

2. Add the flour all at once and begin beating vigorously with a wooden spoon. Continue beating until smooth, 2 to 3 minutes. (The mixture will begin to pull away from the sides of the pan.)

3. Remove from heat and continue beating another minute to cool. Add 3 eggs, one at a time, beating well after each addition. Beat in the vanilla.

4. Line a baking sheet with parchment paper. Transfer the dough to a pastry bag fitted with a 1-inch plain tip and pipe out 4-inch rectangles leaving 3 inches of space between each éclair. Preheat oven to 400°F.

5. Brush with egg wash and bake 30-40 minutes, until the éclairs are golden and sound hollow when tapped. Puncture the bottom of each éclair, return to the oven and allow to dry another 20 minutes with the oven off and the oven door propped open.

CHEW ON THIS

Keep your ears open for an early pre-"Seinfeld" reference to the "Soup Nazi" as Rosie O'Donnell tells Meg Ryan, " . . . he's the meanest guy in the world but he makes the best soup you've ever eaten . . ." while entering Ryan's office at the newspaper. The real life "Soup Nazi," Al Yeganeh, continues to make great soup—and harass customers—at his Soup Kitchen International in New York City.

6. Cut the tops off the cooled eclairs and scrape out any remaining dough on the inside.

7. Whip cream until stiff, then fold together the whipped cream and pudding. Transfer the mixture to a pastry bag fitted with a star tip and fill eclairs. Replace the tops and brush with melted chocolate.

8. After dinner, skip the dishes and try to get some sleep.

Yield: Makes 12 large or 24 small eclairs to remember

Our favorite definition of an éclair is from Chamber's English Dictionary, which describes this confection as "a cake, long in shape but short in duration."

Inside Scoop

1939's *Love Affair*, directed by Leo McCarey, was the movie that launched...a bunch of other movies. After directing the original with Irene Dunne and Charles Boyer playing the star-crossed shipboard lovers, McCarey remade the movie in 1957 as *An Affair to Remember* with Deborah Kerr and Cary Grant. In 1993, Nora Ephron took up the cause, making the events in *An Affair to Remember* a major part of the plot for *Sleepless in Seattle*. Then, in 1994, Warren Beatty produced, wrote and starred, with his wife Annette Bening, in *Love Affair*, another remake of the original.

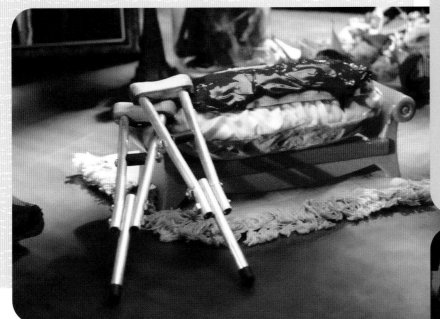

"I have a theory that the romantic comedy was killed by sex. Romantic comedies flourished in a period when you couldn't put sex in a movie. The way people flirted was by going 'Blah blah blah' to one another."
—Nora Ephron (from *Entertainment Weekly*)

Stand By Me
1986

Boys Will Be Boysenberry Pie

This pie is so good, you'll want to start a one-man eating contest.

For the pie dough:

2 ½ cups all purpose flour

1 ½ sticks cold unsalted butter, cut into 1/4-inch cubes

4 tablespoons chilled vegetable shortening

1 teaspoon kosher salt

2 tablespoons sugar

1 cup sour cream

For the boys:

6-8 cups frozen-defrosted boysenberries

1/2 cup orange marmalade

1/2 cup sugar

2 teaspoons lemon zest

1 tablespoon lemon juice

4–5 tablespoons instant tapioca

1/8 teaspoon each cinnamon and allspice

1 tablespoon butter cut into very small pieces

Plenty of root beer, corn chips and a fully loaded pez dispenser

CHEW ON THIS

The biggest hit of former Drifter Ben E. King's career, "Stand By Me" topped the R&B charts and reached the pop chart's top five.

1. In a mixing bowl, combine flour, butter, shortening, salt and sugar with a pastry blender or 2 knives until most of the lumps are no larger than small peas and the mixture has the consistency of coarse corn meal.

2. Dump the mixture onto a clean work surface and flatten it out quickly with a rolling pin. Scrape together, return to the bowl, cover with plastic and place in the freezer for 10 minutes.

3. Add the sour cream to the cold mixture and using a rubber spatula, fold together until the sour cream is evenly distributed and the dough holds together.

4. Divide the dough in two and flatten each piece into a 1-inch x 6-inch disk. Dust each disk with a little flour and wrap well with plastic wrap before refrigerating at least 20 minutes.

5. Preheat oven to 400°F. Roll out one of the disks 1/8 inch thick on a lightly floured surface, fit it into a 8 to 9-inch pie dish, and trim the edges, leaving an even 1/2-inch overhang. Refrigerate until filling.

6. In a large bowl, toss together the boysenberries, orange marmalade, sugar, lemon zest, lemon juice, tapioca, cinnamon, and allspice. Spoon the fruit mixture into the prepared crust and dot with butter.

7. Roll out the remaining dough to fit over the fruit with a 1-inch overhang and tuck the top crust under the bottom. Crimp or flute the edges and brush the top crust lightly with a little milk if desired. (If baking for a pie-eating contest, you may prefer to cut the top crust into 2-inch strips and arrange in a latticework.)

8. Using a paring knife, cut slits decoratively around the top crust (this allows steam to escape) and sprinkle lightly with sugar.

9. Bake in the lower half of the oven for 15 minutes; reduce temperature to 350°F. and bake for another 30-40 minutes, or until the filling bubbles and the crust is pleasantly golden. Cool on a rack at least an hour before cutting.

10. Allow the pie to cool before burying your face in it.

Yield: Serves 8 adults or one contestant

FOOD FOR THOUGHT

You've already made a big mess in the kitchen; why not prepare a few extra batches of pie dough and freeze them. With the dough already made, it's a cinch to throw together a pie with any extra fruit you happen to have.

The great pie crust debate: butter for flavor or shortening for flakiness? We say use both and shut your pie hole.

Stephen King Challenge

Watch some movies based on Stephen King's work and see how many times you can spot the number 237. Reported to be one of King's favorite numbers, it pops up in this movie when the kids pool their money and come up with $2.37 in change.

Inside Scoop

An extremely prolific writer, Stephen King is a major content-provider for film and television. *Stand By Me* was based on King's short story, "The Body." Some of the other memorable films based on his work include:

★ *Hearts in Atlantis*
★ *The Green Mile*
★ *Apt Pupil*
★ *Dolores Claiborne*
★ *Shawshank Redemption*
★ *Misery*
★ *The Shining*
★ *Carrie*

$\mathcal{S}$tar $\mathcal{W}$ars

$\mathcal{O}$bi-Wan Cannoli

For the filling:

2 cups ricotta cheese

1 cup Mascarpone or cream cheese

1/2 cup confectioner's sugar

2 ripe mangos, peeled, seeded and
chopped

1/2 teaspoon vanilla

1 teaspoon finely grated orange zest

For the shells:

2 cups flour

4 tablespoons sugar

1/2 teaspoon salt

1 teaspoon cinnamon

3 tablespoons sesame seeds

2 tablespoons vegetable shortening

1/2 cup Marsala

Vegetable oil, for frying

A pinch of The Force (a little goes a
long way)

Alternate Ingredients

Sissy Spacek was originally under consideration to play the Princess Leia role in *Star Wars*, but opted to do *Carrie* instead. Ironically, the *Carrie* lead was available because front-runner Carrie Fisher had refused to do the nude scenes.

Not very long ago in a kitchen not very far away . . .

1. Place the ricotta cheese, Mascarpone, confectioner's sugar, vanilla, and half of the chopped mango in a mixing bowl and beat as though your life depended on it. Fold in the remaining chopped mango and orange zest. Cover and refrigerate until use. (It will thicken as it chills.)

2. Combine the flour, sugar, salt, cinnamon, and sesame seeds in the work bowl of a food processor. Use the force of the machine and pulse 2 or 3 times to blend dry ingredients. Add the shortening and give the machine a few more short phaser-like bursts.

3. Add the Marsala and continue processing until the dough begins to resemble a ball. (Or better yet, resembles a doomed planet hurtling helplessly through time, space and dimension.) Wrap the dough in plastic wrap and place in the black hole of your fridge at least 1 hour and no more than 1 light year.

4. Roll the dough out on a clean, floured surface as thinly as possible. Cut the dough into 4 to 5-inch discs, using a small saucer as a template.

5. Wrap each disc loosely around a cannoli tube, sealing the overlapping edges with a few drops of Marsala.

6. Heat vegetable oil to about 375°F. Fry cannoli shells one or two at a time until crisp and golden, a little less than 1 minute. Remove shells with a slotted spoon; drain and cool for a few minutes; then slide carefully from the forms while still warm.

7. Spoon the chilled mango filling into a pastry bag fitted with a death-star tip and forcefully fill each cannoli. If using more than one pastry bag, for God's sake, be careful not to cross the beams.

8. Transfer to a platter and garnish with a little sliced mango and confectioner's sugar.

9. Serve proudly, secure in the knowledge that regardless of galaxy, these Obi-Wan Cannoli will taste out of this (or any other) world. Then start another batch—you can bet your asteroid there's bound to be a demand for a whole series of sequels.

Yield: Serves 12 Humanoids or 1 Wookie

Special Equipment: You will need some cannoli forms. These are simple metal tubes roughly 6 inches long and 2 inches in diameter available at kitchenware stores. (I've also been told that old aluminum patio furniture cut into sections works like a charm providing no one is lounging in your chaise when you descend upon it with a hacksaw.)

If cannoli forms and patio furniture are unavailable, substitute by wrapping a few layers of aluminum foil around the handle of a broomstick. If alone in the kitchen, take a moment to briefly wield the foil-wrapped broom like a light saber saying something like, "When I left you, Obi-Wan, I was but the student, now I am the master." Then boldly progress to the next step.

Grain of Salt

Star Wars has earned more than $700 million worldwide and is credited—along with *Jaws*—as the film that ushered in the era of the blockbuster. Ironically, the word "blockbuster," which originated during World War II, was used to describe a bomb that could level a block with its force.

CHEW ON THIS

NASCAR's loss is Hollywood's gain. George Lucas planned to be a professional racecar driver until a car accident just after his high school graduation put an end to his driving ambition. In the hospital after the accident, Lucas came up with the idea for "The Force."

"Leave the gun. Take the cannoli."
—Peter Clemenza, *The Godfather*

The Audience Is Listening

George Lucas used his earnings from the *Star Wars* trilogy to establish his own groundbreaking special effects company, Industrial Light and Magic (ILM), and develop the renowned THX Sound System which revolutionized sound in movie theaters.

Troop Beverly Hills 1989

- 1 teaspoon cinnamon
- 2 ½ cups rolled oats
- 1/4 cup steel-cut oats (a.k.a. Irish or Scottish oatmeal)
- 2 ½ sticks butter, softened
- 1 cup granulated sugar
- 1 cup light brown sugar
- 2 eggs
- 1/2 teaspoon vanilla
- 1 ½ cups all-purpose flour
- 1/4 teaspoon salt
- 1/2 teaspoon baking powder
- 1 ½ cups of chocolate chips, nuts, raisins, dried cherries, or a combination (optional)
- 1 silver spoon in mouth (from birth)

You Go Girls!

Founded in 1912 by Juliette Gordon Low, the Girl Scouts' main goal was to get girls out of their sheltered homes and into the world. Fueled by Low's personal funding (she sold a rare pearl necklace to pay for early operations) by 1920, the organization had its own uniform, handbook and constitution and was gaining popularity across the nation. The girls began selling their famous cookies in 1936.

9021 Oatmeal Cookies

Make this recipe and you'll earn a merit badge for delicious!

1. Combine the cinnamon and rolled oats in a large, dry sauté pan over medium heat. Being careful not to burn it, toast and toss for 5 minutes until fragrant. Remove from heat and set aside.

2. Bring 1 cup of water to a boil, stir in the steel-cut oats and simmer 20 minutes, stirring often. Remove from heat and spread on a plate to cool.

3. Preheat oven to 350°F. Beat the butter until creamy; add the sugars and continue beating until light and fluffy, 2-3 minutes. Beat in the eggs, one at a time, then beat in the vanilla

4. In a small mixing bowl, combine and whisk together the flour, salt, and baking powder, then beat the flour mixture into the butter mixture. Stir in the toasted oats, the cooked and cooled steel-cut oats and any optional ingredients.

5. Form the dough into 1-inch to 3-inch balls and place on parchment-lined cookie sheets. Leave enough room for the cookies to spread as they bake.

6. Bake in the lower third of the oven 20 to 25 minutes, until the cookie edges turn golden brown. Rotate pans halfway through cooking to avoid oven hot spots.

7. After dinner, gather your troops by the sink and let them earn their dishwashing merit badges.

Yield: Makes up to 2 dozen cookies

So, You're Oats

Groats—whole minimally processed oats

Steel-cut oats—thinly sliced whole oats

Old fashioned oatmeal—whole oats that have been steamed, rolled and flaked

Quick or instant oats—old-fashioned oatmeal cut into small pieces for faster cooking

It Looked Better On Paper

In 1989, American Quakers raised objections to the *Quaker Oats*® "Popeye the Quaker Man" advertising campaign. Church leaders felt Quaker Popeye's eager use of violence was antithetical to the religion's pacifist teachings. The fact that Popeye's parrot repeatedly shrieked, "Popeye wants a quaker" couldn't have helped.

According to the folks at *Quaker Oats*®, more people eat oatmeal in January than any other month.

CHEW ON THIS

This was Betty Thomas' final feature film role before switching to a very successful directing career with such films as *The Brady Bunch Movie* and *28 Days*.

Vegas Vacation

1997

4 cups dried figs, apricots, or other
   dried fruit, stems trimmed
1 cinnamon stick
Rind of 1/2 lemon, cut into strips
Rind of 1/2 orange, cut into strips
1/4 cup bourbon
1 cup granulated sugar
2 cups white grape juice
1 stick butter, softened
1/2 cup brown sugar
1 teaspoon pure vanilla extract
1 teaspoon baking powder
1/4 teaspoon salt
1/2 teaspoon cinnamon
2 tablespoons milk
2 large eggs
2 ¼ cups all-purpose flour
1 autographed copy of "Danke Schoen"

Wayne's Newtons

Thank you Wayne, darling, thank you Wayne...
Thank you for all the newts you bring...
They're not big but they're filled with figs...
And they're golden brown...wash them down...
They're so sweet...what a treat...

1. Combine the figs, cinnamon stick, citrus rind, bourbon, 1/2 cup of the sugar, and the white grape juice in a medium saucepan over high heat. Bring to a boil; reduce heat to medium and simmer until all but 2 or 3 tablespoons of the cooking liquid has evaporated, stirring often. Remove cinnamon and citrus rind; set aside to cool.

2. Transfer the warm fig mixture to the work bowl of a food processor and process until smooth, about 30 seconds. Transfer the mixture to a piping bag fitted with a large plain tip and set aside.

3. Cream together the butter, brown sugar, remaining granulated sugar, vanilla, baking powder, salt, and cinnamon until smooth. Beat in the milk, then the eggs one at a time. Add the flour in 3 batches and beat until just blended. Evenly divide the dough into three discs, wrap each in plastic and refrigerate at least 45 minutes.

4. Remove one of the dough discs from the refrigerator, place on a floured work surface and roll out into a 6-inch x 12-inch rectangle.

Inside Scoop

Founded in 1970 by veterans of the *Harvard Lampoon* humor magazine, *National Lampoon* thrust counter cultural humor into the face of the masses, championing a "no-sacred-cows" philosophy that leaves no one safe from parody. Perhaps the most infamous NL cover photo featured a dog with a gun to its head with the headline "Buy this Magazine or We'll Kill this Dog."

Cut the rectangle in half lengthwise and carefully pipe the fig mixture down the center of each strip. Brush the sides lightly with water and overlap both over the filling; press lightly to seal.

5. Repeat with remaining dough and transfer to a parchment lined baking sheet, seam side down. Cover and refrigerate at least 20 minutes before baking. Preheat oven to 350°F.

6. Cut into 2-inch bars and bake about 30 minutes, until very lightly golden but not brown.

7. Wait until the dishes are piled high in the sink, then go on vacation.

Yield: Makes about 24 two-inch bars

All You Can Eat

Though it built its reputation on the 99-cent shrimp cocktail, in recent years, Las Vegas has attracted top chefs eager to open outposts of their famous restaurants in the booming entertainment oasis. Some of our favorites include: Nobu Matsuhisa, Jean Georges Vongerichten, Joachim Splichal, Jean-Louis Palladin and, of course, the two hot tamales, Susan Feniger and Mary Sue Milliken.

Did You Know...

A Fig By Any Other Name—The Kennedy Biscuit Works in Massachusetts gets the credit for what is now the third most popular cookie in the country. After developing a machine that could simultaneously extrude two materials, the intrepid cookiesmiths were able to pump out endless lengths of the fig filled cookie dough. In keeping with company tradition of borrowing names from nearby towns, the new cookies were christened "Fig Newtons" after Newton, MA. (Although they were almost named Fig Shrewsburys.)

FOOD FOR THOUGHT Think figs are a fruit? Don't bet on it. A fig is more like an inverted flower. Some biblical scholars are convinced that figs were the forbidden fruit picked by Eve in the Garden of Eden.

Danke Schoen

Beginning his professional singing career when he was just six, Wayne Newton is most closely associated with the '60s tune "Danke Schoen" but the '70s hit "Daddy Don't You Walk So Fast" was his biggest hit.

CHEW ON THIS

When Clark (Chevy Chase) tells Rusty (Ethan Embry) and Audrey (Marisol Nichols) he hardly recognizes them, he's making an in-joke about the Griswold children being played by different actors in each of the *Vacation* movies.

The Wedding Singer

1998

2 tablespoons butter plus more for greasing the dish

10 ounces French or Italian bread, cut into 1-inch cubes

4 bananas, peeled and sliced lengthwise

2 tablespoons lemon juice

1/2 cup, plus 2 tablespoons sugar

1/4 cup light rum

4 cups whipping cream or half & half

1 cup milk

1 vanilla bean, sliced in half lengthwise

1/3 cup unsweetened coconut

1 pound high quality white chocolate, chopped

4 egg yolks

3 large eggs

All 38 verses of Hava Nagila

Inside Scoop

No stranger to weddings, by age 27 Drew Barrymore had been married and divorced twice.

It's a Nice Day for a White Pudding

Dearly beloved, we are gathered here today in the sight of our chef, to join white chocolate bread pudding and wedding cake in holy matrimony, which is an honorable estate. These foods will not undertake this union unadvisedly, lightly or wantonly but richly, flavorfully, and deliciously. If anyone has reason to object to this union, let him speak now or forever hold his piece . . . of cake.

1. Butter a 2-quart glass baking dish and set aside.

2. Arrange bread cubes on a cookie sheet and place in a 200°F oven for 15 minutes, until dry. Remove from oven and set aside. Increase oven temperature to 350°F.

3. Toss bananas with the lemon juice. Melt butter in a large skillet over medium-low heat. Add bananas and 2 tablespoons sugar; cook slowly (without browning) about 5 minutes, until tender but not falling apart. Add the rum to the bananas and set aside.

4. In a heavy saucepan over medium heat combine 3 cups of the whipping cream, milk, remaining sugar, and the vanilla bean. Bring to a simmer stirring often and remove from heat. Add the coconut and half of the white chocolate and stir until melted.

5. Whisk the eggs and yolks in a mixing bowl and then, a little at a time, add and whisk the warm cream/milk/chocolate mixture (from step 4) into the eggs.

6. Arrange one-third of the bread cubes in the buttered baking dish. Top the bread with one-third of the banana slices. Repeat with the remaining bread cubes and bananas and pour the white chocolate mixture over the bread and banana slices. Cover with foil and set aside 15 minutes.

7. Bake 45 minutes, or until a skewer inserted into the center comes out clean. Transfer to a rack and cool at least 15 minutes.

8. Bring the remaining cream to a boil, remove from heat and stir in the remaining chocolate. Spoon warm pudding onto plates, top with warm white chocolate sauce and garnish with coconut.

9. After everyone has enjoyed their delicious white pudding, magically produce a microphone, accompanist, and a powder blue ruffly shirt. Then proceed to croon out an unending medley of heartfelt songs dedicated to whoever volunteers to clean up. Make it clear that you won't stop until someone does.

Yield: Serves 8

FOOD FOR THOUGHT

The very first wedding cakes were in fact small loaves of bread. In ancient Greece, the happy couple would each take a bite, to ensure a plentiful life together. The remainder was broken over the bride's head. The tradition of wearing a veil was eventually introduced to keep chunks of food out of the bride's hair and face.

He's Our Idol

Born "William Broad" in Middlesex, England, Billy Idol was one of the first rock stars made by MTV. Though his first big hit, 1980's "Dancin' With Myself," was recorded with his aptly named band, Generation X, he soon embarked on a solo career. "White Wedding" was one of two top-40 hits from Idol's self-titled 1982 debut effort.

CHEW ON THIS

Adam Sandler filled a significant hole in our national holiday song repertoire with his release of "The Hanukkah Song" which receives frequent radio airplay throughout the holiday season.

Chapter 8

Breakfast Served All Day

Burglar

1987

1/2 cup kosher salt

1/2 cup sugar

1 tablespoon juniper berries

1 tablespoon fresh-cracked black pepper

1/2 cup chopped fresh dill

Zest of 1 lemon

Four 6-ounce salmon fillets

2 ounces gin

1/4 cup each: hickory chips, raw brown
   rice and brown sugar

4 bagels

Miscellaneous garnishes: tomatoes,
   cream cheese, onions, cucumber

1 airtight alibi

Inside Scoop

**Born Caryn Johnson, Whoopi
Goldberg worked as a bricklayer
and funeral-home make-up artist
to support her fledgling acting
career on Broadway. She eventually
moved to California where she
joined the improvisation group,
Spontaneous Combustion, and
began to polish her comedic skills.**

Whoopi's Combination Lox and Bagel

*Using standard methods, it could take a week to make "lox," the
traditional Jewish version of cured or smoked salmon. But when
your show's only a couple of hours long, you've got to figure out
a faster way. Our solution: a delicious combination of roasting,
curing and smoking that produces lox so tasty you'll pick them over
and over again.*

1. In a small mixing bowl, combine kosher salt, sugar, juniper
berries, cracked black pepper, chopped dill, and lemon zest.

2. Rub the salt mixture evenly over both sides of the salmon fillets,
sprinkle with gin, cover, and refrigerate 30-45 minutes.

3. Meanwhile, place the wood chips in a small bowl and cover
with hot water and soak at least 10 minutes. Line a large, heavy
pot that has a tight-fitting lid with aluminum foil.

4. Place the soaked wood chips, brown rice, and brown sugar in the
pot; lightly oil a wire rack and set it inside the pot, over the chips.

5. Scrape off all excess salt mixture from the salmon and arrange
the fillets on the oiled rack. Cover the pot tightly and place over
medium-high heat.

6. When the pot begins to smoke, reduce the heat to medium and continue smoking another 10-15 minutes, or until firm to the touch. Serve warm or cold with all the trimmings.

7. Criminally ingenious clean-up tip: Make sure to insure all of your dishes, and then arrange to have them conveniently stolen immediately after dinner. "Help, police, I've been robbed!"

Yield: Serves 4

Idea For A T-Shirt: I Saved Your Country And All I Got Was This Lousy Dough Stirrup

Our sources tell us the first bagels were a Viennese invention. Originally made in 1683 to honor King Jan of Poland after he drove off marauding Turkish invaders, bagels were made in the shape of a riding stirrup, or "beugal," because the king was known to be an avid horseman.

D.O.A.

For the gravy:

1 pound country sausage

1 cup sliced mushrooms

1 red onion, minced

3 tablespoons flour

2 cups chicken stock

1/2 cup cream (optional)

1 teaspoon chopped fresh thyme

Salt and freshly ground black pepper
  to taste

Tabasco® sauce, to taste

For the biscuits:

4 cups self-rising flour

3 tablespoons sugar

1/4 teaspoon baking soda

1/4 teaspoon sage

6 tablespoons cold shortening

4 tablespoons cold butter

1 cup heavy cream

2 cups buttermilk

1 ½ cups cake flour, or all purpose flour

1 Last Will and Testament

This movie was based on the 1950
film-noir classic of the same name.

Biscuits to Die for
(with One Foot in the Gravy)

*What would you do if you found out you had 24 hours to live?
We'd cook up some Biscuits to Die For with One Foot in the Gravy.
With plenty of butter, cream, shortening, and sausage this dish is
deadly delicious and would be a great last meal.*

1. Brown the sausage in a large, heavy skillet over medium heat.
Transfer sausage to a plate and set aside.

2. Discard all but 3 tablespoons of drippings from the pan; add the
chopped mushrooms and onion and cook until lightly browned,
about 3 minutes.

3. Add the flour and cook, stirring constantly, until the flour begins
to color, about 3 minutes.

4. Add the chicken stock and cream and continue cooking until
thickened.

5. Add the cooked sausage and fresh thyme and season to taste
with salt, pepper and Tabasco.

Get your biscuits in order:

1. Preheat oven to 475°F. Butter a muffin tin, round cake pan or
pie plate.

2. Sift together the self-rising flour, sugar, baking soda, and ground sage into a large mixing bowl.

3. Cut the shortening and butter into small pieces and work into the flour mixture until the lumps are no larger than a small pea.

4. Add the cream and buttermilk and stir together only until the mixture becomes cohesive. It will be too sticky to handle. Allow the mixture to stand about 5 minutes.

5. Dump the cake flour onto a clean work surface in a pile. Dust hands with flour and pinch off biscuit-sized lumps of dough.

6. Quickly roll through the cake flour and roll lightly between your hands to form a ball and transfer to a well-buttered muffin tin or crowd together into a buttered cake pan or pie plate.

7. Brush with cream or melted butter and bake about 30 minutes or until proud, puffy, and golden. Remove from oven and brush with melted butter if desired.

8. Cheer up: Look on the bright side—death is merely nature's way of telling you to slow down a little and let someone else do the dishes.

Yield: Makes enough to last the rest of your life . . .

CHEW ON THIS

According to Jerry Dunn's enlightening book of workplace slang, *Idiom Savant*, death travels under many different aliases including:

–CTD (Circling the Drain)
–FTD (Fixin' to Die)
–STBD (Soon to Be Dead)
–DOV (Dead on Ventilator)
–DFO (Done Fell Out)
–CD (Celestial Discharge)

FOOD
FOR THOUGHT

On "Dinner & a Movie," it's pretty clear we don't obsess with precision when we cook, but when we bake, we measure carefully. To accurately measure flour, don't scoop from the bag—first spoon it into the measuring cup and then level it out.

Inside Scoop

When Dennis Quaid isn't acting, he frequently tours the country with his band, The Sharks. Also a musical dabbler, Meg Ryan sang back-up on pal Melissa Etheridge's album "Skin."

No self rising flour?
Substitute 1 cup all-purpose flour sifted together with 1/2 tsp. salt and 1½ tsp. baking powder.

Footloose

8 slices thick bacon

1 ½ cups cornmeal

1/2 cup all-purpose flour

1 tablespoon sugar

1 tablespoon baking powder

1/2 teaspoon baking soda

1/2 cup grated cheddar cheese

1 teaspoon salt

1 teaspoon ground pepper

1 egg, beaten

1/2 teaspoon Tabasco® sauce

1 cup buttermilk

4 scallions, minced

1/2 cup corn

3 tablespoons cold water, if needed

Corn oil, for frying

1/4 cup grated Parmesan cheese

1 empty factory with disco sound system and dance floor

1 angry and sensitive (but masculine) solo dance routine

Six Degrees

Talk about your six degrees of Kevin Bacon! In real life, Kevin Bacon's dancing body double (Peter Tram) in *Footloose* was married to the dancing body double (Marine Jahan) for Jennifer Beals in *Flashdance*.

Six Degrees of Bacon and Cheese Hushpuppies

This movie reminds us of a story we once heard about a small Midwestern town where all dinner parties were outlawed after a tragic fondue accident involving a rogue pair of Sunday shoes. Kids were forced to smuggle trays of hors d'oeuvres across the state line. Then, one day, a mysterious stranger rode into town. Armed with nothing but a well-seasoned, cast-iron skillet and this recipe, he freed the people with platters of finger-snappin', toe-tappin' appetizers. There was no turning back . . .

1. Cook the bacon until crisp. Cool and crumble into little bits.

2. Stir together the following ingredients in a medium mixing bowl: cornmeal, flour, sugar, baking powder, baking soda, cheddar cheese, salt, and pepper. In a second bowl, mix together the beaten egg, Tabasco®, buttermilk, scallions, bacon, and corn.

3. Heat 2 inches of oil in a heavy saucepan over medium-high heat.

4. Pour the egg mixture into the cornmeal mixture all at once and stir to make a very thick batter. (Add the cold water only if the batter seems too thick.)

5. Scoop out rounded spoonfuls of batter and drop into the hot oil. (Don't overcrowd; they need room to dance.) Fry until golden brown, about 1 minute on each side. Roll the hot hushpuppies in grated Parmesan cheese and listen to the howls of delight.

Yield: 2 dozen pups

Inside Scoop

Another actor with musical aspirations, Kevin Bacon and his brother Michael have released three albums with their musical group, The Bacon Brothers, which serves up a mix of folk, rock and country.

CHEW ON THIS

No stranger to loose feet, Sarah Jessica Parker danced with the Cincinnati Ballet and the American Ballet Theatre before playing the title role in the hit musical "Annie" on Broadway.

Remember, when hushpuppies are outlawed, only outlaws will have hushpuppies.

FOOD FOR THOUGHT

When in season, we suggest using fresh corn rather than frozen. Unfortunately, the kernels fly all over the place when you cut them. Try sticking one end of the cob in an angel food cake pan. Cut from top to bottom and the kernels will fall neatly in the pan. We find this exciting!—that kind of tells you about our life.

Hook

Peter Pancakes and the Lost Boysenberry Syrup

Here's a happy thought . . . you can never be too old to enjoy pancakes and syrup for dinner!

For the syrup:

4 cups or 1 pound fresh or frozen boysenberries

2 cinnamon sticks

1/2 cup water

1/2 cup sugar

Pinch salt

1 cup light corn syrup

2 teaspoon vanilla

For the pancakes:

1/2 cup pecans

2 cups all purpose flour

3/4 teaspoon salt

1 ½ tablespoons sugar

1 teaspoon baking powder

1/2 teaspoon baking soda

2 eggs, room temperature

1/3 cup melted butter

3/4 cup whole milk

1 ½ cups buttermilk

Pixie dust, to taste

Make the syrup:

1. Combine berries, cinnamon, water, sugar, and salt in a saucepan. Bring to a boil, reduce heat, and simmer 30 minutes.

2. Remove cinnamon and add corn syrup and vanilla. Strain if desired and keep warm until use.

Make the batter:

1. Chop pecans into small pieces and toast in a dry skillet over medium heat for 3 or 4 minutes, stirring and tossing occasionally. Set aside.

2. Sift together the flour, salt, sugar, baking powder, and baking soda into a large mixing bowl.

3. Separate the eggs.

4. In a second bowl, combine and whisk together the egg yolks and melted butter.

5. Add the milk and buttermilk to the egg yolk mixture and mix well.

Inside Scoop

Because Julia Roberts' Tinkerbell was always barefoot and often in the air, Roberts had an assistant whose "sole" responsibility was cleaning her feet.

6. Add the wet mixture to the dry and stir together, then fold in the pecans.

7. Whip the egg whites to soft peaks and gently fold into the batter.

8. Heat a griddle over medium high heat until quite hot and brush lightly with vegetable oil.

9. Pour batter onto the hot griddle 3 to 4 tablespoons at a time and cook until the surface begins to bubble and volcano, about 2 minutes.

10. Flip the cakes and cook another minute and eat promptly.

11. After eating your fair share of these lofty cakes, sing a round of "I Don't Want to Grow Up", take a nap and leave the dishes for the grown-ups.

Yield: Serves 4

Did You Know??

Keep your eyes open and you'll see Gwyneth Paltrow making her screen debut as the young Wendy. The young Peter Pan is played by Dustin Hoffman's son, Maxwell.

Oh, Grow Up!

Ladies, do you know men who exhibit signs of irresponsibility, narcissism, and chauvinism? Steer clear! They may be suffering from the highly contagious and incurable "Peter Pan Syndrome" as identified in the 1983 book of the same name.

CHEW ON THIS

Unlike Peter Pan, child star Charlie Korsmo did grow up. The young actor finished his Jackie Banning role in *Hook* and officially retired from show business (though he made a brief return to acting in 1998). Currently a physics graduate student at MIT, Korsmo also does some very adult work as a special assistant with the Environmental Protection Agency in Washington, D.C.

Hats off to the wily horticulturalist, Rudolph Boysen, who in 1923 had enough chutzpah, moxie, and vision to cross a blackberry, raspberry and loganberry to make a Boysenberry.

FOOD FOR THOUGHT

3 quarts water

3 tablespoons white vinegar

8 very fresh eggs

3 sticks butter

3 extra large egg yolks

3 tablespoons cold water

2–3 tablespoons fresh lemon juice

2 teaspoon prepared horseradish

Salt, black pepper, and cayenne to taste

1 loaf unsliced sourdough bread

Pure olive oil, as needed

1 ½ pounds beef fillet, trimmed
    and cut into 8 slices of equal thickness

2 beefsteak tomatoes cut into 8 slices

1 bunch fresh basil, sliced very thinly

1 union stuntman

Inside Scoop

This movie is filled with inside jokes but our favorite is the title "A Franco Columbu Film" which appears at the beginning of Jack Slater IV. A friend of Arnold Schwarzenegger's since their bodybuilding days, Columbu has appeared in many of his films.

Last Action Hero 1993

Schwarzeneggs Benedict

Many people think of Eggs Benedict as a sophisticated, refined dish. Not the way we make it! Our Schwarzeneggs Benedict features a meaty, muscular fillet topped with a horseradish hollandaise that explodes with flavor. It'll give you all the strength you need for a day of bullet-dodging, bad-guy-hunting, and random acts of Austrian-accented heroism. You'll be back . . . for seconds.

1. Add the vinegar to the water and bring to a low boil. Crack the eggs into a small bowl and slide them one-by-one from the bowl into the boiling water. Cook until the whites are just set (about 3 minutes) and transfer to an ice-water bath with a slotted spoon. Adjust the heat so that the water remains at a simmer and cover.

2. Melt the butter in a small saucepan over low heat. When the butter has melted, ladle off and discard any froth that has risen to the surface, then ladle the clarified butter into a bowl without getting any of the water that has settled to the bottom. Discard the water and transfer the clarified butter from the bowl back into the saucepan. Keep warm until use.

3. Combine the egg yolks and water in a medium saucepan and whisk until frothy (about 1 minute). Place the saucepan over medium heat and continue whisking as though your life depended on it. The mixture should double to triple in volume and thicken dramatically. When this happens, remove pan from the heat and continue whisking until the mixture cools somewhat.

4. Whisk the clarified butter into the egg yolk mixture, a little at a time, until all the butter has been added. The sauce should be thick and shiny. Whisk in the lemon juice and horseradish; season to taste with salt, pepper and cayenne. Keep warm until use over a very low heat or by transferring the sauce to a heated thermos.

5. Heat a large cast-iron skillet over medium-high heat. Cut the sourdough into eight fat slices and trim each slice into a circle using a 3 to 4-inch cookie cutter or an empty tin can. Brush each piece with olive oil and brown lightly on both sides in the hot skillet. Transfer toasted bread to a 250°F oven and keep warm until use. Leave the pan on the heat.

6. Sprinkle salt lightly over the bottom of the hot pan (it should be very hot by now) and lay the beef slices in the pan. Cook for approximately 90 seconds on each side for medium-rare, 2 minutes for medium-well. Season with freshly ground black pepper and remove meat to a plate to rest. While the steaks are resting, return the eggs to the simmering water for one minute.

7. Assemble the Schwarzeneggs Benedict by placing 2 toast rounds on each plate, placing a piece of beef fillet on the toast, a tomato slice over the beef, one poached egg atop the tomato, and hollandaise over the egg. Garnish with thinly sliced basil.

8. Once your guests taste the meal they will realize for themselves the extent of your culinary heroics and absolute fearlessness in the kitchen and they will begin to worship you. Accept all compliments with an "ah shucks, it was nothing" type of humility, then let it slip that there is one kitchen feat that still leaves you mortified beyond words and requires a real pro . . . the dishes. (Hey, it's worth a try.)

Yield: Serves 4

Bean Counting

Critics considered the disappointing earnings of this movie to be proof that the comedy and action genres could not be mixed. A year later, Arnold Schwarzenegger proved them wrong with his highly successful comedy/action movie, *True Lies*.

CHEW ON THIS

The schoolteacher who praises Laurence Olivier's performance is played by Olivier's widow, acclaimed actress Joan Plowright.

FOOD FOR THOUGHT

Throwing a brunch? Poached eggs are ideal for a large group. Prepare them in advance like a restaurant does by half-poaching the eggs until the whites have set but the yolks have not. Immediately transfer to a bowl of ice water and refrigerate. When ready to serve, bring a large pot of water to boil and carefully drop in the eggs. Cook until heated through, about 45 seconds and serve proudly.

Naked Gun 2½

For the bun part:

1/4 cup lukewarm water

1 tablespoon active dry yeast

3 eggs plus 3 egg yolks, at room
  temperature

4 tablespoons sugar

1/2 teaspoon salt

1/3 cup melted butter

1/2 cup lukewarm whole milk

1 teaspoon pure vanilla extract

3 ½ cups all-purpose flour, plus more
  for dusting

For the "schticky" part:

1 cup melted butter, plus more for
  brushing on the dough

2 ½ cups brown sugar

1/4 cup dark corn syrup

1/2 cup maple syrup

3 cups chopped pecan pieces

1 bag of well-worn comedy chestnuts

CHEW ON THIS

Leslie Nielsen didn't exactly come from
a family of jokers. His father was a
Canadian Mountie and one of his
brothers was a Deputy Prime Minister
in the Canadian government.

Lt. Frank Drebin's "Really Schticky" Buns

We were in the "Dinner & a Movie" Test Kitchen listening to the food scanner when we got the call. As far as cooking show work is concerned, every once in a while something comes up that you're just not quite prepared for. Somehow some demented mad chef— probably full of self-hate and possibly a couple of months behind in his rent—snaps and holds back on the schticky topping for his buns. We rushed to the scene of the crime. Victims were choking and puckered after ingesting the brutal, dry buns. We immediately administered emergency schticky and set to work on this recipe . . .

1. In a small bowl, whisk together the warm water, yeast, and a large pinch of the sugar. Set aside for 10 minutes until the mixture begins to bubble.

2. In a large mixing bowl, beat the eggs well, then whisk the sugar, salt, and melted butter into the beaten eggs. Add the yeast mixture to the egg mixture.

3. Use a wooden spoon to beat in the milk, vanilla, and 3 cups of the flour. Continue beating until smooth and elastic, about 3 minutes. (Not you . . . the dough.)

4. Turn the dough out onto a clean, floured surface and knead in the remaining half-cup flour, plus more as needed to keep dough from sticking. Transfer to a lightly oiled bowl, cover, and place in a warm spot until doubled in bulk. (Not you . . . the dough.)

5. While the dough is rising, combine and blend all the "schticky" ingredients. Line a 12-inch cast-iron skillet with aluminum foil and spread 3/4 of the mixture evenly in the bottom of the skillet.

6. Once the dough has risen, roll it out into a 16-inch x 18-inch rectangle and brush with melted butter. Spread the remaining "schticky" mixture evenly over the top, leaving a 2-inch border along one of the long edges.

7. Starting with the edge opposite the border, roll up tightly, jellyroll style, to form an 18-inch long log. Cut into 8 to12 even pieces and pat each down lightly. Lay the buns over the "schticky" mixture in the cast-iron skillet, cover with a clean towel, and set in a warm spot to rise for 20 minutes.

8. Bake in a 375°F oven for 25–30 minutes until the tops are brown and the syrup bubbles up around the edges. Cool for 10 minutes, then place a large platter over the skillet. Put on two oven mitts (one on each hand), take a deep breath, then quickly and deftly invert the skillet and platter so that the platter is now on the bottom and the skillet is on top. Carefully pull the skillet off the buns and serve while still warm, but not so hot as to disfigure your hands.

9. Surely, your guests will know that after eating these fabulous "schticky" buns they should pitch in with the dishes . . . sorry, didn't mean to call you surely.

Yield: 1 dozen

Face it—yeast is mysterious. Perhaps this is because it must be "alive" to do its job. The expiration date on the package is critical; if it has expired, your yeast may have too. If you are uncertain about the health of your yeast, test it by combining with warm (not hot) water and a pinch of sugar. It should foam and bubble. If not, give it a timely burial.

Schtick is a Yiddish word meaning a routine or gimmick, usually associated with comedy.

Inside Scoop

The highly successful *Naked Gun* films grew out of an unsuccessful TV series, "Police Squad!" which appeared on ABC in 1982 and was produced by Jerry and David Zucker and Jim Abrahams.

Stepmom

1998

Divorced Eggs and Broken Home Fries

Marriages have crumbled over smaller issues than what kind of sauce to put on your eggs. We suggest heading trouble off at the pass by making a breakfast that embodies the secret to all successful relationships . . . compromise. Divorced eggs—or "huevos divorciados" as they're known south of the border—uses red AND green sauce, so everyone can start off the day getting their way.

1. Make the red sauce: Combine the dried chiles, tomato, water, salt, and vinegar in a small saucepan over medium-high heat. Bring to a boil and simmer for five minutes, then transfer to a blender and puree until smooth. Strain into a small saucepan, cover and keep warm over low heat.

2. Make the green sauce: Heat an ungreased griddle or cast-iron skillet over medium heat. Place the tomatillos, garlic, and jalapeño on the griddle and roast for about 10 minutes, until the tomatillo skins begin to blister and brown on all sides. Transfer to a blender and add the salt, sugar, and chicken broth; blend until smooth. Strain into a small saucepan, stir in the chopped cilantro; cover and keep warm over low heat.

3. Poach the eggs: Combine the vinegar and water in a medium

For the red sauce:

1 cup dried California or New Mexico chiles

2 medium ripe tomatoes, halved

1 cup water

1 teaspoon salt

2 tablespoons white vinegar

For the green sauce:

1 pound fresh tomatillos, husked and rinsed

2 cloves garlic

1 fresh jalapeño

1 teaspoon salt

1 teaspoon sugar

1 cup chicken broth

3 tablespoons chopped fresh cilantro, plus more for garnish

For the eggs:

3 quarts water

3 tablespoons white vinegar

8 very fresh eggs

Dry Mexican cheese, for garnish

For the broken home fries:

2 russet potatoes cut into 2-inch chunks

1 sprig fresh rosemary

4 tablespoons olive oil

2 cups chicken stock

1 family, strained & separated

saucepan and bring to a boil. Crack the eggs one-by-one into a small bowl, and then slide each egg from the bowl into the boiling water. Cook until the whites are just set, about 3 minutes. Remove from the boiling water with a slotted spoon and place gently into an ice water bath.

4. Cook potatoes: Place potatoes, rosemary, and olive oil in a medium nonstick saucepan and cover with chicken stock. Bring to a boil, reduce heat and simmer until the stock evaporates, about 20 minutes. When the potatoes soften, break apart and continue cooking until brown and yummy. Season to taste with salt and pepper.

5. Serve: Warm the poached eggs by placing into the hot sauces. Serve over home fried potatoes and top with more sauce and crumbled cheese. Garnish with cilantro and serve at once.

6. After dinner, call a good lawyer and arrange to have your guests get custody of the dirty dishes.

Yield: Serves 4

FOOD FOR THOUGHT

If uncertain as to whether an egg is fresh, place it in a glass of water. If the egg sinks, it's still fresh. If it floats to the top, it's not. If it hovers above the surface of the water, it's possessed.

CHEW ON THIS

After peaking in 1979, the U.S. divorce rate has actually been on the decline. Currently averaged at 40 percent, the divorce rate for first-time marriages is even lower as second and third-time marriages are more likely to fail.

Inside Scoop

Susan Sarandon fell into acting by accident after attending a casting call with her then-husband, Chris Sarandon. (They obviously didn't have the recipe for "Huevos Divorciados".) Though her husband was an aspiring actor, it was Susan who won a major role in the film and began her career as an actress. She now enjoys "Living in Cinnamon Buns" with long time partner Tim Robbins whom she met while filming *Bull Durham*.

Witness

1985

Barn Raisin' Bread

Like Kelly McGillis in Witness, *this bread is plain on the outside but has hidden passion—and raisins—just beneath the surface. But no matter how longingly it stares at you with its raisin swirl, resist the urge to give your loaf a sponge bath.*

For the dough:
3/4 cup whole milk
1/2 stick unsalted butter
1/2 cup golden raisins
1 ¼ teaspoons salt
1/4 cup lukewarm water
1/3 cup sugar
1 tablespoon rapid-rise yeast
2 eggs at room temperature
1/2 cup uncooked oatmeal
3+ cups unbleached flour
Vegetable oil for coating

For the cinnamon filling:
2 tablespoons brown sugar
4 tablespoons white sugar
2 tablespoons cinnamon

For the egg glaze:
1 egg, beaten with 1 tablespoon milk
1 big, empty field
Lots of lumber
200 of your closest friends

1. Preheat oven to 350°F.

2. Combine milk, butter, raisins, and salt in a small saucepan over low heat. When the butter melts, set mixture aside and allow to cool to no more than 105°F.

3. In a large bowl, dissolve the sugar in the lukewarm water and sprinkle the yeast over the top. When the mixture begins to bubble, beat in the eggs and then the warm milk mixture.

4. Beat in the oatmeal and 2 cups of the flour with a wooden spoon until fully blended and smooth, about 100 strokes.

5. Mix in another 1/2 cup of flour and scrape the mixture out onto a clean work surface. Knead by hand at least 15 minutes, adding only enough additional flour to keep from sticking.

6. Transfer the dough to a large, oiled bowl; cover, and place in a warm spot until doubled in bulk.

7. While the dough rises, grease a 9-inch x 5-inch loaf pan. Combine the sugar and cinnamon and set aside.

Inside Scoop

If any star is qualified to raise a barn, it's Harrison Ford. Ford supported himself as a master carpenter before his acting career took off and still does it today as a hobby.

8. Punch dough down and pat or roll into an 8-inch x 16-inch rectangle. Sprinkle the cinnamon-sugar mixture evenly over the dough and lightly brush the edges with the egg-milk mixture.

9. Roll the dough up lengthwise and pinch the seams together. Transfer to the greased loaf pan, seam-side down. Cover and let rise to the top of the pan.

10. Brush the loaf with the egg-milk mixture and bake in the preheated oven about 45 minutes, until it is pleasantly golden and gives a hollow thud when tapped on the bottom. Cool on a rack before cutting.

11. Plain tip: Consider inviting a non-Amish friend over to load and operate the automatic dishwasher.

Yield: One loaf

What's Raisin' Your Bread?

When yeast is activated, it hungrily consumes sugars and starches, converting them into carbon dioxide and alcohol. The carbon dioxide bubbles get trapped in the structure of the dough, causing it to rise.

CHEW ON THIS

Though this was Australian director Peter Weir's first Hollywood film, *Witness* contains the clash of old and modern cultures that pervade most of his work. If you like *Witness*, check out Weir's early movies, *The Last Wave* and *The Year of Living Dangerously*, or his highly underrated American film, *Fearless*.

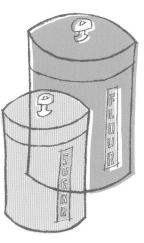

Know Your Terms!

Banana Peel 1) Skin from the fruit of a large tropical plant. 2) Slippery slapstick comedic device.

Beat 1) To vigorously stir to blend ingredients. 2) The pregnant pauses between the important lines an actor has and the stuff the other actors say.

Beefcake 1) Pastry-encased meat of a bovine animal. 2) Well-muscled actor who finds himself shirtless more often than not.

Best boy 1) He who offers to do the dishes. 2) Asst. chief lighting technician.

Blanch 1) To cook briefly in a liquid. 2) Best-known Tennessee Williams character, who claimed to depend on the kindness of strangers. (This Blanche has an "e" at the end.)

Blend 1) To combine and mix ingredients well. 2) What an extra actor does if he wants to keep working.

Bombe 1) Spherical frozen dessert. 2) Cinematic disaster (see *pan*).

Butterfly 1) To split open and spread apart. 2) Something that forms in actors' stomachs prior to their walking on stage and forgetting their lines.

Caper 1) The pickled bud of the caper bush. 2) Popular genre of action-adventure movie.

Casting 1) Process of molding decorative sugar. 2) Process of auditioning decorative actors, occasionally employing use of couch.

Chafing 1) A type of dish used to keep food hot at the table. 2) Painful condition suffered by many actors working in adult films and westerns.

Cheesy 1) Dish using cheese as a key ingredient. 2) Movie containing an overabundance of saccharine moments.

Clam 1) Sweet bivalve. 2) Sour note.

Coddle 1) To gently cook in very hot, but not boiling, water. 2) How a star actor is treated regardless of his behavior.

Corny 1) Dish employing large amounts of corn. 2) Much like Cheesy, but less believable.

Cottage Cheese 1) A fresh, unripened cheese. 2) Good reason for use of a body double.

Curdling 1) Denaturing process caused by enzymes, acidity, or heat whereby milk separates and turns to curd. 2) Type of spine-tingling, high-pitched scream employed by actresses in horror movies.

Cut 1) To divide into pieces with the use of a sharp knife. 2) What the director shouts to stop the cameras from rolling.

Demi-Glace 1) A very highly reduced meat stock. 2) Lipstick specifically formulated to be used under bright lights.

Dice 1) To cut food into small uniform cubes. 2) Clever middle name of former stand-up comedian turned actor.

Emulsion 1) A mixture composed of a suspension of fat globules. 2) Light-sensitive coating on movie film that causes it to capture and retain an image.

Flake 1) To break apart into small pieces. 2) To forget to show up for rehearsal.

Fold 1) To combine ingredients with a gentle, circular motion. 2) What generally happens to a show after unanimously scathing reviews.

Fool 1) English dessert consisting of fruit folded into whipping cream or custard. 2) Word most used by stockholders when describing the studio executive who passed on *E.T.*

Frappe 1) Flavored liquid frozen to a slushy consistency, 2) Fast dance step, quick action of the leg.

Gel 1) To congeal with the use of gelatin or pectin. 2) Color filter used over stage lighting.

Ginger 1) Aromatic rhizome commonly used in Asian cooking. 2a) The one you chose over Mary Ann. 2b) The one you chose over Cyd Charisse.

Glaze 1) To brush a dish with a light coating of sauce. 2a) Look commonly seen in the eyes of Hollywood agents when discussing large amounts of money. 2b) Official doughnut of the teamster's union, Hollywood local.

Grain 1) Edible seed; i.e. corn, rice, and wheat. 2) Tiny particles of light-sensitive material on film.

Grate 1) To cut food into small bits with the use of a grater. 2) The effect that actors crossing over into singing careers have on the ears of the hearing.

Grease 1) To wipe fat onto a pan to keep food from sticking to it. 2) Incredibly popular musical starring middle-aged teenaged actors.

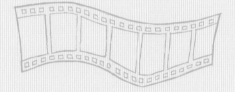

Grind 1) To reduce a food into powder by crushing between hard surfaces. 2) How a $300,000-a-week television actor describes his job after a grueling two seasons.

Grip 1) Handle of a knife. 2) Person responsible for handling, adjustment, and maintenance of equipment.

Hack 1) To forcefully cut with uneven or irregular blows. 2) An actor who's either been in more than one infomercial, or should be.

Ham 1) The cured thigh or hind leg from a hog or pig. 2) Actor who can't differentiate on-stage from off-stage.

Ink 1) Squid excretion commonly used as a flavoring agent. 2) Press coverage, commonly arranged by a favored agent.

Junket 1) A rennet-thickened, milk-based dessert. 2) An all-expenses-paid vacation for the Hollywood press corps in which they're allowed to follow a star around and ask probing and insightful questions.

Legs 1) Streams of wine on the inside of a wine glass that indicate body. 2) Streams of income that indicate the continuing return of large profits; i.e. "This show's got legs!"

Loins 1) The tender cuts of meat taken from the front quarter of an animal on either side of the backbone. 2) Common spot for aching to be felt by characters in the "coming of age" film genre.

Mace 1) Popular baking spice found in the outer layer of the fruit of the nutmeg tree. 2) Popular defensive aerosol used by actresses to keep frisky paparazzi at bay.

Martini 1) First shot at the end of a long day. 2) Last shot at the end of a long shoot.

Milk 1) Nutritious secretion produced by various mammals, often used as food by humans. 2) Squeezing every drop of emotion out of a scene, often used as trick by actors.

Mint 1) Any of several aromatic herbs belonging to the mint family. 2) Cost of an average Kevin Costner spectacle.

Mole 1) Famous Mexican sauce containing, among other things, chilies, chocolate, garlic, and sesame seeds. 2) Trademark facial imperfection.

Mousse 1) Dish consisting of a flavoring base folded into whipped cream or egg whites. 2) Gooey hair product very popular with moody young actors appearing in John Hughes movies.

Nut 1) Edible single seed or kernel, often surrounded by hard shell. 2) Operating expenses to be recovered, often deductible in a contract with the film distributor.

Oscar 1) Classical veal dish garnished with crayfish, asparagus and béarnaise sauce. 2) Official Award of the Academy of Motion Picture Arts and Sciences.

Pan 1) Vessel in which food is cooked. 2a) Universally poor reviews. 2b) Process of rotating a camera.

Pasties 1) Little meat-and-vegetable turnovers. 2) The difference between an "R" or an "NC17" rating.

Pearl Barley 1) A highly polished form of barley commonly used in soup. 2) Highly polished singer commonly seen in old movies.

Roll 1) A small, rounded individual portion of bread. 2) What the director shouts to begin filming.

Saccharin 1) Non-caloric sugar substitute approximately 500 times sweeter than sugar. 2) A shameless display of insincere emotion.

Score 1) To partially cut through the outer surface of a food. 2) Musical composition that, when recorded, becomes part of the soundtrack of a film.

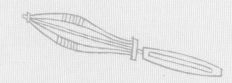

Season 1) Enhance the taste of food through the use of spices, herbs, etc. 2) A recurrent or specific division of time marked by new film and television releases.

Shark 1) Family of edible predatory fish growing up to forty feet in length. 2) See "Agent" below.

Shot 1) One jigger full of alcoholic spirits. 2) One in a series of camera angles.

Spit 1) Metal rod used to skewer and cook food over an open flame. 2) Foamy liquid often found issuing forth from the mouths of emotionally charged actors.

Skin 1) To remove the external membranous tissue from a piece of fish or poultry. 2) The weaker the script, the more of this you're likely to see.

Thickening Agent 1) Any of various ingredients used to thicken sauces, soups, etc. 2) An actor's representative after too many power lunches.

Toss 1) To mix a salad as to coat with dressing. 2) Hosting term: to get back to the Movie; i.e., … and now back to "Prisoners in Love."

Wok On 1) Preheating a Chinese skillet. 2) Minor, non-speaking role.

Wrap 1) Cylindrical sandwich made with thin, unleavened flatbread. 2) To finish shooting.

Bare Bones Essential Equipment

Just have a can opener and a hotplate, but can't quite put your finger on what's missing?
Here's a great list to help get you started:

- One 8-10" high carbon, stainless steel chef's knife (sometimes called a French knife)
- One 4" paring knife
- One 6-8" utility knife
- One 8-10" serrated knife
- 1 oyster knife
- 1 sharpening steel
- At least 2 vegetable peelers (we usually lose one)
- 1 pair kitchen shears
- 1 corkscrew
- 1 bottle opener
- 1 cheese grater
- 1 can opener
- 1 pepper mill
- 3 cutting boards (one all-purpose, one for pastry and one small one just for garlic, onion, chilies, etc.)
- 2 glass measuring cups (one 1-cup, one 2-cup)
- 1 set dry measuring cups
- 1 set measuring spoons
- 1 oven thermometer
- 1 instant-read meat thermometer
- 3 nested stainless mixing bowls
- 3 nested glass mixing bowls
- 1 rubber spatula
- 1 pancake-type turner
- 2 or 3 wooden spoons
- 1 large slotted spoon
- 1 large metal spoon
- 1 fine mesh skimmer
- 1 medium mesh strainer
- 1 colander
- 1 funnel
- 1 pastry brush
- 1 ladle

- 1 pair tongs
- 1 large 2-3 tine fork
- 1 balloon whisk
- 1 rotary beater
- 1 rolling pin
- 10 "Dinner & a Movie" Cookbooks
- 1 kitchen timer
- One 2 qt. saucepan with cover
- One 3 qt. saucepan with cover
- 1 steamer basket
- 1 Dutch oven with cover
- One 10-12 qt. stockpot with cover
- One 8" sauté pan with cover
- One 10" sauté pan with cover
- One 12" cast-iron skillet with cover
- One 8-10" nonstick omelet pan
- 1 roasting pan
- 1 roasting rack
- 1 flat cookie sheet
- 1 glass pie plate
- One 2 qt. glass casserole
- 1 aluminum loaf pan
- 1 muffin tin
- 1 fire extinguisher
- 1 salad spinner
- 1 tea kettle
- 1 blender (with or without goldfish)
- 1 remote control (which conveniently defaults to TBS)
- 1 programmable VCR and lots of blank tapes (in case you miss "Dinner & a Movie")
- 1 TV scheduling guide (to find out if "Dinner & a Movie" is on before or after the Braves)
- 1 charming co-host of choice

Goods to Keep on Hand

Wonder what to keep in your larder? To be honest, we're not quite sure what a larder is, but if we had one, these are some of the things we'd keep in it:

Dry Goods
all-purpose flour
baking chocolate
baking powder
baking soda
brown rice
brown sugar
cake flour
cocoa powder
corn meal
corn starch
dried beans
dried pasta
dry active yeast
granulated sugar
kosher salt
shelled nuts; i.e., walnuts,
  almonds, pecans, peanuts
table salt or sea salt
white rice

Canned and Bottled
anchovies
balsamic vinegar
canned beef stock
capers
canned chicken stock
Dijon mustard
extra-virgin olive oil
honey
hot pepper sauce
ketchup
mayonnaise
pure maple syrup

pure olive oil
pure vanilla extract
red wine vinegar
soy sauce
toasted sesame oil
tomato paste
tomato sauce
vegetable oil
white vinegar
Worcestershire sauce

Assorted Dried Herbs and Spices
(to be replaced at least once a year)
allspice
basil
bay leaves (Turkish)
cayenne pepper
celery seed
chili powder
cinnamon
cloves
coriander
cumin
curry powder
dill weed
dry mustard
fennel seed
garlic powder
ground ginger
mustard seed
mustard powder
nutmeg
onion powder
oregano

paprika (Hungarian)
red pepper flakes
rosemary
sage
tarragon
turmeric
thyme
peppercorns, black
peppercorns, white

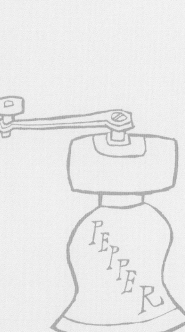

NEW Entertaining & Kitchen TIPS

Be prepared

Take 5 minutes to read any recipe through before starting. Do you have the time, equipment, and ingredients necessary?

Stay seasonal

Attempt, whenever possible, to use seasonal produce. This may even mean choosing a different recipe, but fruits and vegetables ALWAYS taste better and are cheaper in season. (How often do you get that combination?) This, by the way, is why so many great cooks appear so shifty when asked to give a recipe for a popular dish. Although some of them are undoubtedly truly shifty, the remainder know that duplication of their creation is virtually impossible without quality ingredients.

Take a rest

The "resting" of meats after roasting isn't just a snooty term that gastronomes employ to sound superior, (Don't worry, they have plenty of others to fall back on.) It's true, allowing a roast to sit at room temperature for even 5 or 10 minutes after leaving the oven allows any free-flowing juices an opportunity to retreat into the meat. Bottom line . . . you get a reputation for moist meat.

Taste!

The best cooks we know will taste a dish constantly as it cooks (not recommended, of course, for pies and cakes) and before they actually begin cooking. If the apples are exceptionally sour or sweet, they know to adjust the sugar accordingly. One moment, a stew may taste just the way you want it, only to have the flavors flatten out the next. Tasting is the measure of a great cook.

Salt is your friend

Don't be afraid to salt—at the right time. Proper salting can coax out a variety of flavors. Plus a pinch of salt in the kitchen can avoid a blizzard of salt at the table. One word of caution: never salt a dish you intend to reduce. As the liquid evaporates, it will become saltier than the tears you will shed when your guests take one taste and head off to the nearest restaurant.

A good habit

Clean as you work. (I don't, but my wife keeps saying it's a good habit to get into.)

300° or 500°F?

Calibrate your oven (and start your engines!). Actually, calibration is simply placing an accurate oven thermometer in the center of the oven and setting it to 350°F. If after 30 minutes, the thermometer reads more than 25 degrees off in either direction, call the gas company.

Spices

Buy whole spices and grind them yourself. The easiest way is to keep an old coffee grinder around and grind just what you need. The taste difference is amazing.

Show them you care . . .

15 minutes before serving, place plates in a 250°F. oven. It's very little trouble, shows your guests you care and really does help keep food hot at the table.

Counter intelligence

Next time you have a big meal to prepare and not much counter space for ingredients, try setting up an ironing board in the kitchen. (If you don't have an ironing board, take all your ingredients to the cleaners. I'm sure they have one.)

The cold truth

Want to know the cold truth about frozen food? Contrary to popular belief, those good-ies languishing in your freezer are not in sus-pended animation. They are in fact decom-posing very, very, very slowly. Allow us to share a few strategies to help extend the life of frozen items:

- Buy a freezer thermometer and maintain freezer temperature at zero or below.
- Tape a log on the inside of the freezer door indicating when things go in.
- Keep the freezer full of food—you'll use less electricity.
- Probably the most important thing . . . shut the door.

Oh, ginger

Fresh ginger never holds up well in the refrigera-tor. We suggest storing it in a plastic bag in the freezer. When you need some, go ahead and grate it frozen, skin on.

How full is the tank?

How to tell the amount of propane remain-ing in the BBQ tank? Pour water on the out-side of the tank in question. A frost line will appear indicating exactly how full the tank is!

'Cue tricks

Even the most experienced home grill master knows that chicken is surprisingly tricky to cook properly on the grill. It is not uncommon for the skin to blacken while the meat near the joints remains grotesquely bloody. You're left having to shamefully return the meat to the grill to finish cooking while your guests get hungry and grumpy and begin to hate you. Avoid this and gain the admiration of friends and family with perfectly cooked, well-timed chicken by first oven roasting your poultry pieces, then brush with sauce and grill just before serving. No one has to know (and we won't tell if you won't).

Smokey salt

Make smoked salt by plac-ing a pan of kosher salt on the grill. Throw some soaked hickory chips right on the coals; cover and smoke for 20 minutes. Transfer the smoky salt to a jar and cover tightly. Use all year long whenever you want that backyard BBQ flavor.

Don't forget to floss

Try using (clean) dental floss to cut cheesecake, layer cakes and goat cheese. May we suggest the unscented variety.

That's just grate

Everyone knows that freshly grated cheese always tastes superior to the pre-grated packaged stuff. Unfortunately last minute cheese grating too often results in the sacrifice of one's fingertips. Ouch. If you are as fond of your fingertips as I am, try keeping a few metal thimbles in your kitchen drawer. Cover what's left of your fingers with thimbles and grate fearlessly.

Tools
To us, any tool that only does one job is a waste of space. Hard-boiled egg slicers were in that category until we learned recently what a good job they do slicing mozzarella, mushrooms and soft fruit like kiwis.

Boil in a hurry!
In a hurry to bring a stockpot of water to boil for pasta? Pour half of the water into second pot and heat it on another burner. When both come to a boil, combine them in the larger pot. Should be nearly twice as quick.

Lobster lessons
Lobsters must be purchased either live or fully cooked. Never buy one that is recently deceased, yet uncooked. The moment a lobster dies, both bacterial growth and its own natural enzymes begin breaking down the meat, making it unhealthy for consumption.

Fresh fish?
Truly fresh fish should not smell "fishy" at all; ask the clerk for a sniff (of the fish that is) and inspect it. If the fish is whole, the gills should be pink and the eyes clear. Pressed lightly with a fingertip, the flesh should be supple enough to spring back.

Grilling
Please be advised that food scientists now tell us that grilling has been proven to produce trace amounts of certain spooky carcinogens. One can, however, minimize those pesky, fun-busting compounds by marinating meats at least 2 hours prior to grilling, avoiding cooking over high flames and avoiding grilling any foods until so dark as to appear blackened.

Dough sticking while rolling?
If you have trouble keeping dough from sticking while rolling, a good way to cheat is to roll out between layers of wax paper or parchment. It's also easier to transfer after rolling.

Hey, margarita fans!
When buying limes for juicing purposes, look for the ones beginning to turn yellow in spots. These will be ripe and juicy, whereas the vivid green limes are generally immature and dry.

Measuring peanut butter.
Goopy ingredients like peanut butter or shortening can be inaccurate and messy to measure. Try this: Fill a 4-cup measuring cup with 2 cups of cold water. Scoop the shortening into the water until the water rises to the 4 cup mark; you now have exactly 2 cups of shortening. Just pour the water off and use. Tip: Try to do this when other people are watching, they'll think you are really smart.

Spots are good.
Don't search for perfect, unblemished bananas when making banana cream pie, banana pudding,

banana bread, etc. Spots begin to make an appearance as the sugar content increases, thus making those brown spotted bargain bananas better suited for tasty desserts.

Remove onion smell from hands.
Remove the smell of onions and garlic from your hands by rubbing them with a piece of stainless steel. Specialty stores actually sell little stainless steel discs for this purpose, but you can just as easily use the sides and top of a clean, high-carbon stainless steel knife. Be careful not to cut yourself, we haven't found a really foolproof method of bloodstain removal.

Last minute cake decorating tip
Need to pipe out birthday decorations but don't have a piping bag, tips or icing?
1. Chop some chocolate; place in a ziplock bag and seal tightly.
2. Set bag in warm water until chocolate melts.
3. Snip off the very tip off one corner. Slowly squeeze the softened chocolate out as you would a pastry bag.

Onions—sweet, mild, and strong
Onions can be categorized as sweet, mild, or strong. The sweet group includes Maui onions, Vidalia onions, and Spanish onions. Any of these are great sliced thinly in sandwiches and salads. The Vidalia's, native to TBS's home state of Georgia are so sweet you can eat 'em like fruit! Shallots, leeks, pearl onions, and red onions are mild to medium flavored while the good old white and yellow onion are stronger and more pungent, making these ideal for stews, soups, and roasting.

Cooking with cast iron.
With all the high-end cookware available, it is easy to forget about the beauty of the classic, cast-iron skillet. There are plenty examples of these tried and true workhorses being passed down through families for three and four generations. And fried chicken, catfish, cornbread and plenty of other traditional American dishes just seem to taste better cooked in cast iron. Although the seasoning process is a source of confusion, it is quite simple.
1. Rinse the pan in hot water and dry well.
2. Place a handful of Kosher salt and a tablespoon of lard, shortening or vegetable oil in the pan; then use a paper towel or kitchen rag to scrub inside and outside.
3. Brush out the salt and coat again lightly with oil.
4. Place in a 300°F oven for 45 minutes.
5. Each time you use the pan, the patina (black coating) will become thicker, darker and more stick resistant. Don't ever clean a seasoned pan using soap or detergent; rinse with hot water and scrub with salt if needed, then rub with oil before storing.

Be a Flake
One of the prime characteristics of top-notch pie crusts and other so-called flaky pastry is, in fact, its *flakiness*. The trick to achieving this is to break the butter, shortening or other fat into very small pieces.

In order to accomplish this, the fat must be very cold and if the kitchen is warm you must work quickly. If the butter is too soft it will just mush up rather than break apart. If that happens, (heaven forbid) the end product will be tough rather than flaky.

When a pastry recipe calls to have the fat cut in, what they are really asking you to do is somehow manually mix the flour mixture with the fat in such a way that tiny fat particles become evenly distributed throughout the mixture.

This is where the fun begins. Cooks love to argue on the optimum method to achieve this. The simplest method is to *use one's fingers*. Many folks swear by this method and I must assume they are by nature a cold-handed bunch (although I'm assured by good sources they are warm at heart). On the other hand, if you've ever received a steamy handshake from someone with warm, sweaty hands, you can imagine what effect those fiery phalanges would have on an unsuspecting stick of butter. Determine to which category you belong and either dig in or read on.

The next few methods are still manual in spirit with the help of one type of tool or another.

The 2-knife method: The advantage of this method is not having to obtain specialized equipment. Most people have access to 2 knives unless they're either chopstick fanatics or in the Big House. (In which case you might ask a friendly guard to cut your butter in for you).

The cheese-grater method: With this technique, the butter must first be frozen. Simply grate the butter on the largest holes of the grater and work carefully as to avoid having to list knuckle skin as an ingredient.

The pastry-cutter method: Still probably my favorite. An inexpensive tool (usually under $5) that allows you to work quickly with a consistently admirable result.

And finally...It's big and bulky...it's hard to clean . . . and it can make perfect pie crust faster than six grandmothers on a cold day . . . That's right,

it's a food processor, folks. As many of our loyal "Dinner & a Movie" viewers already know, if this appliance was good for nothing else at all, it would still be worth having just to make pastry. If making more than one batch, put the work bowl and blade of the processor into the freezer a few minutes before beginning. As with all of the preceding techniques, make certain the butter is well chilled. You can even go that extra flaky mile and chill the flour too.

Stop Whining

Our opinion is that the greatest error made when deciding on a wine to use in a recipe is choosing a bottle based solely on price. Our central rule is: if it's not good enough to drink, we wouldn't want to cook with it. By the time most of the alcohol cooks off and the wine reduces, what you're left with are simply the initial flavors greatly intensified (and if they weren't yummy to begin with then you're really in trouble). Using wine as an ingredient also embraces one of our favorite, most fundamental cooking principles: Just use ingredients that taste good and you're halfway there.

If cooking with wine for the first time, start by cooking with a wine that you would choose to enjoy with the meal. Unless the main course has fairly rich flavors like roast duck or pork, try cooking with a wine with little or no residual sugar; in other words, bone-dry.

An entertaining experiment is to practice making simple sauces with a few different wines, serving them with something modest like a grilled chicken breast or a piece of poached salmon and then finding out which combinations are personal favorites. You might even be surprised to find that your own tastes run counter to the traditional red wine with red meat-white wine with fish premise with which many of us grew up. The easiest way to do this is by making a simplified wine-butter sauce.

Simply take a cup or two of Cabernet, Pinot Noir, Zinfandel, Sauvignon Blanc, Champagne, Chardonnay, Syrah, Merlot or what ever you can get your hands on and boil it down in a saucepan until only a few tablespoons of syrupy liquid remain. Remove the pan from the heat and immediately whisk in a few tablespoons of butter. It's that simple.

An experiment like this can give you the opportunity to try a number of different wines with different dishes and see what combinations you personally enjoy. After all, who cares what the experts say. The bottom line is personal taste; follow that and you can't be wrong.

Here are a few tips to avoid dumb mistakes when purchasing, storing, and handling raw poultry.

Purchasing: If the chicken is prepackaged, check the sell by date on the label. Avoid packaged chicken with excess accumulated juices. If you're buying a lot of groceries, wait until just before check out to choose your chicken, then head right home and refrigerate promptly.

Storage: Use or freeze poultry within 2 days of purchasing. If not using immediately, store in leak proof containers and never, ever allow raw juices to drip onto any other foods. It's also not a bad idea to hang a refrigerator thermometer in your fridge and spot check occasionally to see that the temperature never rises above 45°F. This also serves to extend the shelf life of all your refrigerated foods especially dairy, meat, fish, and poultry.

Handling: Wash hands after handling raw chicken and before touching anything or anyone else. Be mindful of any surfaces that have come in contact with raw poultry, washing them thoroughly with

soap and hot water or bleach solution before continuing. This includes cutting boards, counters and knifes.

Cooking: Use an instant-read meat thermometer if you are uncertain as to whether chicken is done. Ideally, a perfectly cooked piece of chicken should be fully cooked, yet still juicy. About 150°–155°F for white meat and 165°–175°F for dark meat. It's good to know that dark meat is generally much more forgiving and won't dry out as much as white meat when inadvertently overcooked.

ENJOY!

Index

Index

Index

Index

Credits & Acknowledgements

Designer—Carley Brown
Project Director—Christine Drayer
Cover Photography and Additional Photos—Mark Hill
Unit Photographer—Tom Scheuber
Editor—Kimberlee Carlson
Additional Text—Rick Batalla, Jay Griffiths, Keith Merryman, Robert Taylor

"Dinner & a Movie": Monday Nights on TBS Superstation
Hosted by: Paul Gilmartin, Lisa Kushell, Claud Mann

Special Thanks to:
Mark Allen, Perla Batalla, Eva Batalla-Mann, Piers Bath,
Stephen & Jordan Bedikian, Brad Benedict, Denise Bradshaw, Leslie Brymer, Michael Buckley,
Deb Camponeta, Bobbie & Hillary Carlson, Jeff Carr, I Li Chen, Kelly Cole, Bill Cox, Horace Derricotte,
Tom Evans, Dave Gekler, Andrew Glaser, Anthony Godos, Annabelle Gurwitch; Daniel & Bobby Hawley,
Gary Holland, Travis & Annabelle Johnson, Ingrid Kornspan, Christy Kwon Kreisberg, Kevin Little,
Amy Lovett, Bonnie Lu's, Ward McCarthy, Gina McKenzie, Kathleen McTee, Mike Miller, Deb Murphy,
Jack Pendarvis, Carla Plunknett, Dennis Quinn, Michael Regan, Rachel Ruskin, Cheryl Schayer,
Susan Seyler, Misty Skedgell, Alysa Story, Kurt "Smokey" Tiegs, Richard Turner, Lee Tyo, Liz Weller,
Jessica Wolser, Terrell Yelverton, Nancy Zakreski and the nice people at Absolute Post Broadcast Production
Services, Bruce Austin Productions, Norsemen Productions & Wolff Brothers Post.

TBSSUPERSTATION
www.TBSsuperstation.com

Standard Abbreviations

teaspoon	t / tsp
tablespoon	T / TBL / Tbsp
TBS	the superstation!
Cup	c
Quart	qt
Pound	lb
Ounce	oz

Standard Measurement Equivalents

A few grains/pinch/dash, etc. (dry)	= Less than 1/8 tsp
A dash (liquid)	= A few drops
3 teaspoons	= 1 tablespoon
1/2 tablespoon	= 1-1/2 teaspoons
1 tablespoon	= 3 teaspoons
2 tablespoons	= 1 fluid ounce
4 tablespoons	= 1/4 cup
5-1/3 tablespoons	= 1/3 cup
8 tablespoons	= 1/2 cup
8 tablespoons	= 4 fluid ounces
10-2/3 tablespoons	= 2/3 cup
12 tablespoons	= 3/4 cup
16 tablespoons	= 1 cup
16 tablespoons	= 8 fluid ounces
1/8 cup	= 2 tablespoons
1/4 cup	= 4 tablespoons
1/4 cup	= 2 fluid ounces
1/3 cup	= 5 tablespoons plus 1 teaspoon
1/2 cup	= 8 tablespoons
1 cup	= 16 tablespoons
1 cup	= 8 fluid ounces
1 cup	= 1/2 pint
2 cups	= 1 pint
2 pints	= 1 quart
4 quarts (liquid)	= 1 gallon
8 quarts (dry)	= 1 peck
4 pecks (dry)	= 1 bushel
1 kilogram	= approximately 2 pounds
1 liter	= approximately 4 cups or 1 quart

Approximate Metric Equivalents by Volume

U.S.	METRIC
1/4 cup	= 60 milliliters
1/2 cup	= 120 milliliters
1 cup	= 230 milliliters
1 1/4 cups	= 300 milliliters
1 1/2 cups	= 360 milliliters
2 cups	= 460 milliliters
2 1/2 cups	= 600 milliliters
3 cups	= 700 milliliters
4 cups (1 quart)	= .95 liter
1.06 quarts	= 1 liter
4 quarts (1 gallon)	= 3.8 liters

Approximate Metric Equivalents by Weight

U.S.	METRIC
1/4 ounce	= 7 grams
1/2 ounce	= 14 grams
1 ounce	= 28 grams
1 1/4 ounces	= 35 grams
1 1/2 ounces	= 40 grams
2 1/2 ounces	= 70 grams
4 ounces	= 112 grams
5 ounces	= 140 grams
8 ounces	= 228 grams
10 ounces	= 280 grams
15 ounces	= 425 grams
16 ounces (1 pound)	= 454 grams